❧ The Maiden of Tonnerre ❧

J. Condé Delin.t et Sculp.t

LA CHEVALIERE D'EON.

Née à Tonnerre le 5. 8.bre 1728.

The Maiden of Tonnerre

The Vicissitudes of the Chevalier and the Chevalière d'Eon

Charles d'Eon de Beaumont

TRANSLATED AND EDITED BY

Roland A. Champagne
Nina Ekstein
Gary Kates

The Johns Hopkins University Press
BALTIMORE AND LONDON

English translation © 2001 *The Johns Hopkins University Press*
All rights reserved. Published 2001
Printed in the United States of America on acid-free paper

2 4 6 8 9 7 5 3 1

The Johns Hopkins University Press
2715 North Charles Street
Baltimore, Maryland 21218-4363
www.press.jhu.edu

Library of Congress Cataloging-in-Publication Data

Eon de Beaumont, Charles Geneviève Louis Auguste André
Timothée d', 1728–1810.
[Selections. English. 2001]
The maiden of Tonnerre : the vicissitudes of the chevalier and the
chevalière d'Eon / Charles d'Eon de Beaumont ; translated and edited
by Roland A. Champagne, Nina Ekstein, and Gary Kates.
p. cm.
Includes bibliographical references and index.
ISBN 0-8018-6687-1 (alk. paper)
1. Eon de Beaumont, Charles Geneviève Louis Auguste André
Timothée d', 1728–1810. 2. Diplomats—France—Biography.
3. Spies—France—Biography. 4. Female impersonators—France—Biography.
5. France—Foreign relations—18th century. I. Champagne, Roland A.
II. Ekstein, Nina C., 1952– III. Kates, Gary, 1952– IV. Title.
DC135.E6 A3 2001
944′.034′092—dc21   00-011754

A catalog record for this book is available from the British Library.

FRONTISPIECE

La Chevalière d'Eon, by J. Condé, first published on 1 March 1791 in *European
Magazine.* It is a fairly realistic portrait of d'Eon in her late fifties, living as
a woman but with the Cross of Saint Louis over the left breast.
(Courtesy of the Bibliothèque Nationale, Paris)

ৰু Contents ৯৯

❧ *Acknowledgments* ❧

The editors gratefully acknowledge the cooperation and permission of the Brotherton Collection, Leeds University Library, where the original French manuscripts of this volume's selections are stored as follows:

Box 1, file 1: La Grande Epître Historique de la Chevalière d'Eon

Box 8, pp. 30–33: Extraits de la Seconde Visite de Mademoiselle d'Eon à Notre St. Christophe de Beaumont

Box 6, pp. 5–14: Extraits de la lettre de Madame d'Eon à Mademoiselle d'Eon . . . 28 october 1777 and Extrait de la réponse de Mademoiselle d'Eon à sa mère . . . 3 novembre 1777

Box 8, pp. 1–92: Extrait de l'Epitre de la Chevalière d'Eon à Madame la Duchesse de Montmorenci-Bouteville de mai 1778 à Versailles

Box 7, pp. 983–90: Epître de Mademoiselle d'Eon à Madame la Duchesse de Montmorenci-Bouteville à Londres le 15 juin 1789

Box 7, pp. 991–93: Réponse de la Duchesse à Mademoiselle d'Eon

Box 8, pp. 55–59: Réflections chrétiennes

Box 8, pp. 34–41: Important Document dans mon état présent

Box 8, pp. 1686–1708: Grande Requête de Mademoiselle d'Eon pour demander la petite indulgence . . .

Box 7, pp. 32–136: Les Pieuses Métamorphoses ou Histoire des femmes qui ont déguisé leur sexe pour se consacrer à Dieu et professer la vie monastique

The editors are also grateful to Charly Coleman, James Gallagher, Orest Ranum, George H. Thompson, Richard Woods, and Jeanne Morgan Zarucchi for their help at various stages of preparing this manuscript.

❧ *Introduction* ❧

A Gendered Life

During the final decade of a very long life, the Chevalière d'Eon (1728–1810) made preparations in London to publish an autobiography that he had been working on for more than twenty years. He contracted with a publisher, received a substantial advance, prepared a polished version of the manuscript, and hired a British editor to translate his French into English. He called it *La Pucelle de Tonnerre: Les Vicissitudes du Chevalier et de la Chevalière d'Eon* (The Maiden of Tonnerre: The Vicissitudes of the Chevalier and Chevalière d'Eon). For whatever reason, the translation was never completed and the autobiography was never published. Or rather, not until now.[1]

Certainly d'Eon had much to write about. Born into a prominent French noble family, d'Eon became a diplomat, spy, military officer, and the author of more than fifteen volumes of history, economics, literary reviews, and political pamphlets. But what made him famous was neither his political career nor his written work: rather, since the eighteenth century, he has been known as one of the most famous transvestites in history; indeed, he lived the first five decades as a man and then thirty-two years (from age forty-nine to age eighty-one) as a woman.

There have been twenty or more biographies of d'Eon, along with several historical novels, plays, a film, and even an opera. Because, however, d'Eon's autobiographical writings were largely inaccessible until the 1930s—and even since then available only to those willing to read the manuscript pages in the archives of the University of Leeds library—biographers have ignored what is arguably the most important source for understanding d'Eon's life: his autobiography. But without these memoirs we cannot hope to fully understand the Chevalier/Chevalière's decision to live nearly half his life as a woman.

Having said that, we must admit that the memoirs are not as straight-forward as they might be because d'Eon was playing a double game: he was writing for a contemporary public that thought that the gendered story of his life was in fact the opposite of the truth. That is, d'Eon's contemporaries believed that he was a biological female who had been raised by his parents as a boy and that, consequently, he had lived as a man until 1777, when he supposedly returned to the gender of his birth. As the public would discover upon his death, however, d'Eon was a biological male who lived the second half of his life as a woman.[2] Therefore, d'Eon's autobiography is certainly the story of a transgendered person; but it narrates the journey of a supposed female-to-male transvestite, when the actual situation involved a male-to-female transgendered life.

D'Eon, of course, was caught in a bind. If he told the truth about his life, it would have been impossible for him to continue living as a woman. The publication of a candid autobiography would have meant a virtual suicide for the Chevalière d'Eon. So the autobiography was written on two levels. For contemporaries, d'Eon may not have been telling the truth about his anatomy, but his ideology regarding sexual differentiation, gender and religion, and conceptions of manhood and womanhood were sincerely conveyed. By understanding d'Eon's ideas about gender identity in the context of his behavior, modern-day readers can understand the memoirs as a justification of his extraordinary self-fashioning from manhood to womanhood.

D'Eon's autobiography does not celebrate his political and diplomatic career; it constitutes rather an exploration into early-modern ideas about gender. Like his contemporary and mentor Jean-Jacques Rousseau, whose autobiography became a classic of the Enlightenment when it was published in 1782, d'Eon wanted his readers to see his life as guided by overarching moral and philosophical principles.[3] He wanted us to come away with a respect not only for what he did but more important for what he thought. D'Eon would have liked readers to remember him not simply because he was the century's most famous cross-dresser but also because he was a philosopher of gender.

Perhaps the autobiography's most important theme is the intense Christianity expressed on virtually every page. At first we may find d'Eon's preoccupation with Christian grace rather baffling and distracting, as if it has only marginal ties to his transgendered identity. Indeed, all previous books about d'Eon ignore d'Eon's Christian identity. But as any reader of these essays can see, d'Eon's faith is a key to understanding his life.

D'Eon's autobiographical essays reveal a passionate and heartfelt devotion to the promise of salvation by Jesus. D'Eon envisioned the autobiography as an evangelical book, a work of piety whose purpose was to bring readers closer to God. The retelling of his life was to be a spiritual exercise for both author and reader. The title of the main autobiography — *The Great Historical Epistle* — was meant to evoke the New Testament letters of Saint Paul. The use of quotations from Paul throughout the autobiography and the other essays makes that allusion obvious. Likewise, in "A Special Request" d'Eon explicitly acknowledges that his model was Saint Augustine's great late-Roman autobiography, the *Confessions;* elsewhere d'Eon compares his own mother to Augustine's Monica.[4]

D'Eon embraced an Augustinian version of Christianity that accepts Adam's original sin as the starting point for understanding how nature became corrupt. For an Augustinian, becoming a Christian first meant acknowledging the hegemony of sin in this world. Piety required the renunciation of one's ego, career, desires of the flesh, and worldly aspirations. Throughout these essays, d'Eon argues that women have an easier time than men in understanding this sort of sacrifice.

At times d'Eon sounds like a Jansenist, a sect of early modern French Catholicism that incorporated much of Calvinist theology without rejecting Catholic ritual. For example, Jansenists took from Calvin a belief in predestination, claiming that God had already chosen a few "elect" who were to be saved after death. But it is difficult to read d'Eon's Jansenism as anything more than sporadic and eclectic. One of d'Eon's key religious patrons, the Archbishop of Paris Christophe de Beaumont, was one of France's most vociferous opponents of Jansenism. D'Eon gives us (in Chapter X and then in Part II) dialogues between d'Eon and Beaumont that clearly show the influence of the Archbishop upon the Chevalière.

D'Eon's Christianity focused on the death of Jesus as a model for his own salvation. He believed that this world is hopelessly tainted with sin. Thus d'Eon found fault with religious sects, such as Judaism, that concentrate most of their efforts on this world. Since much of the Torah seeks to show Jews how they can achieve holiness on earth — a project that d'Eon abhorred—the essays sometimes reveal a certain degree of anti-Semitism, which was common in early-modern Augustinian theology.

D'Eon rarely wrote about religion before he became a woman. His rediscovered Christianity surfaced between 1777 and 1785, the very time he began to live as a woman. For example, in the Archives Nationales (Paris) is a diary dating from this period in which d'Eon jotted twenty-five book titles of religious works he found while reading the Jansenist *Nouvelles ecclé-siastiques*.[5] For the next twenty-five years, d'Eon's Christian identity would develop in tandem with his feminine identity. D'Eon's Christianity became an armor to protect and justify his new gender identity.

Charles Geneviève Louise Auguste André Timothée d'Eon de Beaumont was born on October 5, 1728, in the sleepy town of Tonnerre, in the beautiful Burgundian wine country of eastern France.[6] His father, Louis d'Eon de Beaumont, was a royal official in charge of maintaining order and prosperity in the region. Although he was among the wealthiest notables of his small town, Louis d'Eon was only a minor player among France's powerful nobility. D'Eon's mother, Françoise de Charenton, was from a rich noble family in Montpellier. She would live until 1792, well into d'Eon's life as a woman. Louis and Françoise had two children before d'Eon: a daughter, Marguerite-Françoise (who later married an Irish nobleman), and a son, Théodore-André, who died before his first birthday in 1727.

When he was around fifteen years of age, d'Eon left home for one of France's most prestigious schools, the Collège de Mazarin in Paris. There he lived with his uncle, André-Timothée d'Eon de Tissey, who was inspector general of the Paris police, a position that gave him considerable influence. The nephew used his uncle's patronage to obtain an internship in the office of the Paris intendant, Louis Bertier de Sauvigny. By the time d'Eon was awarded his law degree—in 1749, also the year of his father's and uncle's deaths—he was already well known in Parisian aristocratic circles. Soon he secured a post as a royal censor, which gave him an income, thus allowing him the leisure to read books and to work on his own writing.

Like many young and talented noblemen, d'Eon hoped for a career that would take him into public service. To show his talents, he made himself into something of an economist, that is, an expert in France's fiscal policy. In 1753 he published his first book on state finances, followed five years later by a two-volume history of taxation. Meanwhile, he began writing articles and reviews for Fréron's *l'Année littéraire,* before that journal became preoccupied with attacking Enlightenment philosophers. By the time d'Eon turned thirty, in 1758, he was a rising star among the young aristocratic elite who hoped to serve the monarchy in some important capacity.

D'Eon did not have to wait long for such an opportunity. In 1756 Louis XV had chosen d'Eon to become the secretary to the Ambassador to the Russian court of the Empress Elizabeth. He distinguished himself to such a degree that Elizabeth offered him a permanent position in the Russian government. But by 1760 he wanted to follow his patrons, the brothers Comte de Broglie and the Maréchal de Broglie into the battles of the Seven Years' War, where d'Eon became a captain of the dragoons under the Maréchal. At the end of that war, in 1762, d'Eon was chosen as a member of the negotiating team, led by the Duc de Nivernais, that went to London to draw up what would become known as the Treaty of Paris. Indeed, the treaty itself was personally carried from London to Paris by d'Eon in February 1763. Louis XV rewarded his efforts with the highly coveted Cross of Saint Louis (a military medal supposedly given for heroic leadership during the recent war) and also by raising his noble status from sieur to chevalier. Finally, encouraged by Nivernais, the King also appointed d'Eon France's new temporary Ambassador (plenipotentiary minister) to England. The Chevalier returned to England in the late spring of 1763 with optimism, confidence, and power. He had arrived.

Or so he thought. Just at this watershed moment of his political career, his fate began to turn. Back home, d'Eon's patrons had fallen on hard times. The King's cousin, the Prince de Conti (himself a controversial figure and one who had attracted d'Eon's loyalty early on), retired from the court only to anger the King by encouraging a radical opposition. His allies, the Comte and the Maréchal de Broglie, were banished from Paris and forced to live in bucolic boredom on their country estate in Normandy. The resulting political void was filled by the King's mistress, Madame de Pompadour, whose influence became so great that she played an important role in choosing the next foreign minister, the Duc de Choiseul. He in turn rejected d'Eon's candidacy for the permanent post of Ambassador to England, choosing instead his own protégé, the Comte de Guerchy. D'Eon would return to his previous position of secretary.

When word reached d'Eon of Guerchy's appointment, he was furious. Instead of smoothing the way for the new Ambassador, d'Eon began a public feud with Guerchy that spilled into the noisy London press and embarrassed the French government. He even claimed that Guerchy had tried to poison him. In October 1763 the French foreign minister formally recalled d'Eon to Paris. Amazingly, d'Eon refused the recall; indeed, he demanded that Guerchy be the one recalled. For the rest of Louis XV's reign, d'Eon lived in a self-imposed exile in London, while the French government regarded him as an outlaw.

How could d'Eon think that he could get away with such disrespectful resistance to the French government? The reason lay with the King himself. Shortly after Louis XV approved d'Eon's appointment as plenipotentiary minister he also made him a spy in a network so secret that even the monarch's own ministers, including Choiseul, did not know about it. "The King's Secret" had spies throughout Europe's capitals, testing options that were too dangerous to be handled by the military. D'Eon was the King's man in England. As plenipotentiary minister he was expected to comply with the Treaty of Paris, which he himself had helped to negotiate. As a spy, he was ordered by the King to scout sites on the English coast for possible landings in a surprise attack. It was d'Eon's role as a royal spy that gave him the temerity to resist the foreign minister's recall order.

Despite his questionable status after 1763, d'Eon continued to spy for Louis XV, writing secret reports regularly until the King's death in 1774. D'Eon proved an invaluable source of information about political conflict in the House of Commons, especially during the crisis surrounding British member of Parliament John Wilkes during the late 1760s. Perhaps no one taught the French King more about England during this decade than d'Eon.

When Louis XVI ascended to the throne after his grandfather's death, he insisted on closing down The King's Secret, retiring its spies with comfortable pensions. But d'Eon proved a special case, not only because the Foreign Ministry considered him an outlaw but also, more importantly, because the government was convinced he was a woman.

The rumor regarding his sex began in 1771, when suddenly everyone from the French King to readers of the London dailies were buzzing about it. We will never know for certain what caused the rumor, but clearly d'Eon encouraged it from the start. He refused to comment and would not allow a physician to examine him. Most important, he never denied the rumor,

either to the press or even to his friends. This silence only encouraged speculation, and gamblers bet over £200,000 on the issue. When a spy was sent by
the French King in 1772 to discover the truth about d'Eon's sex, he returned
to Versailles with the report that d'Eon was a woman. Thus when Louis XVI
became king, he and his ministers were certain that they were dealing with
a woman. In 1777, when gamblers sued each other in court, Chief Justice
Lord Mansfield declared that so far as English law was concerned d'Eon was
a woman.

Meanwhile the new King sent an unusual emissary to negotiate d'Eon's
retirement: the flamboyant playwright Pierre Caron de Beaumarchais. By
the time of d'Eon's London trial, he and Beaumarchais had signed a lengthy
agreement that provided for d'Eon's safe return to France, official royal recognition of his gender as a woman, and a pension that would allow him to
live his life as a wealthy, aristocratic lady.

For the next eight years, from 1777 to 1785, d'Eon lived in France,
and the memoirs focus more on the first months of his return than on any
other period of his life, perhaps because this transition from manhood to
womanhood was the most difficult phase for him. At first he tried to retain his dragoon uniform, but within a few months the King ordered him to
wear appropriate dresses, made especially for him by the Queen's wardrobe
director, Rose Bertin.

These months are marked by his journey from London to Versailles,
where he lived in the home of the chief administrator of foreign affairs,
Jacques Edme Genet, and gained counsel from social lights such as the
Duchesse de Montmorenci-Bouteville. During this period d'Eon also seriously considered joining a convent. He felt restless and was confused about
how to live as a woman. When France joined the cause for American inde-
pendence in 1778, d'Eon begged the foreign minister, Vergennes, to allow
him to lead an army of women into battle. Finally, Louis XVI ordered d'Eon
to retire to his placid estate in Tonnerre, where he lived with his elderly
mother and produced fine wine from his valuable vineyards.[7]

Prevented by the King from living in Paris, d'Eon began to miss the
vibrant life he had known for so long in England. In 1785 d'Eon returned to
London, where he lived as a woman until his death in 1810. He participated
in fencing tournaments until he became too old and frail. D'Eon probably
planned to return to France. However, the French Revolution broke out in

1789, and by 1792, when Louis XVI lost his throne, d'Eon knew that returning would be foolish and dangerous. Besides, the monarchy's fall had left him with no pension, and his financial condition and his frail health kept him home much of the time.

Sometime during the 1790s he moved into an apartment with Mary Cole, the widow of a naval admiral. The last years were miserable ones for d'Eon, as he spent most days in the cold, damp apartment poring over his autobiography. He watched his spending very carefully, eating only what was necessary to stave off illness. On May 21, 1810, Mary Cole found d'Eon's dead body and also discovered that his body was unambiguously male.

The earlier facts and the narrative that links them together are provided mostly intact by d'Eon in his autobiography. But d'Eon adds certain tall tales to his life story, and the reasons for these fibs are not difficult to discover. D'Eon did not simply want to be known by his public as a woman; he wanted to be known as a certain kind of woman: Amazonian, pious, virtuous, patriotic; a woman in the mold of the Maid of Orléans, Joan of Arc. Indeed, d'Eon's self-fashioning was successful insofar as one of France's premier journalists, Simon Linguet, called d'Eon "a modern Joan of Arc." Perhaps more impressive, d'Eon received countless poems and letters like the following from fans across Europe:[8]

> *Jeanne d'Arc eut besoin d'un siècle encore gothique*
> *Pour s'acquérir un nom*
> *Mais ce siècle philosophique*
> *Rend un double hommage à d'Eon.*

> [Joan of Arc needed a century that was still Gothic
> in order to make a name for herself
> But this philosophical century
> Pays double homage to d'Eon.]

To present himself as an eighteenth-century Joan of Arc, d'Eon invented at least four major myths about himself regarding his childhood, his diplomacy in Russia, his trial in England, and his conversations with his mother between 1777 and 1779.

First, d'Eon concocted the tale that a relative had left an estate to a son born to Louis d'Eon, the Chevalier's father. When d'Eon's older brother died in infancy, shortly before d'Eon's own birth, Louis's grief and worry caused him to adopt the plan of raising d'Eon as a boy. This myth had the effect of blaming d'Eon's supposed gender change on his parents, thereby deflecting criticism from a potentially critical public.

D'Eon's next story concerned his first diplomatic assignment to Russia. The King's cousin, the Prince de Conti, recruited d'Eon to become more than a junior secretary to the Ambassador; in addition to that, Conti supposedly asked d'Eon to dress as a woman and become the French reader and close confidant of the Russian Empress Elizabeth. D'Eon wrote that he performed this incredible role with such success that he became the conduit of a personal correspondence between Elizabeth and Louis XV. Clearly this story was invented to show how d'Eon's cross-dressing had served France.

D'Eon's third tall tale was invented to explain how his supposed female gender was discovered while he was living in London. In several of the Leeds manuscripts he tells the same story: while he was riding his horse across Westminster Bridge one rainy day in the 1770s, the horse slipped and fell, throwing d'Eon onto the cobblestones. While blood gushed from his groin, rescuers cut into his pants, discovering d'Eon's biological sex. This narrative functioned on at least two levels: first, it demonstrated that it was not d'Eon himself who began the rumors about his sex, which dogged him between 1771 and 1777; and second, it served as a reference to Saint Paul's own conversion experience.[9]

Finally, the autobiography quotes whole letters and conversations between him and his mother, portraying the mother as urging her "daughter" to give up manhood for womanhood—even though his mother could not possibly have believed that d'Eon was female.

These stories are fictional. But at least they are solid historical fiction. D'Eon used real characters, actual locations, and genuine—if somewhat exaggerated—relationships. For example, although d'Eon's parents certainly did not raise him as a girl, they had, as d'Eon says, lost his infant brother the year before his own birth. Likewise, although Conti did not send d'Eon to Russia as a woman, the Prince was a patron of d'Eon and probably secured a similar post for him. D'Eon's story of the Westminster Bridge also rings true, because d'Eon certainly crossed the well-trafficked bridge during this period. The fall could have happened even if not in the way he narrates it. Finally, d'Eon had conversations with his mother when he said he did, even if they are not accurately depicted.

From the moment his contemporaries accepted the discovery of d'Eon's womanhood as a fact, they besieged him to reveal his life story. The London dailies were full of so many false stories (including one about his giving birth to the baby of John Wilkes) that d'Eon was determined to set the record straight when he returned to France in 1777.[10] Within two years a short volume appeared in print in Paris under the title *La Vie militaire, politique, et privée de mademoiselle d'Eon* [The Military, Political, and Private Life of Mademoiselle d'Eon], which was supposedly written by La Fortelle. D'Eon either wrote the work entirely or contributed much of its substance. In contrast to d'Eon's autobiography, the La Fortelle biography focused exclusively on d'Eon's military and political career before 1777, virtually ignoring any psychological or spiritual reasons that may have motivated d'Eon to live as a woman. The book served as an authorized biography, and newspaper articles about him generally took it as gospel.[11]

The biography presents the first of the d'Eon myths—that his parents raised a biological girl as a boy—but it does not mention the three others. D'Eon's diplomatic mission, for example, is explained without any anecdotes regarding cross-dressing. From this early biography, then, we can presume that d'Eon had not yet invented the tales about cross-dressing in Russia, the fall from his horse on the Westminster Bridge, or the conversations with his mother. These all came later, probably shortly after 1777. On the other hand, La Fortelle's biography demonstrates that the story about his gender-bending childhood is likely the first myth that he told to explain his transvestism.

In any event, the biography did not satisfy d'Eon's public. His new friends in Paris—especially the aristocratic ladies who ran Paris high society—demanded more. So d'Eon seems to have started writing his memoirs almost immediately upon returning to France. At least that is the impression given by the title, which probably indicates the date of first composition. But as soon as d'Eon finished one draft he would move on to another or revise the earlier one. The Leeds archive includes different versions of the same narrative. Indeed, it is likely that one of d'Eon's primary activities during his thirty-plus years as a woman was writing and rewriting his autobiographical essays. D'Eon lived nearly half his life as a woman by writing his way across the gender barrier.

This volume contains three types of documents from the Leeds archive. In Part I we present the most polished version of d'Eon's autobiography, the one for which he signed a contract with the Richardson brothers in 1805 and which he seems to have completed in French around that time. Part II includes fragments from earlier versions of the autobiography in addition to more autonomous pieces from other files and boxes that d'Eon himself seems to have arranged. These essays reveal d'Eon's convictions more forcefully, precisely because his prose is in a rougher state and his tone is more natural. On the other hand, because they are more draftlike, these pieces tend to be less polished and therefore somewhat less readable, with odd transitions between sections and some repetition.

Part III presents a different sort of document altogether. It is not a memoir, though it is found in the same boxes as the autobiographical manuscripts. It is a relatively polished, short, book-length manuscript narrating the history of women who lived considerable portions of their lives as men, usually for religious reasons. This book, with the title *The Pious Metamorphoses; or the history of women who disguised their sex in order to consecrate themselves to God and to adopt the monastic life and who have been recognized as saintly by the Greek and Latin Church,* constitutes a series of historic examples that were meant to serve as models for the Chevalière d'Eon and to justify "her" own transvestism. Many of the women included were saints, whose cross-dressing was endorsed by the Catholic Church. Thus d'Eon used these examples not only to create a social context and historic tradition for his transgendered life but also to give it legitimacy and spiritual meaning. Clearly d'Eon meant this work to serve as an appendix for his autobiography, and we have thus included it as such in this volume.[12]

Autobiography and History

Autobiography, writing about the life of the self, has a complex relationship with history. Both are influenced by the need to tell a story. On the one hand, facts and artifacts ground history so that its story connects these elements in a structure that explains the past and provides causal explanations. On the other hand, autobiography is centered on a speaking subject telling a story that mythologizes the facts and artifacts of history within the context of the life of the speaking subject. While history proceeds from the facts and artifacts, autobiography begins with the speaking subject and manipulates historic facts and artifacts for its own ends.

The historic facts of d'Eon's life are used to identify the nonhistoric: the four myths that structure d'Eon's autobiographical text. In fact the entire autobiographical epistle can be read as an inversion of history: instead of history's male writer who adopted the role of a woman for the last thirty-two years of his life, d'Eon gave us a female raised as a male, who was finally forced to return to his "natural" state of womanhood. D'Eon's autobiographical epistle stands history on its head. In so doing, it engages the reader in the problems of gender crucial to the nature of the self. A whole new conceptualization takes place in the autobiography of Part I. This conception is corroborated by the documents in Part II and modeled in Part III by stories of women who have been declared holy, some even canonized, within Christianity.

The autobiography's mythologizing function is related in d'Eon's case to a need to place himself among the major historic persons and events of his day. That place necessarily entailed the highly structured monarchical universe of the *ancien régime.* His autobiography—and his life—blur the distinctions that defined that universe: those between men and women, those between nationalities, and those between the privileged and the not privileged. D'Eon challenged these distinctions and consequently lost his historic place. Through his autobiography he instead invented a historic role for himself.

The move across the gender boundary was manifestly complicated and difficult. Signs of struggle are everywhere, from his reluctance to wear a dress as commanded by the King, to the male-coded Cross of the Military Order of Saint Louis that d'Eon always wore with his dresses, to the orthographic confusion of the words *cour* (the royal court) and *coeur* (heart), suggesting the ambivalent and interchangeable character of the political and the personal, as well as his own historical, public aspirations. His autobiography thus bears witness to his profound ambivalence concerning gender. While forced by society to be either a man (1728–77) or a woman (1777–1810), d'Eon's natural state seems to have been far more indeterminate and unstable. Perhaps most interesting, d'Eon played out much of this struggle in a public rather than a private realm.

The Cross of the Military Order of Saint Louis is emblematic of the complexity of d'Eon's gender construction. First, it was a relic of the privileges that his male identity had earned. Ironically, the Chevalier d'Eon was awarded this medal not for military bravery, as was normally the case, but for spying for Louis XV. Hence the medal was an ambivalent sign: d'Eon earned it for crossing boundaries between nations as a spy, yet it was a sign of male, military honor. The Chevalière thus openly wore the badge of her repressed male self while knowing that it represented her ability to cross boundaries denied to most members of society. This boundary transgression extended to the narrative construction of the autobiography.

D'Eon's grammar is a key to the gender transformation he narrates. In French grammar, agreement is made between nouns or pronouns and adjectives; in certain cases, there is agreement between subjects or direct objects and past participles. In the eighteenth century the former agreements were universally applied, while the usage concerning the latter was inconsistent. Within both categories, d'Eon shifted frequently between male and female when identifying himself. To give the reader a sense of the ambivalence with which d'Eon "marked" his own gender, we the translators indicate each instance with an *m* or an *f.* Specific examples are illuminating. In 1778 d'Eon wrote to the Duchesse de Montmorenci-Bouteville that he "was bold and paid for it personally" (Part II), with "bold" being marked as feminine. His boldness, a quality admired by dragoons, was incongruous in one who wanted to be a woman. This choice suggests a transgendered identity. His conversion to the virtues of womanhood, therefore, was not as absolute as he outwardly claimed it to be in addressing the Duchesse. Thus through d'Eon's ambivalent sense of gender his autobiography transforms the historic facts and artifacts of his life to project a new historic space for himself.

As a dragoon and a diplomat, d'Eon was accustomed to wearing certain prescribed clothing—or if you will, costumes. When identified by the English law and the French monarch as a woman, he donned yet another costume, this time a dress. Interestingly, during d'Eon's lifetime, masquerade parties were very popular in France, England, and Russia. Therefore, it is hardly surprising that d'Eon saw costume as a way of experimenting with identity. In the *Pious Metamorphoses* (see Part III), examples abound of women who disguised their sex on their way to pious, exemplary lives. These examples provide models that d'Eon emulated, as transgendered disguise is shown to be a crucial component of holy, respected lives. Pope Joan— whose example recurs throughout *The Great Historical Epistle,* the miscellaneous writings, and the *Pious Metamorphoses*—created with her masculine disguise a space for herself at the pinnacle of Christendom. During Joan's reign as pope, her female gender reasserted itself with the astounding and public spectacle of her illegitimate child's birth during the pomp of a male religious procession. Thus although she crossed gender lines (through costume and demeanor) convincingly enough to attain the male pinnacle of her position, her female sex could not be entirely erased.

D'Eon's Christianity gave spiritual significance to his gender transformation. We can surmise easily enough that d'Eon's decision took much courage, especially as the days turned into months and years. His theology gave him the confidence to trust only in God and to ignore earthly powers. This is the message of one of his pieces in Part II, the brief "Christian Reflections." He believed fervently that he belonged to God's elect. "How happy is the lot of women" who have the "sweet smell of Christian virtues." D'Eon's ambivalence about being "forgotten or ignored by . . . our great cabinet ministers in Versailles" was compensated only by living as a Christian woman wholly devoted to God.

D'Eon was thus born again *simultaneously* as a Christian and as a woman. Christianity helped d'Eon cross the gender barrier; it gave him the spiritual strength and mental courage to live as a woman among the same people who had known him as a man. It also gave him the inner conviction that what he was doing was no lie or trick—even if it obviously required a level of deceit—but rather constituted a moral regeneration. Far from being a sin, switching gender was a way to purify oneself and become closer to God.

Within the Church, the traditional space reserved for women was the convent. D'Eon was attracted to the convent as a place where his virginity would be seen as a virtue and where women have authority outside the male hegemony. Although he chose not to enter a convent, the convent was still a powerful metaphorical space for d'Eon. In his autobiography, d'Eon created a virtual convent, a protected space where he could experiment with male and female attributes and still retain his virtuous virginity. Here again, autobiography adapts history in that d'Eon's writings modified the actual space of eighteenth-century convents by creating a psychic space within which he could explore his ambivalence toward gender. For this reason the autobiography's discourse often resembles seventeenth- and eighteenth-century convent literature, such as the Duchesse de la Vallière's *Lettres,* of which d'Eon owned the 1767 edition.[13]

Especially important for d'Eon in this new realm was the notion of virginity, a virtue usually ascribed to women. Throughout his writings, d'Eon took as his model Joan of Arc, in whom virginity combined with male, military valor. D'Eon's own virginity as a male might have been highly suspect among his peers. As a woman, however, d'Eon mythologized his virginity as a virtue while at the same time his public status as a virgin allowed his gender experimentation to remain free from the suspicion of perversion. Within the convent of his writings, he could explore how his feminine voice could make use of his virginity as a virtue and lead to his salvation within Christianity. In his myth of the fall on Westminster Bridge, d'Eon had the doctors who examined him—and who discovered he was a woman—declare him a virgin. Thus links were established among virginity, virtue, grace, and Christianity, links that tied d'Eon's gender conversion to religious conversion.

As with the dragoons and the diplomatic corps, Christianity provided d'Eon with the satisfaction of being received by a community of peers. Both d'Eon's mother and the Duchesse de Montmorenci-Bouteville served as models of Christian virtue for d'Eon. Implicit in d'Eon's choice to address his autobiographical epistle to the Duchesse was his own call to a community of Christians, his need to be praised for his feminine virtue. Within the conventual community of his writing, d'Eon was seeking communal recognition of the virtue of virginity among women and his consequent salvation. The Chevalière presented himself as a virtuous Christian, a woman whose chastity was the primary reason for his being saved along with other Christians. D'Eon's Christian conversion and gender conversion were similar "events," justified within the rhetorical scheme of the autobiography, in which d'Eon moved between genders. Having become converted as a Christian woman, forgiven, and saved, he now was on one side of the line looking at the other side—his male, sinner's life.

D'Eon's rhetoric served to convince the Duchesse and other potential readers seeking to be convinced by verifiable, historic events that this was a feminine voice speaking from a position of certitude about religious and gender identities, both being imposed by a bolt of lightning from above (God, the law, the King). His inner dialectic between male and female genders was revealed by his style, in which we find reiterations of the *mauvais garçon/bonne fille* opposition. This tension throughout his writing indicates his entrapment in the duality of genders; that is, as d'Eon revealed an affiliation with one gender, then the self's alliance with the other gender was both concealed and implied in the same affirmation, and vice versa. These gender double binds are flip sides of the same coin called d'Eon. For example his "method" of choosing either the left or the right side of a page in the Bible to answer questions about his future, and implicitly his gender, was completely arbitrary. Biblical hermeneutics, the science of interpreting the meaning of the Bible, was mocked by this arbitrary search for an answer to gender identity. D'Eon signaled the problematic nature of any such appeal for certainty by multiplying his biblical searches.

Thus ambivalence reigned supreme. While the Chevalière claimed several times to have buried his dragoon self, the autobiography literally resurrects him. And the d'Eon who is resurrected is beyond the categories of male and female and is saved—through virginity, through grace, and through compliance with the dictates of authority.

1.

Grande Epître Historique
de la Chevalière D'EON
En 1785
A Madame la Duchesse de Montmorenci Bouteville

_____

Infelix Regina jubes renovare dolorem.

_____

Chapitre I

* petit village,
agréable situé
à l'entrée de la
grande forêt
de Maine
dépendante du
Comté de
Tonnerre.

† du 5. octobre
1728.

Mon pere ayant perdu son fils unique, à Villou *
en nourrice à Villou * où il est enterré, au pied du
maître autel dans le chœur de l'Eglise. étoit dans
un chagrin, planté par des raisons paternelles, que
par des raisons d'intérêt de famille, l'equité y a de
remarquable, à un naissant en que Ce trouvée exercé
Je suis née Coiffée, ma nature. s'est trouvée exercée
in nubibus. n'importe trois jours après ma naissance
mon pere ◊ me fit baptiser par son cousin et son ami M.
Borde Doyen de Notre Dame de Tonnerre et
ma paroisse sous les noms de Saints et de
Saintes de peur de se tromper.
ma grand-mere et ma mere grandes devotes
et leur intérêt furent long-tems entre elles à
hésiter et à mediter si ou feroit de moi une
fille ou un garçon. mon pere vouloit que je fusse un
je fusse garçon et ma mere que je fusse une
bonne fille. grande querelle intérieure de menage,
mais le bruit ne passoit pas au delà de la
chambre à coucher.
Après la révolution de mes études à Paris, et à
l'académie du cheval et des armes on a fini par
faire de moi un Cornette de Dragons, puis je
suis devenu fille malgré moi. le monde
crie au miracle, mais où est-il sinon dans la
nature de la bête qui a été trompée comme une poire

PART I

The Great Historical Epistle by the Chevalière d'Eon, Written in 1785

To Madame the Duchesse of Montmorenci-Bouteville

Infelix Regina jubes renovare dolorem

Chapter I

About the main incidents in my life from my birth, to my youth,
to my old age

My father lost his only son while the latter was an infant, sent away to
Villon to be wet-nursed.[1] The child is buried there at the foot of the main
altar in the choir of the church. This event saddened him profoundly both
as a father and because of the interests of the family. What distinguishes my
birth is that I was born ᶠwith a caul ᶠand that my sex was hidden *in nubibus*.[2]
In any case, three days after my birth on October 5, 1728, my father had me
baptized by his cousin and friend Monsieur Borve, the dean of my parish
of Notre Dame of Tonnerre, with the names of both male and female saints
in order to avoid any error.[3]

My grandmother and my mother, both extremely pious women, hesi-
tated and meditated a long time about whether I was to be treated as a girl
or a boy. My father wanted me to be a (bad) boy and my mother wanted
me to be a (good) girl. There was a great quarrel between the couple, but
the noise was limited to their bedroom.

After the completion of my studies in Paris and at the military academy, I was finally transformed into an officer in the dragoons and later became ᵐ a girl against my wishes.[4] The world cries out that it is a miracle,
but where is this miracle if not in the very nature of a foolish girl who was
tricked to go along like a foolish ewe. Something similar happened to my
relative Madame Dodun of Tonnerre, who until the age of sixteen was raised
in boys' clothing by her father, a Lieutenant Colonel of the dragoons. She
finally listened to nature and became a mother of two boys and nine girls.[5]
That is much better than inflicting death on the living.

One of my father's favorite excuses for raising me as a boy was his
need to have me replace my brother, who died so young. And one of my
mother's favorite excuses was that she had received twelve thousand francs
from her mother, Madame Delaud of Charenton, in the form of a mortgage

on the house, which Madame d'Eon would receive if she gave birth to a boy. This mortgage was the property and the responsibility of the Baron de Bon, the first president of the Court of Finances in Montpellier.[6] The Abbé Jean Chanoisse of Montpellier was the agent and guarantor of this arrangement. My father and mother may have had other excuses, either good or bad, which I am not obliged[m] to reveal or make public. But what I can tell truthfully and without risk is that when I returned from London or from Versailles in 1777 to be with my mother at Tonnerre, she herself requested that I once again wear a dress to get her out of trouble, and here is what she said to me: "Since your father has been dead for twenty-eight years, the entire responsibility now falls upon your mother, who sinned in spirit and who must in good faith make up for it now by having you dress as a woman in the place of your birth. Having been unable to send you to school when you were a child, we spent the time as best we could in the country under the pretext that you were still too young for schooling and that you didn't have the stamina to apply yourself."

Although during my childhood the works of Jean-Jacques the Citizen of Geneva did not yet exist, my father, educated — as I was to be later — in Paris at the College of the Four Nations, acted the philosopher and had me brought up by my mother in the spirit of Jean-Jacques, if you accept it as his style to allow children to run around on "all fours."[7] Rousseau, born for our generation, came too late for my father. Rousseau's character, like his genius, called out for a new kind of man but would not have required a new kind of woman had he only known my mother.

I will not say anything about all the concerns and all the cares taken by my father and mother in raising me at home under their scrutiny day and night. Born[f] with a frail constitution, I became[f] strong[f] through nourishing food, good wine, and the healthy air of Tonnerre. Tonnerre is situated among the vineyards, the mountains, and the woods of the Armancençon and the Armence Rivers, which irrigate a long, pleasant valley running from Joigny to Lemur and Dijon.

Neither my body nor my mind was worn out from studying when my father took[m] me to Paris at the age of thirteen. At that point, I knew only how to read and write, and not well at that. I, however, fell into the hands[f] of my uncle and aunt who made[m] me feel ashamed[m] of my ignorance and who motivated me to study. Furthermore, they alerted and warned me that if I revealed the truth of my sex I would be locked away[f] in a convent forever. The very word "convent" made me tremble, and I knew that my uncle, because of his position, had a dossier full of *lettres de cachet* without any names written on them.[8] Imagine my fear! My father, to keep me in line and in the proper religious spirit, had placed[m] me under the tutelage of his friend the Abbé Rigaud, the first vicar of the parish of Saint Sulpice, the area in which I lived. This Abbé was also the prior of Grisel, in the Department of Tonnerre, where my grandfather and my father were delegates with plenary authority of the administrator of the Generalité of Paris.[9] I feared this saintly Abbé Rigaud even more than my father.

During the course of my studies in Paris, I unfortunately stumbled upon the lives of the saints and the hermits of the higher and the lower Thebaïd.[10] Having then neither good judgment nor any experience, I got[m] it into my head to imitate as much as I could the harshness of the one group and the austerity of the other. I deprived myself of half of my lunch and dinner in order to give the food to the poor. During the coldest part of winter, without making any noise, I lay on the floor and prayed ceaselessly and fervently until I was so cold that I was obliged[m] to seek refuge in my bed. During those days I was so heated about going to heaven that I would have come down[m] from Mont St. Bernard or Mont Blanc to sleep on the snow in the valley.[11]

I became accustomed[m] in time to bear the cold as well as the heat, hunger and thirst, late nights, hard work, and prayer. For many years I wore a horsehair undershirt. I will not report the details of the fasting and repentance that I underwent from my tenth to my twenty-first year. No one would believe me, or I would be called mad,[f] although it is an abiding truth before God and mankind.

During the period of my studies, the War of 1745 broke out.[12] All Paris was filled with placards, drums, trumpets, officers, soldiers, and recruiters for various military groups: the infantry, the cavalry, the dragoons, the hussars, and volunteer armies. The Maréchal de Saxe, a great protector of my uncle, was the commander-in-chief and was renowned in France and Europe for his exploits. This rekindled the inclination or the passion that I had had during my youth to join the army, but I had not yet finished my studies and was still too young.

I did not have the patience to wait for the end of my studies before giving myself over to the practice of weapons and the use of horses. I worked so hard[m] at these skills that my efforts were rewarded by great success, as is only too well known in my case.[13] Despite this, my love for studying and for religion was not diminished in its zeal.

Although I did all my schooling in Paris, I was taken to the theater only four times and to the opera twice. I never wanted to go to a ball or to masquerade parties. I never picked up cards for the purpose of gambling, but because of my profession I did pick up bullets many a time in order to kill.

Willingly I have remained[m] for periods of three months, six months, and entire years at a time in my library in Paris, in St. Petersburg, and in London without ever going out. I usually work fifteen out of twenty-four hours. When I have money, I eat and drink as any other would. When I have no money, I stay in bed and work from morning to night. I survive on bread, cheese, lettuce, vegetables, and fruit. As a consequence of this philosophical diet, I have had the misfortune to bury many friends as well as numerous doctors I have known.[14]

Never did a girl or boy in Lacedemonia or Sparta have a harsher or a more industrious life than mine.[15] Riding horses, practicing weapons, hunting, traveling four times from one pole to the other, and moving day and night, all made[m] me indefatigable.[16] During the war in which I was engaged in Germany, I never slept on any other bed than my large bearskin spread out over straw. I took off only my boots and my uniform jacket; I kept on my tunic and my other articles of clothing. I wrapped myself in a large Russian fur coat made of fox or Astrakhan sheep.[17] At the first drum roll or bugle call, I was ready[m] in an instant. Danger made me adaptable and imperturbable. My life is really good only for terrifying a Parisian hero, a minister of foreign affairs at Versailles, and a special Ambassador to London.[18]

Immediately after finishing my studies in Paris, I lost my father, my uncle, and their fortune all within five days.[19] From Tonnerre, I wrote to the Comte d'Ons-Enbray, the Lieutenant-General in the King's Armies, about my father's death in order that he inform my uncle, who was a good friend of the Comte.[20] On the day he received my letter, the Comte was having the evening meal at my uncle's home. Despite the caution he observed in learning about my father's death, my uncle was so grief stricken that his servant found him dead in his bed the next morning. He had made my father his sole heir, but since this heir died five days before my uncle, the will was ipso facto declared null and void by the tribunal of the Châtelet of Paris in October 1749.[21] This unexpected misfortune quite suddenly deprived me of my two closest advisors. So important were they to me that I might call them my "Aulic" Council because they were led by the now deceased Prince de Conti, the King's cousin and friend, who had his own reasons for protecting me.[22] This irreparable loss plunged me into sadness and generated endless reflection. I recognized the danger of my position.

I had been educated as a boy, and I dressed as one. I blushed when the mere word "girl" was mentioned in my presence.

I had two personalities. My mind tended toward tranquility, solitude, and study. Prudence told me that this was the wisest and simplest way to shield myself, but my heart loved the clash of weapons and the display of all the military drills. Unable to consult either man or woman, I consulted God and the Devil and, so as not to fall into the water, I jumped[m] into the fire.

I cannot describe the anguish of both my mind and my heart when faced with deciding upon a career at that point in my life. I had been raised[m] very piously. I confessed and took communion once a month. My devout confessor often asked me what I was doing with myself or what I planned to do. I answered: "I do not have any idea what I am about. And I do not yet know what I want to do." He often asked me about the sins I did or did not commit. I often answered: "I do not know what you are talking about, Father." Then he would stop the conversation and say: "These then are all the sins you confess. Say your *mea culpa* and go in peace. I absolve you even as you go from doubt to another, vacillating between contradictory resolutions."

Contradictory resolutions troubled me day and night. At times I wanted to enter a convent of nuns, at other times I wished to hide beneath the banner of the dragoons, for which I had great propensity ever since my youth, when I had been excited by the uniform, the horses, and the military drills of La Rochefoucault's dragoon regiment, which had its winter quarters in my native Tonnerre.

I would say to myself: "After having grown up[m] and studied in Paris, if I enter a convent, there will be a scandal; if I enter a monastery, I will be found out[m] during my novitiate. If I become a nun, I'll have to take my vows after a year; and I may come to regret having lived and died as a wet hen.[23] It would be better for me to hide among the dragoons. You don't grow old there, so I will retire when I want. I will serve only as an officer; given the way they bed down at night; and the precautions I will take, it will not be easy to find me out.[24] During the day I will act in such a way that no one will be able to tell whether I am a girl or a boy. If I am wounded[f] I will not be dishonored[f] in having been a warrior. If I am killed[f] I will be shrouded[f] with the dust of military glory." It was only to go off to war that I took so much trouble to learn to use weapons and to ride a horse.

Religion was the only voice telling me to go off and withdraw to a nunnery. My whole heart told me to go off and join the courageous dragoons. I believed my conscience to be clear because a military career is the career of kings and princes. The military is a proper and honorable choice since, in the Scripture, the Supreme Being is always called the God of armies.

Unable to consult anyone about my situation, I decided to go pray at the tomb of my patron saint, Geneviève, in the underground chapel of the Abbey that bears her name in Paris. In vain I called her name, prayed to her, and implored her. Deaf to my prayers, she did not reply. Unable to say silly things to her, nor beat her, in my impatience, I determined my fate by drawing lots, by pointing to the most beautiful letters in the New Testament with my right hand and my left hand. That is, if the verse chosen by opening to the New Testament with my left hand began with the closest letter to A, it would mean that it was the will of Heaven that I hide my sex in a convent, and a letter farther from A would tell me to hide my sex in a regiment.[25]

When I first opened to the New Testament with my right hand, I encountered this verse: Mark 3:35, "For whosoever will do the will of God is my brother, my sister, and my mother." When I opened it with my left hand, I found this verse: Matt. 22:30, "For at the Resurrection, women will not marry or be married: men will be like the angels of God in heaven." Right away I said, here are two "for"s [*car*] that begin the two selected passages. I have to begin again. This drawing of lots is nullified, ipso facto.

In the second drawing, I encountered this passage with my right hand: Matt. 15:28, "Then Jesus answered her: 'Woman, your faith is great; may it be done unto you as you wish.'" [26] With my left hand, I found this verse: Luke 3:11, "And he answered and told him: let anyone who has two garments give one to someone who has none at all." [27]

Then I said to myself that I certainly won according to the letter that is closest to A, but the meaning of the two verses defied my understanding. At the same time, my uncertainty about my destiny was increased rather than diminished. In my anguish, I said: "I want to try asking the Lord for a decision about my future with a last stab at the New Testament." Upon opening the book, I found that the first verse on the left side began with the following words: "Now let the person who has a purse keep it, and the same for the person who has a wallet; and let the person who has no sword at all sell his or her own clothing and buy a sword" (Luke 22:36).

So I said to myself: "Here's a passage that speaks more clearly both to my mind and to my heart. If a spirit or an angel has spoken to me, I will not go against the will of God." I quickly left the dark, subterranean Chapel of Saint Geneviève, and I went up into the immense dormitories to find Dom Bernard, a canon of this Abbey and also a great preacher in Paris, as well as the confessor of the Duc d'Orléans, who died in grace at the Abbey. Dom Bernard was also the friend and confessor of my uncle, the Chief Secretary of the Duc d'Orléans. I found Father Bernard alone in his cell. Without explaining anything about the particulars of my case, nor about my naiveté in searching for a decision about my destiny in the chance openings of the pages of the New Testament, I said to him: "Very Reverend Father, since the death of my uncle, who was your friend, and since the death of my father, both within a period of five days, I have felt serious doubt about which career to choose."

He said to me: "Do you know what your father and your uncle wanted for you?"

I replied: "No. A week after my arrival in Burgundy, my father and my uncle died within five days of each other. I did undertake to make a novena to my patron saint, Geneviève, in the hope of gaining insight, since the name Geneviève was given to me at baptism by my godmother, the sister of my father and of my uncle."

Dom Bernard said to me: "I am greatly saddened about the loss of your uncle. I am not the only one here who feels this way. The Duc d'Orléans also misses him and often speaks to me about it." Then he added: "Your Saint Geneviève is certainly a great saint, but I know a saint even more powerful in heaven and on earth: Divine Mary, the glorious mother of Jesus Christ."

My reply was: "I know that the mother of all saintliness is called 'Star of the Morning Sky.' For that reason, my mother had the Archbishop of Sens, Monsieur Languet, give me the name Marie at my confirmation at the Church of Saint Sulpice in Paris. However, I use the name Geneviève because I was baptized [f] with it."

He smiled at me: "With those two names you are bound to go to heaven. You should have first said your novena at Notre Dame in Paris or in Hautvervilliers.[28] Confess your sins and take communion with a clear conscience. Then go on a retreat in some religious community, and God will enlighten you. Who is your confessor?"

"The Abbé Lebel, a doctor of the Sorbonne. I have known him for a long time. He is knowledgeable and pious. I will go see him and talk to him." And so I left [m] contented [f].

I did as he advised me to do. After finishing my novena at Notre Dame and taking communion in the chapel in back of the chancel, I began [m] again, but for the last time, to divine my destiny by choosing pages in the Gospels as I had done in Saint Geneviève's Chapel. My first selection was: Mark 10:38, "And Jesus said to him: 'You don't know what you are asking. Are you capable of drinking from the same cup from which I must drink?' "[29] The second selection was: Matt. 27:35, "They divided my garments among themselves and they drew lots for my robe."

I quickly remarked how bizarre it was that the Gospels spoke more clearly to me at the tomb of Saint Geneviève than at the foot of the altar to the divine Mary. I see that I am even more stupid than I am naive for Saint Paul says that the letter kills and the spirit gives life.

Nonetheless, I cannot be accused of acting purely out of superstition because it is also said that at the First Council directed by Peter, the choice of appointing either Joseph the Just or Matthias to be an apostle was decided in the latter's favor by drawing lots. Thus Matthias was added by consensus to the other eleven Apostles (Acts 1:26).

Upon the death of a pope, his successor is elected by the conclave only by means of a system of lots cast. Upon the death of Our Lord, his robe was subject to the drawing of lots to determine to whom it would belong (Matt. 27:35; Mark 15:24; John 19:24).

I found in the Epistles of the Apostle to the Gentiles more light and more of the salt of true wisdom than in all the speeches by the Doctors of

Navarre, the Sorbonne, and Saint Geneviève. However, I did not want to dismiss the advice I had received from Dom Bernard, from Doctor Lebel, and from his brother the Abbé Lebel, the former rector of the university. The Abbé Lebel had also been my professor of rhetoric at the Collège Mazarin and had taken a great liking[m] to me because I had won the prize for memorization by reciting the whole book of the Gospel according to Saint Matthew while making only three mistakes. He claimed that I was the brightest of his students. However, there was among us the young man who has since come to be known as the wise Target, the famous lawyer of Parliament.[30] In any event, the Abbé Lebel declared in class: "I will excuse the errors of those of d'Eon's friends for whom he asks forgiveness."[31]

As a result of the advice from Dom Bernard, the Doctor, and the Abbé Lebel, I went on a number of pious retreats in various places. I wanted to visit La Crupe, Orval, Septfons, Montserrat, and the Conobites of Montliban, of whom Saint Euphrosyne became the General and where Saint Marina hid as a nun and lived with her father until her death.[32] But I didn't have the money to embark on trips to such distant places. I had to make do with short retreats at the Carthusian monastery in Paris, at the order of the Camaldules in Grobois, with the hermits in the forest of Senar and at Mont Valerien with the community of priests in the order of Calvary. I finished my short period of retreat at the Benedictine Abbey of Noëfort in the suburb of Meaux, about forty kilometers from Paris. Pious persons surely will say that it was dangerous to undergo this new experience of a retreat from both perspectives.[33] But to resolve this delicate question I wanted to use the resources available to me nearby. Having weighed the positive and negative factors and seen the differences in lifestyle from one religious order to the next in the same religion, I concluded that it would be foolish to submit to rules established by men. I did not have any difficulty realizing that what monks and nuns practiced were for the most part observances of devotion and foolishness invented by men rather than the precepts of the doctrine of Jesus Christ. I returned[f] to Paris to live in tranquility at home with my philosophy and my books.

I worked night and day to learn about the organization of the internal administration of France. I volunteered or worked without compensation in the offices of Monsieur Bertier de Sauvigny, the intendant for the Généralité of Paris to which my father and my uncle had been delegates. I soon thought myself well-informed and produced for public consumption several works in Latin and in French, for example: *A Historical Essay on the Various Positions of France Regarding its Finances from the Regency of the Duc Mortehuyrs to 1754*, and a short historical treatise on the functions of intendants and receveurs généraux of finances in the provinces.[34] Since these two short works were successful in the literary and financial worlds, I temporarily dropped my religious and military plans. I often went to consult the wise director of la Bleterie—the Académie des Inscriptions et Belles Lettres—who was the verbose Abbé Raynal, author of *The Philosophical History of the Two Indies*. I also dined three times a week at the home of the famous critic Fréron, the author of *l'Année littéraire*, who had become a good friend. These two critics disparaged my considerable piety and opened my eyes philosophically. My perspective was so broadened that I even worked up the courage to frequent more assiduously the Prince de Conti who had been my father's and my uncle's patron and who had his special reasons for protecting me as well.

In those days the Prince protected most particularly a Scottish gentleman connected with the Pretender, who used the name of the Chevalier Mackenzie Douglas.[35] When the Pretender was arrested in Paris upon leaving the opera, the Prince de Conti sent the Chevalier to the former's property at Liladan, where the Chevalier Douglas took refuge under the name of Monsieur Michel.

Since Monsieur Michel Morin was bored staying at an estate that its owner hardly ever visited, the Prince de Conti proposed to bring him back to Paris under the name of Monsieur Michel as the tutor of the only son of Monsieur Bertier de Sauvigny, who would one day become very wealthy. Monsieur de Sauvigny was the nephew of Monsieur Orry Pontvoleu, the General of Finances, as well as the son of the intendant of the Généralité of Paris and of Madame de Sauvigny (the daughter of the elderly Duruey d'Harnancourt), who had been the intendant of Grenoble and of the Prince de Conti's army. Monsieur Bertier de Sauvigny sought to please the Prince de Conti because everyone in Paris knew that he met twice a week with the King both before and after the royal meetings with the Ministers. Monsieur de Sauvigny accepted the proposal, as did the so-called Monsieur Michel, to bring him out of isolation.

In 1755, the Prince de Conti had the idea to reconcile France and Russia; the two countries had been oddly estranged since the notorious adventures of the Marquis de la Chétardie, the French Ambassador to Russia. He thought about sending Chevalier Douglas to Russia as a Scottish traveler without informing anyone that he would be going there, to probe the opinions in the Russian court about the possibility of a genuine diplomatic reconciliation with France.

Chevalier Douglas — after having become good friends with the Vice-Chancellor, the Comte de Vorontsov, who was the best and most honest of men, and after having earned the respect of the beautiful and virtuous Comtesse de Vorontsov, the cousin and first lady-in-waiting to the Empress Elizabeth, confided to the Vice-Chancellor that he was carrying a personal letter addressed to the Vice-Chancellor from the Prince de Conti. But since the Chevalier had been uncertain whether this letter would please or displease the Vice-Chancellor, he had delayed giving it to him until that day. The Vice-Chancellor avidly read this letter and saw that it represented Louis XV's personal desire to reestablish a harmonious relationship between the two sovereigns — the Empress Elizabeth and King Louis XV — as well as a solid understanding between the two empires. The letter proposed a direct correspondence between them, whether by secret courier or by mail in code. The Vice-Chancellor said: "Give me several days to give you a definite response to this matter."

After three days, the Vice-Chancellor told him: "The Empress has always liked Louis XV. She accepts with great pleasure the offer of a secret correspondence. But how will it be handled? She cannot confide this secret to anyone. She does not know how to write in French very well. Where could she find a woman who could write French well enough to express the responses of her court to the King, encode the letters, and decode the answers? The Empress, to cover her actions, would like to find an honest and pleasant French woman who is well educated and who can function as her reader of French. The Empress would employ her to write, encode, and decode this secret correspondence."

The Chevalier said: "I do not know of any woman who might meet the needs of the Empress, but I will communicate the Empress's wishes to the Prince. He will certainly be able to find, perhaps in Paris, a lady such as the one the Empress seeks."

Soon after the Prince de Conti said to Douglas: "It is not possible to find a modest, circumspect young woman in Paris. The more Parisian women are circumspect, the more they are ignorant and stupid. If a Parisian is intelligent and of good moral character, she soon becomes mean spirited. Regarding her knowledge of the world as a young woman, she brings nothing but a mastery of the social world, fashions, and the concerns of women. Not a single one knows any Latin, nor how to write French well. Where would we find one who knows how to word succinctly a dispatch, how to decode and encode, and is well-informed about the politics of the European courts? We would need one or two armies to prepare a young woman for such work. And our secret correspondence between the King and the Empress of Russia is urgent in the present circumstances. Nevertheless, you and I both know a young man whom I am protecting and who is himself more circumspect and more knowledgeable than all the young women in Paris. This is our d'Eon, who is a dragoon of virtue.[36] I cannot send him as a reader for the Empress, but I can send him as the secretary to vice-chancellor Comte de Vorontsov for his correspondence in French with the various European courts. If young d'Eon does not suit the vice-chancellor, he will remain with you as secretary of the legation because I have so much confidence in your zeal, dexterity, and talent that I believe your secret mission will soon become public. Such is my hope for your prompt success."

Since much of what happened here is secret, lengthy, and warrants a long chapter, I will simply tell you that the result of my first secret mission to Russia was that I did not become the Russian Empress's reader simply because of vice-chancellor Comte de Vorontsov's fear of the drunkenness, vigilance, and malice of high chancellor Comte Bestuchev DuDrumin. Bestuchev was his personal enemy, and the enemy of France and the French, while being a great friend of England and Prussia. Both countries frequently paid him off because he was the instigator of the disgrace and expulsion of the Marquis de la Chétardie, the Ambassador from France.[37]

Instead of being the Empress's reader, a short while later I became[m] the secretary of the legation for the Chevalier Douglas who was appointed plenipotentiary minister from France to St. Petersburg. I then became[m] in succession the Secretary of the Embassy of the Marquis de l'Hôpital, Ensign, Lieutenant, and Captain of the dragoons—what I always wanted to be— then Captain in charge of the army's volunteers, Aide-de-Camp for the Comte and for the Maréchal de Broglie. Then I became Chief Secretary for the Duc de Nivernais's mission in London, which undertook the negotiation of the Treaty of 1763. After his departure, I was appointed plenipotentiary minister. Next I faced the unfortunate German quarrels that the Comte de Guerchy (a friend for thirty years of the Duc de Praslin, the Duc de Soubise, and the Marquise de Pompadour, as well as a great enemy of the Maréchal and the Comte de Broglie ever since the Battle of Kaufen in Westphalia) stirred up for me to deal with in London.[38] Guerchy left the city as Horace left the field of battle, *Relicta non bene Parmula*.[39] He departed London precipitously on July 17, 1767, and left this world on September 17, 1767, without ever explaining his actions to his master the King, who had sent him to England. The King immediately exiled him to his estate in the provinces. He died overcome by shame and despair at not having been appointed Duc and *pair* as had been his predecessors and as his old friend, the Duc de Praslin, had promised him. Louis XV, who was well informed about all that Guerchy had done and not done in London, was inexorable. Far from signing the ducal documents that the Duc de Praslin had drawn up in advance and that the latter presented to the King for his routine signature, the King glanced over them rapidly, folded the parchment neatly, and said dryly to the Duc de Praslin: "You will bring the parchment back to me when I ask for it." The only special favor that this friend of thirty years could obtain for Guerchy was the permission for him to return to his house in Paris to obtain assistance in his declining physical state, and there he died.[40]

Since my return to Paris, I must say in respect for the deceased that after he confessed, took the last sacraments and communion from the pastor of his parish Saint Sulpice, a letter was written by the honest and respected Comtesse de Guerchy to the Duc de Praslin to tell him that his friend was on his deathbed, that he would not likely survive the night, and that he would like to see the Duc, speak to him, and repair part of the wrong unjustly done to Monsieur d'Eon in London. But the Duc de Praslin was in good health and had no desire to admit that he had made serious mistakes because of his anger and pride and thus preferred to avoid the troubling presence of a friend of thirty years who was at death's door and had thirty reproaches to make to him. A certain Comte de Choiseul, appropriately nicknamed "Blackbird" since his youth, answered that it was impossible for him to leave Versailles that day, because there was a meeting of the Royal

Council that evening, but that he would definitely return to Paris the next morning. When he arrived, he found his friend dead, just as he foresaw, and my situation remained *in status quo*. That was exactly what "Blackbird" wanted.

To my great misfortune, Louis XV, my greatest secret defender in France, died in 1774, and I had a fatal fall on the Westminster Bridge at midday after having thoughtlessly forced my young Arabian horse to run to avoid a rainstorm that had caught [m] me by surprise along the way.[41] As his two front legs slipped, I fell [m] with my mount and was wounded [m] in the head, the knee, and the kidneys.

Louis XV's death, the discovery of his secret papers, and my fall and injury all greatly contributed at that time to the revelation of my sex and led to my trial in London and in Versailles, which had me declared a girl and condemned me to wear a dress once again.[42] These origins of my misfortunes were the source of all the bad and all the good that I experience today.

It was then that a new theater of confusion and glory opened before me and swallowed [f] me alive [f] in my skirts at Versailles, where I was kept [f] as an honorable prisoner [f] of war in the household of Madame and Mesdemoiselles Genet, ladies-in-waiting to the Queen, who endeavored to have me emulate their dress, their work, their conduct, and their virtues. They had to please both their mistress, who was a sovereign, and their husbands, who dominated them. For I who have neither husband, nor master, nor mistress, I would like to enjoy the privilege of obeying only myself and good sense. Far from wanting to surpass these women, I did not even seek to be their equal.

These ladies worked together to make me assume their moral standards, their habits, their fashions, their pastimes, and their activities. If I don't imitate them in all respects, I am criticized [f] and blamed [f] wholly, although I am only partly to blame. What torments me is that they often have me get dressed three times over before I am deemed [f] worthy of going with them to the château, whereas I would vastly prefer to remain peacefully in my robe near a fire reading or writing.

Aspiring to live in the good graces of these women, even if I am not forced [f] to keep up with them, I am obliged [f] to agree to whatever might bring me closer to them. They have removed me from the sites of my former freedom to weigh me down with the golden chains of my new slavery, which they embellish with the high-sounding words: decorum required at Versailles. In the name of this decorum they have me play all the roles necessary to teach me how to behave at all times like an important noblewoman, whereas in reality I am only a zero in the pecking order of the Court, and I would rather be on the outside than on the inside.

I prefer the sun and the wines of Tonnerre (Chablis and Veaumorillon) a hundred times more than the shade of Versailles and the water of Arceuil, Villedavré, and Passy, which are good only for giving me colic and a face the color of cheese, yellow or pale like an Englishwoman returning from the waters of Bath or Bristol. I have not adapted very well to all these fine arrangements nor to all the perfect details that the little women at a great court are capable of creating. But these ladies, to bring me to my predetermined point of perfection, make me suffer martyrdom so as to transform me into an elegant woman.

In winter, as in summer, I find myself dressed in muslin with my arms uncovered up to my elbows, my shoulders bared, and my chest covered with a gauze so light and transparent that it is not worth wearing or even mentioning. I have a difficult time getting used to revealing what I hid for so long. These lovely ladies speak to me about their dresses, their hair, and their finery without ever mentioning their love, which I can tell they dream about night and day. This amused me for a while; now it bores me. But you know that time and necessity bring many changes to the unhappy fate of our lives, and in the eyes of society the female sex is as changeable as the moon. Do you honestly believe, Madame, that with my style of life and my personality, I am well suited to a life filled with having a good time, dressing, undressing, chatting, sewing, and embroidering all day long with the vestal virgins of the Court!

I leave it for you to judge how all this must please me. I could not contain my impatience were I not restrained[f] by my gratitude to our just and good King and my gratitude to the Queen, who is so full of wit, mercy, and generosity. The armies and the great power of the prime minister intimidate me.[43] Madame de Maurepas's age and seriousness make me pale. The Comte de Vergennes's thrift, which is as great as his own integrity, would have left me to die of hunger if Louis XV and Louis XVI had not stipulated the details of my fate and my treatment.[44] The austerity of the Archbishop of Paris and the saintliness of Madame Louise force me to comply.[45] But the kindness of the Queen's women-in-waiting, to whom my new education was entrusted, gives me confidence and ties me to them. They claim that my success will be partly a function of the rapidity with which I assume the condition of a woman. This new condition has modified my attitudes and habits as much as my dress and my face. Obedience to the King and submission to the law have guided the path I have taken. Such was the great *coup de théâtre* that transformed my appearance and my nature under the eyes of the Court.[46]

For two years my situation was very difficult.[47] Since then it has improved through habit and the passage of time. But it is you, Madame, who have performed the greatest miracles on my behalf. You alone showed me the example and the practice of maintaining peace in my soul during good times and bad with the patience, gentleness, modesty, and the pleasing manner that you exhibit in company as well as by the Christian virtues that set you apart, you who already enjoy such a distinguished rank in France, while waiting to be named to the highest rank in Spain and in the next world. As for me, I will be content to embroider your portrait on the canvas of my gratitude, as that of my kind benefactress in this life.

Since all that has befallen me in this life has happened to me only by God's decree, the King's command, or the enforcement of the law, I must thank God for everything. Misfortune surrounded[m] me only to give way to the enveloping presence of good. Given that nothing can change my destiny, I no longer expect any justice from men; and I spare myself the useless pain of asking for it. Since I no longer see anything that can tempt me, what remains in this life is a matter of indifference to me.

My presentation to the King, the Queen, and the ministers of the Court gave me the courage to fly the banner of my sex and that of devotion, and to pray aloud *cum et pro devoto femineo sex* [with and for devotion to the female sex].

⁂

Chapter II

*A continuation of the principal events in my life, including my
private audience at Czarkocelo with his excellency the Comte
de Vorontsov, Lieutenant General of the Armies of Empress
Elizabeth of Russia and her Chancellor of the Department of
the Interior and Foreign Affairs of this vast Empire*

You may try to remove the uniform of a dragoon; you can never leave
the dragoons behind. You are possessed. Let him who is on his feet take
care not to fall because, whether he wants to or not, he must pay his debt
to nature and to truth according to time, place, and circumstances.[1]

In every country where I have lived, your little d'Eon has been called
a great dragoon of Virtue. This useless title contributed more than a little
both to my glory and to my humiliation by giving rise to suspicions concerning my sex.

After having spent a long time in St. Petersburg with an excellent
reputation for discretion, I was dispatched in the midst of a terribly cold
winter by our Ambassador, the Marquis de l'Hôpital, to Czarkocelo, the
magnificent country palace of the Empress, to communicate the summary
of a pressing and important message from the French Court to the High
Chancellor, the Comte de Vorontsov. After dining with the Comte, who had
a great deal of respect for the Marquis de l'Hôpital and much friendly affection for his little d'Eon, he ushered me into his study to discuss the response
he would give me for the Ambassador, and said: "Do you have a personal
letter from the King for me to give to the Empress or perhaps a secret letter
from Monsieur Tercier for me concerning the Duc de Choiseul's request?"[2]

I replied: "No, your excellency, but there may be a message for me on
its way. While waiting you could answer the Ambassador that, before giving
a definitive reply, you must have time to consult the Empress and her Privy
Council."

The Chancellor accepted my evasive reply for a while. Being in a good mood, he said to me either for his own enjoyment or to arouse my interest: "Do you know that there is a young French woman here, about 34 or 35 years old, who is the teacher and tutor of one of the Frêle Princesses in the Empress's service?[3] She has been whispering to the ladies in the palace that she knew you when you stayed with the Benedictine Sisters in the Royal Abbey of Noëford in Meaux.[4] She swears and can prove that you are the same young woman who was well liked by all the nuns and residents of this Abbey for your gentleness and good disposition."

In reaction to this unexpected statement, I blushed to the roots of my hair. I sensed that this discovery would make my dragoon uniform lose its luster in the eyes of others.[5] Keeping my wits about me, I said: "This young lady is mistaken: it's my sister whom she probably knew in this convent. It is true that she resembles me a great deal in size, hair, eyes, nose, and the tip of the chin. Often brother and sister resemble each other from afar."

At this point the Chancellor said: "This young lady remarked to Madame Vorontsov and to my niece the Princess Asthoff that she remembers very well that Mademoiselle d'Eon has a small wine-colored birthmark on her left cheek near her ear, that at the convent in Meaux she wore gold-drop earrings, and that if Captain d'Eon has this wine-colored birthmark on his left cheek and that if he has pierced ears, you can be sure that this is the Demoiselle d'Eon whom I knew[m] in the convent."[6]

At this point the Chancellor added: "I can state categorically that my wife and my niece have noticed that you not only have the wine-colored birthmark and pierced ears but that you have no beard and that your legs, feet, and hands are not those of a man."[7]

Then I said: "Since the great ladies of Russia are such fine observers of the human form, they, as well as your Excellency and several other Russian nobles, must have noticed that, when I was at the home of his excellency Ivan-Ivanitz Shovaloff, Comte and First Chamberlain who occupies the apartment next to that of the Empress, I participated in several fencing matches with the German fencing master from the Academy of Moscow and with the other German fencing master from the cadet corps in St. Petersburg. I fought, defeated, and even thrashed them as if they were mere cadets from good families. Do you think that I learned this in the convent of the Benedictine sisters of Noëford with your French lady who is presently in St. Petersburg? If I were not certain that she is an honorable woman, I would whip her as if she were a drowsy, flighty girl who dreamed that the moon was made of green cheese. If your Excellency can find in this vast empire a girl who is capable of doing what I do, then I will say that that girl is ready to fight not only all the noble girls in the convent of St. Petersburg, those in the monastery of Saluski but also all the dragoons of the devil."[8]

After this short digression, the Chancellor Vorontsov, the most just and honest man in the entire Russian Empire, came to the following conclusion: "Everything that Captain d'Eon says is true in our opinion, and everything that the French lady says is also true in the eyes of Madame de Vorontsov, her niece, and the most respectable women in the Empress's palace. It is not a crime to be a girl or a woman. But it is forbidden to hide or to deny one's gender, no matter how courageous one might be because of the gifts of nature or the force of practice. Confidentially I must say that my spouse and my niece believe that Captain d'Eon could well be Lady Louise Auguste, whom the Prince de Conti proposed to send to me about four years ago as a reader for the Empress and as secretary for her French correspondence in Europe. If these suspicions are correct, as I suspect they are, you have nothing to fear in spite of your disguise. Right now I am trying to replace the High Chancellor Bestuchev, who has been imprisoned for life in Siberia, a serious loss to Russia but one that we hope can be repaired. You have nothing to fear, I tell you. Your circumspection and knowledge would be very useful to the Empress. Wear a dress once again and go off for only a month or two to the convent for well-born girls established by the Empress in Petersburg, and the position of reader will be yours."

I replied: "Your Excellency's offer is very tempting. But unfortunately I am not worthy of such an honor since I am an ensign [a junior-grade officer serving as an aide to the ranking colonel] in the dragoons of France and chief secretary of the Embassy of the Marquis de l'Hôpital, former Lieutenant General of the King's armies, etc."

"This is all true," the Chancellor said, "but the Marquis de l'Hôpital himself says that you make up in mind what you lack in body. In other words, you are more girl than boy. Did you not know that the Marquis de la Chétardie, the Marquis de l'Hôpital's predecessor, had with him a young girl disguised in the costume of a page?"

I answered vigorously: "I am aware of that, and I also know that the Empress found that to be a good reason for sending the Ambassador and his page back to France. I have no desire for the good and venerable Elizabeth to have me thrown out of her empire."

He answered immediately: "Your case is very different. What you do proves your virtue. What the Marquis de la Chétardie did proved his vice. He was intelligent, but he was an old sinner."

I responded: "I know through experience that the great Elizabeth is just in all matters and that justice reigns in her heart as the absolute monarch of her imperial virtue."

On this subject you may consult the third part of my memoirs, printed in London in 1764 by Jacques Dixell, printer in St. Martin's Lane, in which you will find a distillation of the letters that were exchanged between the Marquis de l'Hôpital, who was the French Ambassador to Russia, and the Cardinal de Bernis, the Minister of Foreign Affairs at Versailles. These letters served to convey the King's permission for me to enter the personal service of the Empress Elizabeth in whatever capacity she might choose to employ me. These are the conclusive public proofs that I wanted you to see. As for the secret proofs, they were voluminous, but Louis XV had them taken from me during my last trip home from Russia. Because of the King's order, which was shown to me by the Comte de Broglie and Monsieur Tercier, all I have is a reconstruction of those proofs. I do still have in my possession some fragments, which were declared authentic in a court of law. In my dragoon head, I have organized everything in good battle order. And although one has never given birth from the head, I will do so if you can provide me a field of battle where I might do it freely and securely.

The edition of my work published in London has become hard to find these days, because of the self-interested zeal of their excellencies the Duc de Praslin and the Comte de Guerchy in keeping it from being sold in France and in clandestinely buying up all available copies in foreign countries. I will both satisfy you and save you much trouble and effort by enclosing herewith a faithful excerpt from the correspondence between the Marquis de l'Hôpital and the Cardinal de Bernis, without any need for commentary from me.[9] The text, in its purity, is worth far more than my impure commentary. This is similar to the commentary on the customs in Orléans that is more obscure than the original text. Let anyone critique my words as much as they like; there is no commentary to be made about my actions.[10]

Despite all this, since I saw that my gender was so intensely suspect at the imperial château in the eyes of both M. Condoidi and M. Poissonnier — the primary physicians of the Queen — and in the eyes of the older and the younger women of the Court with their acute sense of smell, my stay in St. Petersburg became a burden, which saddened my dragoon soul.[11] This fateful discussion — whether a matter of a shared secret or an indiscretion — introduced a fatal poison in my overexcited head. I sought an honorable pretext for leaving the Russian Court. I cleverly took advantage of a malady of the eyes accompanied by scurvy, which befell me at that time, so as to retreat in good military order to Maréchal de Broglie's camp in Germany. As I rushed off, I told myself: "Here is an example of when divine influence is quite simply whatever one has decided to do."

Maréchal de Broglie then obtained from the Minister of War the necessary passes to allow me to go from his regiment to that of the Marquis de Beaumont d'Autichamp, his nephew and also the nephew of the Archbishop of Paris. In this transfer, I was promoted to the rank of captain.[12] This justifies the saying that every cloud has a silver lining.

I think that you, Madame, will find hilarious the correspondence between the Marquis de l'Hôpital and the Cardinal de Bernis because since that time I have served so publicly both in Paris and in Versailles as your respectable lady-in-waiting, so well treated in the house of Montmorenci, the head of the family and the first Christian baron; and in the house of the Duc Montmorenci-Laval, Maréchal of France, my former general, etc. If I did not have the advantage of being a lady-in-waiting having come from the honorable corps of the fourteen dragoon regiments of France, would I still today be your lady-in-waiting at Versailles, in Paris, and at your country estate? I would be a willful sinner at present if, after having learned from my illustrious and pious Duchesse to do virtuous actions, I did evil things.

Can I ever forget how much it has cost me to learn to do good while casting my uniform aside? In this sad state, I came to understand my own weakness as never before. I wailed about all the troubles that were going to befall me. I don't want to disparage the law at all because, if I judged the law, I would not be an observer of law, but a judge. I preferred to wash my hands and my heart so that I could once again wear my first dress of innocence. I humbled myself before the Lord. He raised me up; he so changed my sadness into joy that today, in my humble state, I glory in my true elevation. What difference does it make how goodness has reached me? Since

He totally alleviated my distress and since I know that this will lead to my salvation through your example, your prayers, and the eternal help of the spirit of Jesus Christ, I expect at present that I will be confounded by nothing but the firm belief that the force of the all-powerful grace of our Lord will be glorified in my body, whether by my life or my death. My loss is thus a gain for me.

If I had not put on a dress of my own free will, I would have been forced to do so, all the more because of the authority that the King and his ministers exercised over me as well as that of Madame Louise de France, the Archbishop of Paris, the Comte de Maurepas, and the latter's chaste spouse. They were publicly named benefactors and directors of this lost sheep who was found among the dragoons and returned to the Good Shepherd of its soul so that it might be included in the flock of the Daughters of Holy Mary and in the company of the women of our Illustrious Queen, *per vias augustas* [by means of those lofty ways], which are those of the Gospel. How narrow is this path, and how few are they who find it! But nothing in this world can prevent what has been decreed by Providence, by order of the Law and of the King. God measures the wind according to how closely the sheep is shorn.[13] If, along the way, I have improved my lot, it is only by comparison with my origins. Therefore, the advantages I have as a woman should no longer be attacked by ignorant people, for I have become a woman of peace and have the honor of being a faithful companion and lady-in-waiting to Madame the Duchesse de Montmorenci who has rekindled in me faith, hope, and charity so that your glory may grow greater through me. I want you to know therefore that all that has happened to me has worked only to further my advancement on the narrow path of the Gospel. Knowing that the test of faith produces patience, that patience requires a perfect effort on my part in order that I may succeed and that nothing be neglected in my new profession. My case has become famous not only in the courts of London and Paris but also in the congregation of the Daughters of Holy Mary, in the company of the Queen's women-in-waiting, and also in the entire illustrious and ancient House de Montmorenci, whose very name constituted praise in centuries past and will continue to do so in the years to come as long as there will be Montmorenci, that is, perfect Christians, on earth. May I never forget, Madame, how much I have suffered in body and soul. All that I know is that my transformation has made me into a new creature!

Now my soul is troubled. What can I say? The wind of the spirit of God blows where it will. One hears its sound; but one does not know its origin nor where it is going. It is thus with every being born of the spirit. I am like the grain of wheat that falls on fertile soil and that doesn't die. It remains alone: but if it dies, it becomes fruitful. Similarly, he who loves his life will lose it, and he who hates his life in this world will gain eternal life.

What I am writing here is not for the feeble souls of this century who love only this world and who prefer the glory of men to that of God. I write only for the stomachs that are stalwart in their hope in God and strong in their confidence in Our Lord. *Qui moriendo necat mortem, et qui resurgendo nos ad astra secum Dux vocat* [By dying the leader overcame death, and by resurrecting he called us to heaven with him].

⁕

Chapter III

Continuation of the principal events in my life:

> *The trial concerning my gender in London at the King's Bench in Westminster Hall;*

> *My sudden return to France in August 1777 as commanded by my master, the King of France;*

> *My trip to St. Denis, my visit with Dom Boudier, the former general of the Benedictines and now the prior for the Royal Abbey of St. Denis;*

> *My visit with Madame Louise, the superior general of the Carmelites of France, residing in St. Denis;*

> *My warm but fateful welcome at Versailles and the King's command to immediately cease wearing men's clothing;*

> *The command to Mademoiselle Bertin, the Queen's wardrobe mistress, to have a complete set of women's clothes made, as is done for a young woman who is to be sold or married as she leaves the royal school of St. Cyr, and all at the expense of the King, and thanks to the generosity of a woman who will remain anonymous;*

*The King's permission for me to see my mother in Ton-
nerre, Burgundy, whom I had not visited since the death of my
father on November 1, 1749, that is, twenty-eight years previously, while Mademoiselle Bertin worked on my new uniform
that would accomplish my transition from the company of the
dragoons and the army volunteers to the congregation of the
Daughters of Holy Mary and the company of the ladies-in-
waiting to the Queen;*

*All this was for the salvation of my body and soul as a
legitimate heir*ᶠ *to the kingdom of heaven.*

I will not give you an extended description of the long trial concerning my sex, which was found to be not long enough, at the Court of the
King's Bench in Westminster Hall.[1] They were amused by the boldness of
my virginity, which hid itself among the dragoons so as to keep more secure.

I do not want to be so vain as to repeat to you the kind and generous
speech made by the late Lord Count Mansfield, the chief justice of this royal
court, to the jury on my behalf and about the uncommon nature of such
a trial.[2]

It would be too cruel and too flattering to me to make such a report here because it would injure natural feminine modesty. It is the natural
boldness of men to take everything for themselves, leaving women only the
pain of having given birth to them, and placing themselves above public
opinion. Yes, it is only greed or curiosity that guides the kind of men who
want to know everything, who are not any more mistaken by the small details than they are by the grand facts, and who find my story to be spicy
because of the circumstances and because of natural curiosity. Let such masculine impudence, which is brazen and without shame, check the official
records of the King's Bench of England for the date of July 2, 1777, and
all that the famous Linguet reported about it in his political and historical
Annals on that specified day, for he was present at the time of the verdict.[3]
As for me, like another Pilate, I publicly wash my hands of the matter as
far as the public is concerned. My whole case was examined by the King's
Bench of England and by the King of France, printed clearly, engraved in
mezzotint with a chisel and etchings. For my purposes here, I will limit my-

self to the change in my situation, which is as extraordinary as the trial itself and for which there is no precedent among the twelve tribes of Israel.

What might be the purpose today of telling you the sad story of the fateful fall of my Arabian horse, Bucephalus, on the Westminster Bridge, the horse that our honorable Maréchal Ligonier gave to my respected friend Mr. Tynte, a colonel in the First Regiment of the Guards of the King of England, and who gave this handsome horse to me?[4] The horse could see clearly during the beginning of the full moon, but its eyesight dimmed with the waning moon. Not realizing[f] this, I confidently mounted the horse. A short while later, I discovered my foolishness when, attempting to escape a storm of rain and sleet, I hurried my horse along as he was coming off the Westminster Bridge. Stumbling and falling, my horse threw me over his head far in front of him.[5] I will not enumerate my injuries, but I will forever feel deeply the terrible shame that resulted, for as a consequence of my fall, I had a serious episode of seemingly unstoppable bleeding, which severely tested the loyalty or rather the disloyalty of my trusted physicians, who exhibited the patience of Job on his pile of manure.[6] Although I paid them well, they kept my secret only as long as no one asked them anything. But when they were summoned to tell the truth before the august court of the King of England, fear took hold of them. They talked as much as their dear wives would have done in a public market or in the office of a "man-midwife," or that of an apothecary without sugar.[7]

After my trial at the King's Bench and the verdict of the jury, the fatal judgment of July 2, 1777, was pronounced:[8] Lord Mansfield, the well-known judge of the King's Bench and the chief justice of the twelve judges of England, read the sentence that she who had called herself the Chevalier d'Eon until that day was an individual who did not possess what the appellation "man" promised and that she was a "virago" disguised in a uniform. For what reason? He did not know; however, according to the reports of doctors and surgeons, it seemed that, given my sober behavior, neither Mars nor Venus was implicated in the mystery.[9] This last comment was the only consolation for a maiden who during the last war with Germany hid her chastity among the courageous dragoons to keep it secure from the enemies on the outside and within.

I had felt in advance that the sudden death of Louis XV (1774) would be a fateful event in my life as a man and that it would inevitably lead to the discovery of my sex and of my secret correspondence with the King. In fact it brought about the downfall of my status as a man. It led to the trial that had me declared a woman in England and that had me proclaimed a virgin[f] in France. Soon recalled[f] to Versailles, I understood that the closer I came to the palace, the nearer I drew to my undoing. Nevertheless, I obeyed. I preferred being a woman to rebelling against the voice of my master, who had named as his first minister an elderly and intelligent mentor whose character bespoke honor, integrity, and gentility.[10] Nevertheless, I took the precaution of having sent to me a safe conduct pass from the King signed by him and countersigned by the Comte de Vergennes, who was the minister and secretary of foreign affairs, sealed with the Great Seal, and written on parchment, to guarantee my security and safe passage. I thought that, because of my obedience and my former titles of Chevalier de Saint Louis and of Plenipotentiary Minister, on my return to France I would be allowed to wear men's clothing, particularly since the King had permitted me to keep the Cross of the Royal and Military Order of Saint Louis as well as my pension, which he had remitted to me in England. I thought that continuing to wear men's clothing would be the most honorable arrangement for me to take upon my return to France.

The opposite happened, however. Since that time, I fear *Danaos et dona ferentes.*[11] Arriving at St. Denis, I was required[f] to remain there for twenty-four hours. I am obliged[f] to go on at some length about my stop at this safe way station because, as you will soon see, in the Royal Abbey of St. Denis and in the Carmelite Monastery there were three important individuals: Dom Boudier, the former general of the Benedictines and the present prior of St. Denis; Madame Louise de France; and her ex-Jesuit Confessor. All three separately and together greatly influenced the King and the Queen, Mesdames Adelaide and Victoire de France, the Archbishop of Paris, Monsieur and Madame de Maurepas, Monsieur de Vergennes, and the Maréchal de Broglie, who, although a skillful general, had dipped his valiant sword into the holy water of his relative Christophe de Beaumont, the Archbishop of Paris.[12] This saintly cohort worked together to robe the poor Captain of the dragoons in the first innocent dress of Mademoiselle d'Eon de Beaumont, who had taken a false turn[f] and hidden[f] among the dragoons of the regiment of the Marquis Beaumont d'Autichamp, the nephew of the Maréchal de Broglie and the Archbishop of Paris. What mattered was to have the Chevalier d'Eon voluntarily or forcibly recant his errors and take up wearing a dress, which would be the assured harbinger of his future happiness and his fortune. According to them this event should make a strong impression on the minds of several French women who, like Mademoiselle d'Eon, were of a mind to not follow *uterinâ sed de furore bellicâ* [according to their wombs but according to their warlike fervor] in carrying arms against the enemies of France.

My stay at St. Denis was for me the next to the last one in my life as a man. Having reached[m] the door of the Abbey of St. Denis with my traveling companion, the Sieur le Seine de la Chèvre, in order to stop briefly to see Dom Boudier, the latter had us get out of our carriage and told us: "I have been waiting for you for two days." He welcomed us with great joy; but, as a special consideration for me, which caused me considerable pain, he put me in an apartment reserved for women who came to visit their sons who were monks in this old and wealthy Royal Abbey. We were served an excellent meatless dinner. Appreciative[f] and yet painfully embarrassed[f] at being treated[m] like a mother while in uniform, I wanted to leave after the coffee. He stopped me and said: "I will not let you leave without first presenting you to Madame Louise, who is very interested in your fate because of the interest that Louis XV took in you."

Obediently, I allowed myself to be led to her. When we arrived at her reception room, before she pulled up the green shade covering the grill, she asked Dom Boudier: "How is Mademoiselle d'Eon dressed[f]?" He answered: "Madame, she is passing through St. Denis on her journey from London to Versailles. She is still wearing her traveling clothes, that is to say, her uniform." "Alas," she said, "has she forgotten that her name is Charlotte-Geneviève-Louise-Auguste-Marie d'Eon? When she has taken to wearing a dress once again, she may return. I will receive her then with pleasure." Dom Boudier answered sadly: "Madame, soon Mademoiselle d'Eon will be made worthy[f] of being presented[f] to you."

For my part, I said: "Madame, don't charge me with this sin. I was raised[f] like this. Your illustrious father knew it and made use of me. But now that he is dead, I have become[m] a useless servant[f]. However, our dead King is worth as much as any living king. I know what I will do. I will get up and go to my mother and tell her: 'My good mother, I have sinned against heaven and before you, and I am no longer worthy to be called your son; but soon my sin will be washed away, and she who was hidden[f] among the dragoons and the army's volunteers will soon, either voluntarily or by legal edict, be called[f] your dear daughter and your beloved[f] both at Court and in the city. I am closer to salvation than when I left[m] London. My night is over, and day is coming when I will be stripped of my dragoon uniform, my weapons, and my works of darkness. I will soon be clothed[f] in the light and the virtues of your dress in order to conduct myself respectably in the full light of day.'"

Madame Louise then said: "Mademoiselle d'Eon, kindly go into the next room. I want to speak to Dom Boudier."

I immediately went into the next room. A half-hour later, Dom Boudier came to appease my worries. I was afraid of being taken by surprise[f] and being made[f] a prisoner[f] of war in this holy monastery. Dom Boudier, who was as sad as I was perplexed[f], brought me by carriage to Madame Louise's ex-Jesuit confessor.[13] This clever Reverend Father of Loyola, unfortunately a colleague of Malagrida, told us: "Given the extraordinary situation in which Mademoiselle d'Eon finds herself, Madame Louise could not act otherwise."

Quite naturally the Reverend Father Tabourin gave me a fine speech on the need to convert my red outfit into a pure and spotless dress of white satin. At that point Dom Boudier told me that Madame Louise was to write to her nephew the King in Versailles that very evening in order to speed my conversion and to put an end to the scandal of seeing in pants the woman who was known[f] to have been secretly protected[f] by her renowned father. He went on to say that the fact that she still wore men's clothing was extremely indecent in the eyes of the public and that the Archbishop of Paris would forbid her from entering any church in his diocese if she was not soon forced to wear a dress.

I then said to Dom Boudier: "If I continue to visit the holy men and women of St. Denis, I will soon be excommunicated[f] *ipso facto.* People will call to me at the door of the church: *sancta sanctis foris canes* [get out of the holy of holies, you dog]. If I go to see Voltaire, my uncle's former friend, he is going to tell me: 'The priests are not what a vain populace thinks it is; its gullibility constitutes the extent of its knowledge.' I don't know what to do nor which male or female saint to ask to protect me."[14]

Thereupon I received yet another stinging reprimand. The reverend said to me: "Take care not to see Voltaire. He will corrupt you. You should consult the Church. Outside the Church, there is no salvation."

After this imperious statement, I left unconsoled[f] but very pensive[f] and lost in thought[f]. Along the way, I said to Dom Boudier: "This is an awe-inspiring knock on the door of my heart and, at the same time, a mortal blow to the drawbridge of my pants." He replied: "Don't talk this way, Mademoiselle. What Madame Louise said to you is more serious than you think. Let's go into the choir of our church to pray at the tomb of Louis XV. We will ask God to intercede and illuminate the new path you must take."

After doing this, he had me return quickly to the separate apartment intended for women visiting this Abbey. He spoke in private to my traveling companion, the Sieur le Seine de la Chèvre, who was from his region and whom he had known for a long time: "I have made a serious mistake in bringing Mademoiselle d'Eon in men's clothing to call on Madame Louise without her permission. Mademoiselle d'Eon for her part unwisely took advantage of the freedom to roam around in our garden, our cloister, our chapter, our refectory, and dormitory unbeknownst to me. She indeed demonstrated the curiosity of her gender. I must immediately write a note to the King apologizing for this matter."

La Chèvre hurried to inform me about the good Father's concerns. My response was simply to shrug my shoulders in pity: "The King," I said, "has many other things to think about. I believe that he does not trouble himself with the trifling affairs of monks and sparrows, popes and butterflies. *De minimis non curat pretor* [One does not care more for the least important]. He has many other dogs, generals, ministers, and functionaries to thrash. Oh, if I were to dazzle the Pope with the fact that I went to Germany many times by foot and on horseback with my dragoons, with my young friend the Marquis de Richechouard and my old friend Colonel Monet to visit and guard day and night the famous women's Abbey of Gandersheim and the former Abbey of Benedictine women at Willebadessen, four miles from Daderborn, our holy Father would have impatiently sent me to confess to Popess Joan or to walk to the shrines of Saint James in Galicia, or in Coventry; or he would have thought he was doing a worthy deed by sending me off forever to protect the good nuns day and night as I had done against the assaults of General Luckner's volunteers or against the daytime attacks of the Black Hussards of the King of Prussia and against all the nighttime surprises of General Gribeauville's White Sailors.[15] Ha! Alas! If our Holy Father the Pope knew the story of what happened to me at the holy Abbey of Willebadessen, whose abbess is a princess of the Holy Roman Empire, without consulting the devil's lawyer, he would have me canonized in the court of Rome without my paying huge sums to the Datar.[16] And he would laugh about it with Popess Joan loud enough for the angels to hear."

After having produced his well-written epistle to the King about my dragoon faux pas, Dom Boudier came to tell us: "I have ordered our dinner in private."[17]

I said to Dom Boudier: "I am overwhelmed[f] by your hospitality and your generosity, but I am sorely tempted[f] to order the horses readied to return to London because, from what I see here, I don't want to know what awaits me at Versailles. I am afraid I will be sent[m] to the Trappist Reformed Abbey."[18]

Lifting his hands to heaven, Dom Boudier immediately replied: "May God keep you from ever carrying out such a plan. You are no doubt unaware that, since Boulogne, where you got off[f] the boat from England, you have been closely followed. If you turn back, you will be immediately arrested[f]. It is your men's clothing that clouds your mind and brings death to your soul. Wear a dress once again: it will give you your life back through submission to your duty. It will deliver you from your temptations and all your hardships. It will secure forgiveness for you from God, the King, and the Queen. It will inspire a great interest toward you in the pious Madame Louise's heart and in the Archbishop's. You will become once again a Christian woman. The Lord will be with you. He will shower you with gifts and glory. All this I foresee for you."

I listened to every word that Dom Boudier spoke to me. Understanding that he was more learned than I was, my heart sighed and my body trembled right down to its depths. After a moment of reflection, I said to Dom Boudier: "I accept your words as words of life. I will no longer stubbornly oppose the spirit that inspires you. I will do as you have told me. I see that I have crossed the Rubicon. I will be like Caesar, I will not be demoted. It is not a matter here of saving the Republic. It is only a question of saving a poor woman who had been protected by the late King. I have never run away[m] from a field of battle. I have never acted like my friend Horace, *relicta non bene parmula*.[19] I will not run away on the road to Versailles. I am assured[f] of finding in Versailles a generous King and his beneficent ministers. I have had lunch here. I will have dinner and sleep at Versailles. Long live the children of Saint Benedict.[20] If I eat them, they will not eat me. They are not as dangerous as the dragoons."

My positive attitude pleased the old general Dom Boudier, who said: "Since I have made you brave, I want to offer you some good wine from your region of Tonnerre. I will invite Dom Roussel, who was recently the prior of the former Benedictine Abbey of Saint Michel at Tonnerre, and who is a friend of your mother, your sister, and your whole family, to have dinner with us. It's only been a month since his return from Tonnerre to St. Denis."

Dom Roussel, who had heard much about me without ever having seen me, soon arrived and appeared to be overwhelmed with joy. At dessert Dom Boudier said: "I am curious to know what prayer Mademoiselle d'Eon said at the foot of Louis XV's catafalque."

I answered: "My prayer was the one that was appropriate for a heart full of appreciation for his benefactor and of sadness for my position, which was not knowing whether I was still alive."

"Tell us your prayer."

"Here it is: 'Lord, forgive the sins of your good Louis XV who equally did both good and evil. His ministers and his courtiers are more guilty than he is. Have pity on me who was able to do neither good nor evil.'"

Dom Boudier told me: "This is a good prayer, but it is very short. It is biting."

I answered: "*In vino veritas! Brevis oratio penetrat cielos, longua potatio ebriat potos* [In wine is truth. A short prayer penetrates the heavens; a long drinking bout leads drinkers to inebriation]. If you want me to compose a prayer as long as that of a pious Benedictine or an emaciated Carthusian monk, then I will address heaven as follows, *Deo optimo maximo* [To God, the best and the mightiest]. 'My God, our Creator and Protector, Supreme Being, supremely Good and Almighty, I offer you, I give you, I devote to you my heart. Please take it so that no other creature may take it and run off with it. Glory be to the Father, the Son, and the Holy Spirit, as it was in the beginning, as it is now, and as it will always be. *Dixi: Benedictus, Benedicat nos* [I said this: O Blessed One, Bless us].'"

Immediately Dom Boudier said: "I am delighted and beside myself with pleasure to hear your words."

Dom Roussel exclaimed: "Who would believe that so much wisdom, religion, and humility could come from the little town of Tonnerre, where minds are as heady and scintillating as the white wine of the region."

I replied: "Do not be so surprised. Madame Louise, her confessor, and Dom Boudier put some holy water from St. Denis in our wine from Tonnerre. Guided^m by God's grace, he then brought^f me here, no doubt to be led^f with my hands bound at the feet of the great Confessor of Notre Dame, who will wash away the sin of my red uniform, which I still wear, to prepare me for the whiteness of my first dress of innocence."

When this group retired, I bedded down in the small part of the building separate from the Abbey and that was intended for the mothers and sisters of the religious who come there to visit them. The young and old monks and all the lay and hooded brothers of the convent were surprised or scandalized to see a dragoon captain and chevalier of Saint Louis tiptoe off to sleep in the apartment intended only for women. The elderly Dom Boudier, the former general of the order and the present prior of the Abbey, said to them: "Stop being scandalized, my brothers. This Captain of the dragoons and the volunteers of the army, who so boldly enters this sacred apartment, is the courageous Chevalière d'Eon on her way from London to Versailles."

Even though my name was pronounced, the astonishment did not end. It even increased with such fervor that I thought I was seeing the Black Hussars of the King of Prussia at my heels once again.[21] The next morning, as I was descending the stairs to go to my carriage, I saw in the vestibule and in the courtyard a crowd of young and old brothers led there by their curiosity. In their astonishment they were all eyes and reverence. I was completely silent^m as I left in sadness by carriage on the road to Paris and Versailles. I had little hope left in my heart, for I could not hide my fear, which had first begun to blossom in the Abbey St. Denis and at the window grill of Madame Louise's reception room. Along the way, I said to Sieur le Seine de la Chèvre: "The wine has been drawn, I will drink it to the dregs."

He responded: "I want to share with you Dom Boudier's last words. He told me: 'Our Captain is a lady who doesn't use her sleeve or her foot when she blows her nose. She replies quickly and adeptly to everything one says to her. Her mind is not easily controlled. No doubt she will become more flexible when she redons her cornet, her dress, and her skirt: when she is under the tutelage of women in a convent or in a respectable home learning the modesty and decorum appropriate for her sex. I hope that she will lose the attitudes of a captain of the dragoons and the volunteers of the army.'"

During my journey I was lodged with my friend, Monsieur Falconnet, a famous lawyer of the Paris Parlement who had a kind, respectable, and knowledgeable wife. I told myself that the husband would defend me with the eloquence of his feathered quill and his chaste wife would cover me under her feathered down blanket. There, I sounded out the atmosphere at Versailles. By mail courier I wrote to the Comte de Vergennes, the Minister of Foreign Affairs, to tell him that I had arrived^m in Paris on that day and that the next morning at ten o'clock I would be^m in his office in Versailles and at his service.

I kept my word. My arrival appeared to please him and to give him great satisfaction. Since he had long been under the secret command of the Comte de Broglie from the time when he, the Chevalier de Vergennes, was Ambassador to Constantinople, he maintained in his heart a great esteem for Broglie and an attachment to me. He spoke to me at great length about the cordial feelings of friendship for me held by the Marquis de Chavigny, his uncle, who had been a very successful ambassador from France to most of the courts in Europe. He also spoke to me about the elderly Maréchal de Bellisle and his friend Cardinal de Bernis, both of whom had protected me in my youth. He finished by conferring with me about my secret correspondence with the Prince de Conti and Louis XV. Then he said: "I congratulate you upon no longer being the Chevalier d'Eon but rather Mademoiselle d'Eon." He finished by embracing me. He then continued: "I want to introduce you to Madame Vergennes."

He had the maid called. She told him: "Madame has not yet risen."

The Comte answered: "Then she is being lazy. In that case, let us go into her parlor."

There I encountered two gentlemen. Monsieur de Vergennes said to them: "I am honored to introduce Mademoiselle la Chevalière d'Eon, who has just arrived from London and whom you have been awaiting for a long time."

Then turning to me, he said: "These gentlemen are Monsieur Lienteau, the King's principal physician, and Monsieur de la Sosne, the Queen's principal physician, who have been charged by the King with paying you a little visit that will affect you and will be interesting."

As soon as he had spoken, he began to leave. I said to him: "Comte, why are you leaving? My exceptional case depends on your administrative department."

Nonetheless, he left without saying anything and went to the apartment of his chaste oriental spouse.[22] I will stop here. My modesty prohibits me from saying much more. Suffice it to report that in the presence of these two respectable chief doctors, the ghost of Captain d'Eon disappeared like the shadow of the moon or, if you prefer, like virginal wax exposed to the fire of a streetlight. Their surprise was as great as my embarrassment. When the minister returned to the parlor, the two coroner's inquests said to M. le Comte: "We have visited the nether regions of our courageous Captain. They are in as good order as if they had always been protected by the House of Austria."[23]

Immediately the delighted Comte said to me: "Mademoiselle, you save the Court from a difficult situation."

Having kissed me on two cheeks once again, he added: "Don't worry. Everything that the King will do for you will be for your well-being, tranquility, and happiness. Stay here and await my return." He took his hat and his sword and went straight to see the Comte de Maurepas, the King, and the Queen.

After an hour and a half, he returned and had me enter his private office, where he politely told me: "Mademoiselle, I bid you to return immediately to wearing a dress and thus subject yourself to common law, earning women's affection and men's respect. This necessary change will add to your character and your behavior the moderation expected of a woman. It will be a positive portent of your future tranquility and happiness."

The Comte de Vergennes, finding me uncomfortable with the idea of taking such prompt measures, said to me: "Mademoiselle, I deliver and put in your hands the King's order, which doesn't allow much of a delay in your speedy compliance."

This order made me add water to my wine but did not prevent me from publicly complaining about the violation of my safe conduct permit.[24]

The most the Comte de Vergennes could offer by way of consolation was to say: "It's not you who are leaving men's clothing, it is men's clothing that are leaving you. A girl must return to her dress by necessity, reason, and religion, according to the law and the King's mandate and also in the name of the new order of things being established within you. The King and Queen in their generosity and beneficence have had the order given to Mademoiselle Bertin to make you dresses and to make up a complete trousseau for you.[25] You must not show up at the château or anywhere around here in uniform or in men's clothing. You would then be arrested[f]. But you will soon be making your appearance in your dress according to proper decency with the help and cooperation of Mademoiselle Bertin. Tell me, I bid you, Mademoiselle, how were you able to hide your sex for so long and to fight with so much courage among men?"

"Comte, all I did was to hide myself from the eyes of girls and women, boys and men, soldiers, officers, generals, ambassadors, and ministers of war and foreign affairs. They are not the ones who decode the messages nor do the people who serve them, but it was my job to do such decoding for them."[26]

Lifting his hands toward heaven, he said: "That is as marvelous as it is courageous and virtuous! I can neither invite you to dinner, nor do I want you to dine elsewhere, neither at Versailles nor in Paris. Go into my private office, where you will find Monsieur Moreau, your former studying companion in Paris and the nephew of Monsieur Tercier. He will quickly have bouillon and chicken brought to you. Monsieur Moreau will give the order to your servant to be here at exactly two o'clock and to return you by carriage to your lodging in Paris, where Mademoiselle Bertin will measure you for your dresses."

I said to him: "Comte, since the decree of Providence, the King's will, and the rule of law have so imperiously decided my fate, while waiting for Mademoiselle Bertin to begin and finish my new wardrobe, allow me at least to go by carriage to greet my mother, whom I have not seen at all in many years, and to put my domestic affairs in order."

He told me: "I cannot personally give you permission, but I can ask it from the King for you, provided that you give me your word of honor to return in two weeks to Paris to submit to the King's order."

The next day after my return to Paris, Mademoiselle Bertin came to tell me: "I have received an order from the Court about which you probably already know everything, Mademoiselle. The Queen has commanded me to provide you with all that is necessary for your change of state and condition. Let us work together to determine exactly what it is that you need."

I answered: "Truthfully, Mademoiselle, I do not yet know exactly what I need. I only know roughly that I need what you have too much of, especially your good heart, your patience, your wisdom, and your prudence. I only know that it is more difficult to equip a lady than a company of dragoons from head to foot."

Mademoiselle Bertin, after having formed the *calpin* of my new wardrobe, said to me: "All that is left now is for me to take your detailed measurements."[27]

I will not bore you here with the discussion in the War Procurement office between Mademoiselle Bertin and myself about the extraordinary case of my glorious and sad military and political adventure. To cut it short, I will simply say[f] that two days later the Comte de Vergennes sent me the permission to go by carriage to see my mother, whom I had not seen for so many years during which I was carried away by the frenzy of war and politics. I confided only in my mother the destiny that awaited me upon my return to Paris under the inexorable scissors of the Fate Bertin, for me more bitter than pills of bitter aloe.[28]

⁂

Chapter IV

My arrival at my mother's house in Tonnerre in September 1777

Surrounded by her relatives and friends, my mother was waiting for me in her armchair at the entrance to my home. When she saw me still in uniform as I slowly got out of the carriage, before I could cross the yard to embrace her, she had already fainted. I immediately helped carry her to her room, where my female cousins took care of her. I had her take a strong whiff of *Eau de la Reine de Hongrie* and then swallow several drops of it in a glass of water.[l] I said to my cousins: "If you leave me alone[m] with my mother for a short time, I will speak a few words in her ear. I am sure [m] that she will come around shortly."

I pinched her hard in the palm of her hand and said to her: "My dear mother, it's really me. Don't be afraid. I am not coming home by carriage from London. I come from Versailles, and tonight I will tell you why I have come by carriage to see you."

A minute later she answered me: "I am very much afraid that you have come here on a sudden whim or fancy to surprise me dressed as you are, thinking you would make me very happy. But I greatly fear that you, and even I, will soon be arrested. It's the mixture of pleasure, joy, and fear all together that has caused me to feel faint."

I reassured her. I called my female cousins and told them: "I have revived my mother." Soon she was able to return to the reception room, where a number of local acquaintances were assembled.

At this point, I will not tell you that a large crowd of the town's inhabitants had come up to me, armed with guns, shooting them off in front of and behind my carriage, that they had terrified the carriage horses, and that they were on the verge of toppling the horses, my carriage, me, and my servant into the two branches of the Amençon River between the footbridge and the Pont de Notre Dame. This event seemed to me to be a mysterious symbol of the overthrow of my status and fortune in France.

That night, tired [m] from my trip and my magnificent welcome in Tonnerre, I went to bed at ten o'clock. When everyone had retired and the domestic help had bedded down, my mother came to my room and, placing herself at the head of my bed, she said the following to me: "D'Eon, if you think you are someone important although you are really nothing, you are fooling yourself. Think about what you are and that soon you will return here as my cherished daughter whom your father and I have hidden [m] since your childhood with so much effort and care. But all that makes no difference now. The hidden mystery is more than unveiled because it has been revealed openly. Everyone believed and whispered that, upon your return to France, you would be obliged to wear a dress again. If you are as prudent [f] and intelligent [f] as I think you are, my dear daughter, follow my advice and stay quietly in your bed, pretending to be ill for two or three days. During this time, Mademoiselle LaTour, my seamstress, her sister, and I will silently prepare a room upstairs [and] all that is necessary for your change and adornment. I myself—in the presence of the Dean of Notre Dame de Tonnerre, your family, and all the important people in town attending—will dress you in my own dress in order to put an end to your agitated life, which is causing such a stir in polite society and which fills me with such fear for you and alarm for myself."

I answered: "It is certain, my dear mother, that after having passed[m] through the hands of the Harpies in London and at Versailles I can no longer live but as a woman either in the world or in a cloister.[2] But let us not go to work so quickly. Be reassured that there is nothing to fear. Do you believe that in my situation I would have come[m] here like a madwoman? I have in my pocket a valid permit from the Court. Here it is. Read it. I still hope that, during my absence, the Maréchal and the Comte de Broglie will persuade the King to grant me the privilege of remaining in uniform since I have been allowed to retain the Cross of Saint Louis and all my pensions. It is true that in the meantime Mademoiselle Bertin is under orders to make me a new wardrobe; in a month I must return to Paris or Versailles to make use of the new clothes. This is why I am so sad night and day despite my apparent happiness today. Soon I'll have to bend to the will of the King. What makes me so despondent is that the First Minister wants me to be presented[m] to the King, the Queen, and the Court in order to invest me[f] legally with my new status. They say that this official presentation will confer upon me the prestige, stability, and respect that you cannot give me even though you are my legitimate mother."

Immediately, my mother said: "The Court is absolutely right. I cannot conceive of why you would want to continue wearing your uniform. Can't you see that people are laughing at you? Since everyone knows that you were declared[m] to be a woman in London and at Versailles, this masquerade serves only to perpetuate rumor and scandal. You have to be either one or the other. You are destined to be a woman; accept it. Since you had the weakness to wear a uniform in war, you must have the strength to wear a dress during peacetime. How can you still have the folly to think that you will be exempt[m] from this universal law?"

In my frustration I replied: "What? Even my mother is against me today! She who in my youth put me[m] in pants now is in a hurry to put me into a skirt. If you understood Latin, I would say to you: *non etenim satis esse putas ornasse sororem ni pariter naturu verte decente tegas* [indeed, you think that your sister is not dressed well enough, and you insist that she is not equally subject by birth to being treated differently]. Since, according to you, the Court is always right, you must therefore resign yourself to the imminent death of your pitiful dragoon. His days are numbered. He has only a few weeks left to live in men's clothes."

My mother, as a good Christian, wept and said: "Blessed be God, may His will be done, as well as that of the King and the Law. I would now rather see you dead[f] than in men's clothes."

I answered: "I would prefer, dear mother, to live with you wearing a wimple and a skirt than never to see you again while wearing a hat and pants."

In tears, my mother said to me: "You are still my dear daughter sitting in the darkness and the shadow of death. But you will be reborn, my daughter, without fear or reproach, to live and die peacefully by your mother, who loves and will always cherish you. For your salvation and our mutual happiness, I have long prayed for the misfortune that befalls you." She wiped her tears against my face and returned to her room. I hid my face under the covers in order not to see or hear anything. I was even troubled by my own presence in the darkness of night.

In the morning the sight of the sun tormented me. I counted on my fingers the small number of days I had left to live as a man. I did not even dare go into my mother's room because she was surrounded by dresses, bonnets, and pieces of cloth that made me tremble for the appearance of the captain of the dragoons, while her milky way had dried up. The next morning, at ten o'clock, Monsieur Deschamps the elder, the town mayor, along with his municipal magistrates, clerks, and advisors, all very happy to see me and waving branches, came to congratulate me on my return to France and my hometown with all the honors of a returning warrior. The commander of the corps of mounted police with his horsemen, all the soldiers from the highest to the lowest rank, as well as all the important people in town including the dean, the parish priests, the vicars, the canons from St. Peter's and from the Royal Hospital, the Benedictines from St. Michel, and even the minims all had the kindness, the generosity, the courtesy, or the curiosity to congratulate me as well. I won't mention the parties in my honor and those that I gave; they would be difficult to digest within my narrative. All the ladies were on my side, and upon examining me from head to toe, they praised all I did and did not do. But among themselves, they whispered: "Isn't he handsome? Come and see him. And he is such a pleasant man. He is courageous, but he has neither facial hair nor beard. Look at his skin and his neck. Who can't tell that, without his uniform, he has everything needed to be a young lady who will do honor to the mothers of our good town of Tonnerre, where all the girls have as warlike a spirit as the boys?"

I endured all this without saying anything because I wanted to follow exactly the advice given to me by the wise Comte de Vergennes as I was leaving. When I was alone[f] with my mother, she reported to me all that she learned from her conspiratorial friends in the good and bad society of the city. And the truth is to be found in Tonnerre's good wine. She couldn't stop telling me: "I would prefer a hundred times more seeing you wear a dress than to see you suffer thus and be a mute object of public scandal. A little bit of kindness, and it will all be over. Put on your dress again and you will live happily and at peace near me."

She tormented me day and night. And to encourage me she gave me all her beautiful dresses and lacework. I told her: "If I accepted your gifts, it would soon make my sister jealous of me. There has been enough jealousy already between us, especially on her side, since my childhood. Don't increase it. Keep everything for yourself and for her. Our kind and generous Queen has given orders to Mademoiselle Bertin. I will not want for anything. I have already seen the dresses, the lacework, and the diamonds that she has prepared for my return to Versailles."

She said: "Since that's the way it is, your situation has been taken care of and is in good order. You will have to change your tone of voice and your demeanor in order to be a woman at Court and in the city. How are you going to do this?"

"I have no idea," I told her. "God tempers the wind to the shorn lamb. Come with me to Paris and Versailles. You will teach me how to overcome evil with good."

My mother said: "I can easily instruct you about how to live in Tonnerre with the circumspectness, prudence, and decency of a Christian young lady from a good family. But I am too old to leave my home, my property in the country, and my vineyard. Having lived only a short time in Paris long ago and having never lived at Versailles, I am not in a good position to prepare you to go to Paris and Versailles to live among the great ladies there. She who has never seen the Court has never seen anything. Mademoiselle Bertin, the Queen's chambermaid in charge of your wardrobe, will instruct you according to the style of the Court for the year, the month, the week, and the day. Our dresses, customs, example, and good company will take care of the rest. I wish to God, my dear daughter, that you had spent your youth near your mother as I had wanted, then you would be happier today. But your father wanted to raise you in the tradition of Jean-Jacques to make you into a boy, a doctor, and a would-be philosopher!"[3]

I responded humbly: "This is true, but once it's done, it's done, and there's nothing more one can do. I have won for myself the glory of not having faltered[f] along the way, and that cannot be taken from me. I have the rare advantage of having seen many city men and many dealings, both ordinary and extraordinary, both in war and in peace, and I have seen ministers who did not know how to read and ambassadors who did not know how to write."

My mother replied: "Happier is the girl who, like you, has seen her nether regions and who, like you, has defended them to the death."[4]

I answered: "As you can see, mother, I did not die[f] among the dragoons, and I have never gotten fat in the wrong place."[5]

Embracing me, my mother said: "In this matter, you are certainly right. Your good behavior assured me in the past and reassures me about the future. Continue in the same spirit on the road to perfection. With the help of God, the grace of Our Lord, the authority of the law, and the protection of the Queen's influence, you will not want for anything."

Finally, for the sake of my mother's complete consolation, I ended by saying: "This is exactly what I am working for, while struggling with the force that acts powerfully within me. I am not Saint Augustine, but you are my mother Saint Monica, who will convert me by your prayers and example."

While on this subject, I reported to her all that had happened during my stay in St. Denis and in Madame Louise's parlor. Her maternal heart was touched to tears.

During the last week of my stay in Tonnerre, I received by mail from Auxerre a letter from the Comte de Broglie, which suddenly made me very depressed and put me in a very bad humor. My mother would not leave me alone until she learned the reason for my mood. Seeing her so troubled and disturbed, I told her: "Since you want to know everything, come into my room and have a seat next to me. It's a letter from the Comte de Broglie that is causing me so much torment. In this letter, he says: 'My last letter to the King about you did not have the effect I had expected. Still, my brother and I have taken all the appropriate steps. If we have not been as successful as was hoped, it can be blamed only on the nature of your case, which has received so much attention. The Comte de Vergennes did not hide from me that what had most swayed the attitude of the King and the principal members of his privy council was a letter from the Lord Count Mansfield to his nephew Lord Stormont, the English Ambassador in Paris. Mansfield noted in the letter that, after the public decision of the King's Bench, which is the highest sovereign court in the three British Kingdoms and which passed judgment concerning the sex of the Chevalier d'Eon, if the Court of France does not oblige her to wear women's clothing upon her return to France, this inaction will be seen here as public scorn for the decision by the King's Bench of England:[6]

> The public is scandalized and seeks a just and convenient satisfaction for the injuries they have received from the female captain in the society at large and in the different courts, biased upon the part of her conduct which has given most offense to our government in the face of Europe and civilized nations. The attention of the public has been fixed on her arrival and reception at Versailles at the present juncture. The existence of Mademoiselle d'Eon in men's clothes is reprobated as contrary to every principle of religion and every dictate of morality. In these circumstances, his Christian Majesty, supported by the most solid principles of a wise policy, ordered that the female captain shall put on petticoats in a nunnery for her female instruction with the formality prescribed by the law.'"

I explained in detail to my mother the contents of the letter from Lord Mansfield to his nephew Lord Stormont in Paris. All my mother could offer in consolation was: "Do everything the Comte de Broglie tells you to do. He has been guiding you for a long time. Who better than he can know the intentions of the past and present Kings concerning you. You cannot falter as long as you obey the command of our royal master."

"Well," I said to my mother, "I see that regarding my dress, I cannot expect any indulgence from the King. I know what I will do. I will make a decision like a courageous captain. I will retreat to a convent in prayer to await the outcome of God's, the King's, and the law's plans. There, the memory of good works never perishes. This is the most honest, honorable, and safe decision for me. But I want only my mother to know this, and I'll leave Tonnerre without saying a word to anybody. In the past, Regulus, a prisoner of war, returned to Carthage on his word of honor, certain of being placed in a barrel pierced with large arrowheads and being hurled down from the city's highest mountain. I came [m] to Tonnerre to visit my mother, having given my word of honor to return to Paris. Do you think a Christian girl will be more timid than the pagan Regulus getting into a hoopskirt! I will go where honor calls me and pushes me even if my heart should be pierced by a thousand darts."

Right then my mother jumped up to hug me and in her enthusiastic joy said to me: "I recognize today that you are the worthy daughter of your father and mother, who did not raise you [f] to be timid. Follow the road of honor, and may nothing stop you. When your initial embarrassment has passed, you will bless the day when you put your dress on again. What is today your affliction will be your consolation tomorrow."

I said to her: "Mother, you have taught me everything. I will recall your precepts in order to act upon them without postponing any longer. Your Charlotte-Geneviève-Louise-Auguste-André-Timothée d'Eon de Beaumont, through the power of her emancipation and her coming of age, and by the authority of the law and the King, as much the King of England as the King of France, will thus finally become a girl, using and rejoicing in her rights. *Ad majorem Dei gloriam!*" [7]

Chapter V

The episode that occurred between my arrival in Tonnerre and my sudden departure for Paris during the month of October 1777

Vires acquirit eundo. [(Rumor) acquires strength through motion.]

VIRGIL

I will present a short version of some of the events that happened in the period between my arrival in Tonnerre to visit my mother and my return to Paris so as not to impose upon the time of those who are kind enough in my associations with Messieurs Amelot, Sartine, and the Comtes de Broglie, Destaing, etc.[1]

I will tell you confidentially, Duchesse, that despite my mother's discretion, the fate that awaited me upon my return to Paris had already become known in my hometown, and no one wished to see me return in men's clothing. But everyone, including my best friends, were so circumspect and tactful toward me that not one of them wanted to say anything for fear of troubling me to no purpose, at a time when most people were delighted to see me return to my hometown looking fit and in uniform. There were only a few people, and they had at least one foot in the grave, who had the courage to throw stones in my garden, in other words, to speak to me about the matter in a direct or indirect way.

The first one was Mademoiselle de Lespinasse, a maiden of noble and great merit, who was then about fifty years old and who had published some brief, light works in Paris and who, for reasons of finance and virtue, had retired to the Ursuline Convent in Tonnerre. She came to me on behalf of the Mother Superior to ask that I become godfather to the child of a couple from Tonnerre who had been married in Epineuil, a nearby town. This woman was weighed down by poverty and children, and the Mother Superior took a special interest in her welfare. I said to her: "Mademoiselle, I have sworn never to be a godfather to poor children. Since, however, this poor woman has such a pressing need, here are five louis.[2] Give them to her on my behalf with the condition that she say nothing, except to the Lord, who has given me this money so that I may aid women, widows, and orphans."

The next day Mademoiselle de Lespinasse came to ask me urgently, on behalf of her Mother Superior, to go to see her because she wanted very much to consult with me about a request she was to have presented to the Queen to obtain help for her convent, which was poor and heavily in debt.

I went. This Mother Superior, no doubt annoyed by my refusal to be godfather and cut off from me by the double grill of her reception room, had the courage to say: "Monsieur le Chevalier, I am touched by what you have done for the poor woman I recommended to you. I thought that you would see fit to be the godfather or godmother of her child."

I blushed as would a novice, but to get back at her, I said: "Madame, I have never been godfather or godmother. I did all I could do for your unfortunate woman. If her child is legitimate, have the male or female servant of her pastor hold the child at its baptism. If the child is a bastard, let her have him held by Monsieur Bastan, the Chief of Staff for the King, a man so charitable that he is a colossus at Versailles, the grand chaplain of France. As for your request for the Queen, I cannot present it myself, but I have a good connection at court in Madame Campan, the Queen's first lady-in-waiting, who has earned my confidence; and since her father's name is Monsieur Genet, born in Dammoine, just outside Tonnerre, it seems natural that she should take an interest in the poor Ursulines of this town. Her influence with the Queen is vastly greater than my own." This good Mother Superior, a saint by profession, thanked me for the good advice and the offer I made her to approach Madame Campan in this matter.

My reconciliation with the Mother Superior was facilitated even more by the fact that I was a friend ᵐ of her nephews, the De Viviers, the nobility of the town by that name, located two leagues from Tonnerre.³ I really must ᵐ tell you at this point that, even though I hate to say it, most of the people in our little town of Tonnerre and its surrounding area were divided into two factions concerning me. The first was composed of secular and regular clergy, who wanted the Court to force me to wear a dress. The other faction was made up of notables of the area and the members of the military, who strongly advocated that I be allowed ᶠ by the court to keep the privilege of wearing my uniform and to continue my military service.

This small civil war generated various anonymous letters, which I received by mail from Auxerre. I will limit myself to a very short extract from an epistle by a clergyman who had the charity to say to me: "Although we have great affection for the Chevalier d'Eon and his family, we ask and entreat her to no longer visit our churches in a man's uniform, because all the attention of the faithful, which is due only to God, is redirected solely to our Chevalière, who, despite her virtue and courage, has not yet been canonized by the Roman Curia."

The other anonymous letter, which came from the military point of view, said: "Our dear[f] compatriot, the courageous captain of the dragoons, whether you are on foot or on horseback, pay no mind to anything priests and monks may say or write. They are more enlightened by their large paschal candle than by the light of Christian charity. Continue to wear the uniform that you have honored among us in war. Know for certain that no matter what costume we see you wearing, you will always be cherished[f] by your faithful compatriots of the town and region of Tonnerre."

The last letter said: "Our dear[f] and courageous heroine[f], why do you delay so long, for the sake of your honor and our glory, the moment when you wear a dress again? The ladies and the young women impatiently await that moment to open both doors, not only the door of their homes but also the doors of their naturally affectionate hearts."

I urgently asked my mother not to say anything about the receipt of these letters to anyone. I said: "In my position, I must silently and patiently accept both the favorable and the unfavorable winds. I don't want any argument with the priests. They are vindictive, and my hand is quick to the sword. One of us might lose his *calotte,* the other his *culotte.*"[4]

My mother, always cautious, took advantage of the situation to say to me: "You can see from what has occurred that men, who fear your courage and your skill with weapons, use women, who are safe from you, to provoke you."

"Mother, why do you neglect to say 'by men who are worse than women'?"

The request that seemed most to warrant my attention was the one from Father LaBernade, who was about eighty-four years old and the keeper of various Minimes convents, notably the one in Tonnerre. He was at that moment on his deathbed and asked me to go and see him immediately since he had something to confide in me that concerned us equally. To please this upright old priest who was dying I went to see him the next morning. He told me that he was responsible for making a restitution of one hundred écus from his fees from Masses to the Sacristy of the Minimes in Rome.[5] He said that he no longer knew anyone in Rome, that I was well acquainted[m] with the Cardinal de Bernis, our Ambassador to Rome at that time, that I would be doing him a great favor if I could get the money to the Cardinal so that it would reach its destination, and that he had complete confidence in me. Although Father LaBernade has since died, he saw before he died that

I loyally carried out his request. I have at Tonnerre the letter and receipt from Cardinal de Bernis.

The good Reverend Father finished with these words: "I have something on my conscience, and it must surely weigh on yours as well. I don't know how to go about talking to you about it."

I answered him: "Be courageous, Father. I am neither a confessor nor a doctor, but I am your friend^m and I can see by the fire still burning in your eyes that your illness is not terminal. I intend to send you some good bouillon, good poultry, good wine, good tobacco, and good mustard from England to revive your appetite and the lethargic sleep that overwhelms you in your old age. My mother and I will come to visit you in your solitude."

This appeared to enliven him. He then said: "You realize that I was your grandmother's confessor until her death in 1738, and you also know that I am still your mother's and your sister's confessor. Why am I not yours? I could bring some relief to you in your present state."

I said to him: "Father, I am not prepared^m for that. I confess to God before I confess to men, for it is not men whom I have offended."

"But," he said, "you have a habitual sin from which I would like to see you free."

"What is that, Father?"

"It is the one of wearing men's clothing. You must certainly surmise that your birth and education hold no mystery for me."

I said to him: "Don't judge people according to appearances but employ your good judgment. If through the confessional you know something negative about me, you must remain silent. If you know that I am a female because of my trial in London and in Versailles, I know as much about it as you do and the public knows as much as we do. Let's be patient and not work so hastily. Let the Court explain the details since the Court follows the Roman orator's maxim: *de minimis non curat Pretor* [the magistrate does not concern himself with trifles]. The time will come, in fact it has already arrived, when nothing will be covered up that needs to be revealed, nor anything hidden that ought to be known. In the spirit of the liberal practices of the Anglican Church, I followed its example of confessing to God before confessing to the foxes, the Scribes, and the Pharisees who are in the habit of taking advantage of confession for themselves or for their Church. By God's grace, having neither pillaged, nor stolen, nor raped, I can give my complete confession to the principal drummer of my Regiment and have him publicize it in all the encampments we had in Hesse, Wetteran, West-phalia, Prussia, and Germany. Therefore, today, my most Reverend Father, it is without any difficulty that I confide in you without your holy seal of auricular confession, what I regard as a circulating news item, that I have scarcely more than a dozen days to live in men's clothing. If I have worn the military uniform, it is by permission of the King for my service in his army executing secret and public missions in various foreign courts. No one except he has the right to inquire about it.

"Do you not know that the Lord is real and that he is in awe of no one and has no consideration for the outward appearances of men?[6] Do you not remember what Our Lord said to the Jews: 'At the resurrection of the dead those who will have believed in God and in Jesus Christ will be like the angels. They will have no gender; they will not marry' (Luke 20:35–36)? While waiting for that time to come, let us sleep tranquil in our knowledge and our ignorance, for it is said in the Scripture: 'Let he who has two coats give one to him who has none' (Luke 3:11); 'Let he who has no sword sell his garment and buy a sword' (Luke 22:36); 'If someone takes your coat, don't prevent that person from also taking what you are wearing underneath it.'"[7]

I finished my meeting with this pious religious man by having him admit that auricular confession was a Catholic matter or rather a modern device that was not likely to strengthen the union among Christians, who were divided and subdivided by much more important issues.

"I praise my mother, my grandmother, and all the female relations in my family for their religious zeal, but I cannot praise them in all respects. They have their models; I have mine. I think that one should have the wisdom of wet hens who don't confide too much in the fox who comes to wipe them clean with a white handkerchief in hand. We have seen wolves dressed in lamb skins. We have even seen the angels of darkness wearing the wings of the angels of light.

"Auricular confession has always greatly separated Christians in this world. A donkey placed between two paths doesn't know which one to follow. It is therefore not surprising to hear this donkey braying until the arrival of some doctor, preacher, or confessor who lures him by offering him hay. Unfortunately, the wretched donkey doesn't have the presence of mind to say to him: 'Sir, I don't want to deprive you of it.'

"Because a confessor is in a confessional passed on to him by his predecessor, he believes himself to be in Saint Peter's shoes. But he is very far from it because Saint Peter had been dead for four hundred years when the auricular confession was founded and invented. The truth about so ticklish a subject warrants being researched carefully in a pure source. So one has to research it in the authentic documents of the first four centuries. But if you bring me the written documents of the Greek monks, the Caloyers of Mount Athos, then I will say to you *qui vult decipi, decipiatur* [he who wishes to be deceived is deceived]."[8]

Poor Father LaBernade raised his hands toward heaven and perked his ears up to listen to me. He rubbed his eyes three times before telling me: "My honest chevalier or chevalière, I believe you have stolen all the knowledge of the professors of Oxford and Cambridge to fight with what is left of a poor Minim on his straw bed. You are in truth more knowledgeable than I, who taught theology for ten years."

I answered: "My Reverend Father, I don't consider you a *grabataire*, since you baptize others.[9] I in no way claim to be a doctor well versed in sacred things. Although I am a doctor of civil and canon law at the University of Paris, I am constantly afraid of stumbling. I realize that, in the words of the Docteur Chauvine à Kempis, *melior est rusticus quam superbus philosophus* [the rustic is more virtuous than the haughty philosopher]."[10]

This good priest survived this illness and, a few years later, he went to die in a house of his religious order in Vittaux, ten leagues from Dijon. He was respected and missed by monks, who generally congregate without knowing each other, live together without liking each other, and leave each other with no regrets. Well before his death he had the consolation of seeing that everything that I had told him came to pass exactly as I had said, so much so that he died altogether amazed at the miracle visited upon me.

My small religious encounter with the good priest LaBernade only serves to show that in many cases auricular confession has its good side and its bad side. It is sometimes a confession to a holy fox, who will use it to his advantage.

I am speaking to you, those of the devout, feeble, weak, and often foolish sex who reflect only after the deed is done.

As a result of my philosophical and Christian reflections, I am living in great tranquility; and I find myself settled in an attitude of great faith in

Divine Providence and perfect dependence on divine plans and divine will. God is never sought uselessly when the search is sincere. One can find God even at the last moment. But who knows if one will be able to look for God at that last moment? And who does not understand that one can seek God only through a grace that is owed to no one but that everyone can obtain by asking for it with a humble, ardent, and penitent heart.

Let those who are from this world love the things of this world. Let the Christian whose birth and spirit are from heaven only desire to return to heaven and judge only according to the spirit of heaven.

❧❦❧

Chapter VI

My sudden departure from Tonnerre to meet Monsieur Bertier de Sauvigny the younger, subintendant of the Queen's financier, in his château de Sainte Geneviève, four leagues beyond Fontainebleau, for a meeting he had set up when he left the district of Tonnerre; Written at the château de Persey in October 1777.

I escaped Tonnerre at three o'clock in the morning without saying anything to anyone. I only went to kiss my mother goodbye in her bed. With tears in her eyes, she pressed me against her bosom and said to me: "Leave and let nothing stop you. I give you my blessing. May it please God on this day to lead you without sin. You are going to be afflicted[f] because of your nature, and I will be consoled because of mine. The propitious day has arrived for you to make a point of your virginity. You may rightfully use it as long as you give glory to God and continue to consider the Comte de Broglie as your wise mentor in both war and peace."

I kissed my mother for the last time and said to her: "My good mother, I confidently submit to the will of God and the King's orders. Divine Providence, which has led me by the hand through all the dangers of my life, will once again in this urgent situation help me find a way to overcome evil with good. Whoever believes in God and in Jesus Christ will never be lost."

Without delay I climbed into my English carriage to go off to meet

Monsieur Bertier the younger who at the time was in his beautiful château de Sainte Geneviève where he had agreed to meet me on October 19, 1777.[1] I stopped along the way only for lunch at the château de Dorsey, the home of the Marquise LaCamus and her daughter the Comtesse d'Auilly, both very good friends of Monsieur Bertier. For dinner, I stopped at Soigny at the home of my friend Monsieur Basile, the royal mayor of the city, and for supper at the home of the subdelegate of the intendant of Paris. The following morning I took off with Monsieur Goudot, the Commissioner of Wartime Directives, to spend a day at the château of M. Radix de Chevillon, the elder brother of my friend Radix de Sainte-Foi, whose father had bought the old DeCourtenay estate, which had once belonged to Louis le Gros. And so everything in the world devolves right and left. The following day, I dined at la Rochette, the home of the chief architect of the intendant of the Généralité of Paris and his wife, and that evening I went to supper and then spent the night in M. Bertier's château de Sainte Geneviève where I also found Madame Bertier and all her children.

It was there that I learned from Monsieur Bertier himself that he had just had returned to him a letter that he had sent me in Tonnerre by direct order of the First Minister. He had asked Monsieur Girardin, his subdelegate in Tonnerre, to go to my home to deliver the letter to me in person, but since this letter arrived two days after my departure, the subdelegate returned the letter to him. As I transcribe it here, this letter that Monsieur Bertier gave me at Sainte Geneviève will speak better than I can.[2]

The letter is still with my papers at the home of Monsieur Adair, but I will soon have them when I have gotten rid[m] of this dreadful cold. For the edification of my readers, I will write here what I know and what Monsieur Bertier could have known but could not say in his letter. Perhaps he did not even know it.

The secret nature of the sudden order from the First Minister had its roots in a letter that I wrote from Tonnerre to the Comte de Broglie in care of a third person in Paris. In this letter I said to the Comte de Broglie that I would extend my stay with my mother as long as possible so as to give him the time needed to get together with his brother the Maréchal to make one last effort to have the young King understand the public obscenity of wanting to put skirts on a former Knight of Saint Louis and Plenipotentiary Minister of France etc., while being kind enough to allow me the right to wear publicly the Cross and the Red Ribbon of the Royal and Military Order of Saint Louis, which would look much better on the uniform in which I earned it with my wartime injuries.[3]

My letter was only a mere hint of the relationship and the proper position that things and persons in question ought to have with each other. It was only an allusion to the so-called decency of that rambling Patriarch, the First Minister of France, and of his chaste spouse, who saw the world only from the bottom of a bottle or through her respectable spouse's old bladder. This First Minister Maurepas didn't much like and was really afraid of the Comte de Broglie and, having heard about my secret but perfectly normal relationship with the former secret Minister of the late King, he decided, in order to rid the King immediately of the unwelcome entreaties of the Comte or the Maréchal de Broglie, to rush through the case of my wearing a dress again so as to determine my fate by a *coup d'éclat*, a distinguished action.[4] It was hoped that this decision would have a great influence on my mind and heart and would give me the impulse appropriate to my new-found status as a maiden, a maiden who would be brought back to Versailles for her own good and to force her to acquire before the eyes of the Court the perfection that she lacked.

At this moment, Madame, I will not examine either the good or the bad reasons I had for remaining at my mother's side. But to be completely open with you, I have the courage to admit that having been the first to mislead others about myself, I have not stolen but have well deserved to wear, despite my own inclination, my cornet, my dress, and my skirt. This *coup d'éclat* was for me a *coup de conversion* and for the public a *coup de langue* and conversation, and thus a subject of great and small speculation. This natural event has been linked to many supernatural conditions past and present. In every court, there are always those of us who are worried, some of us lazy, and some who are contemplative. And in cities such as London and Paris, there are always the great and the minor prophets of Boismibroda who aren't worth any more than the canons of Alcantara or the Arab astronomers of Amucantarat.[5]

In my hometown, men and women, being good provincials, cried out together: "Mademoiselle d'Eon is wrong to have fled[f] Tonnerre without saying a word to anybody. Why does she insist on wearing men's clothing despite the law and the King? She would do much better to be proud to have been declared an unsullied maiden while living among the dragoons and to stay with us who love her and admire her virtue and courage. Where is one ever better off than in the bosom of one's family, friends, and native land?"

They said to my aging mother: "Madame, what can you say against the law? What can you do against the King? Your dear son is by nature a good daughter. As long as she wore the uniform of a dragoon captain, she would have remained[f] as courageous[f] as a demon and would have poked fun[m] at anyone on foot or horseback."

At his château de Sainte Geneviève, Monsieur Bertier said to me, either to convert or confuse me: "Despite your uniform, I am required to address you as Mademoiselle because your return to a dress is an urgent matter; it is on the agenda in the office of the First Minister. You have reached[f] the end of your military and political career. However, on the day you stop wearing men's clothing, your glory as a woman will begin. You will earn the goodwill of the Court, the respect of men, and the esteem of women. Thus will you gain both your repose and your freedom. Otherwise, you run a strong risk of spending a long time in repose in a dreary convent."

I answered him: "Monsieur, today you have proven to me the sincerity of your friendship and your interest in my happy or unhappy fate. One must always choose the lesser of two evils. *Pauca intelligenti sufficit, si gratia Dei non deficit* [A little intelligence suffices if God's gift is present]. Since you are leaving tomorrow morning for Fontainebleau, allow me to use your office to write a short letter to Monsieur the Comte de Maurepas."

Monsieur Bertier said: "Of course, and I will personally hand it to him as soon as he gets up tomorrow."

A copy of the letter from Mademoiselle d'Eon to Monsieur the Comte de Maurepas, the First Minister of the King. Written in the office of Monsieur Bertier on his property of Sainte Geneviève near Fontainebleau on October 19, 1777 at ten o'clock at night.[6]

Monseigneur,
Since my arrival in Tonnerre to visit with my mother, whom I had not seen for twenty-five years because of my relentless work, I expedited more matters in two weeks than I could have done in Paris in six months. Nevertheless, I was besieged and afflicted on all sides, by battles on the outside and fear on the inside. But God, who consoles demoralized hearts, gave me the courage to come as far as Monsieur Bertier's château de Sainte Geneviève, which bor-

ders on Fontainebleau on the right and Paris on the left. I am thus on the direct route of obedience to carry out without delay the order of our good master.

Mademoiselle d'Eon has only one more step to take to bury her brother the captain of the dragoons with the full honors of war. When I was in Tonnerre, I did not take my mother to be an old clock that displayed the day and the hour. On the contrary, she only helped to make me forget the day of the month and the hour.

I place my hopes in the noble heart of the Comte de Maurepas that he will judge my case with indulgence, a case that does not come up four times in a thousand years. Tomorrow without fail I will inform Mademoiselle Bertin of my return to Paris and tell her to bring with her feathered aides-de-camp to deplume me and to sew the dragoon's skin to that of a girl who is worn out from bitter disappointment with her own skin. This girl has the greatest need of her help to be trimmed, readied, and fitted out by her skillful hand in order that I may walk with unworried assurance along the narrow path of virtue, as is befitting a Christian maiden raised in the liberties of the Gallican Church and who in her early youth has been declared an adult in the legal system of France, and who furthermore has voluntarily left England with a personal safe-conduct from the King.

Monsieur Bertier has promised to hand my letter to you, Monseigneur, as soon as you arrive tomorrow and to tell you in his own voice further information pertaining to my letter. Meanwhile tomorrow morning I will continue on my way to Paris to find Mademoiselle Bertin and her storehouse of dresses, which I will use until I come to know the taste of Madame the Comtesse de Maurepas so that I may conform to it. I am, with the most profound respect,

Monseigneur,

Your very humble and devoted female servant,

The Chevalière d'Eon

This letter appeased the First Minister when he first heard from me. Two days later Mademoiselle Bertin arrived at my house early in the morning and I calmly submitted[f] to the law.

Three months after my obedience to the King's command, I could truthfully say, I give thanks to God for having chosen me from the very beginning, from the moment when I was in my mother's womb, for salvation by the sanctification of the spirit, by good doctrine, and by good deeds so that I may possess the glory that Our Lord Jesus Christ obtained for us. "He who will transform our base flesh to make it conform to His glorious body thus exerts the power to subject all things to Himself" (Phil. 3:21).

꧁꧂

Chapter VII

My return from Tonnerre to Paris. Grand ceremonial visit from Mademoiselle Bertin to Mademoiselle d'Eon on October 21, 1777, the feast day of Saint Ursula, virgin and martyr, a memorable day chosen by Mr. Christophe de Beaumont, a great minister to our souls in Paris, in order to divest without pity the Captain of the volunteers of the army, the aide-de-camp of the Comte and the Maréchal Duc de Broglie, of his weapons of darkness and to clothe him with the weapons of light so that the Captain of the dragoons might pass over into the congregation of the Daughters of Holy Mary and that of the ladies-in-waiting to the Queen, ad majorem dei gloriam [to the greater glory of God] according to the law, the will of the King, the pleasure of the most Christian Queen, and for the edification of all the good women of the court and the city

If the law says it, the King wants it;
if the King wants it, the law says it.
Lex est Rex putens, Rex est lex loquens.
Anyone who does the will of God, of the law, and of the King lives
eternally and is transported from death to life.

MARK 4:9; JOHN 9:17; JOHN 1, 3:14

Curiosity is rampant among ordinary women, even more so among great ladies. My dear and inquisitive Duchesse, you would like to know the details of the meeting between Mademoiselle d'Eon and Mademoiselle Bertin with her feathered aides-de-camp on that memorable day when the Captain of the dragoons exchanged leather pants for the white satin skirt of a Daughter of Holy Mary. Certainly, such a sudden crossing would even for Caesar be as formidable as that of the Rubicon.[1] Extravagant detail about this event, however, would be too much and not very proper for you, for me, or for any sensitive ear steeped in exemplary piety.

The pen of an old captain of the voluntary army, accustomed to calling a spade a spade and Rollet a rascal, is not like Voltaire's, which can even make fun of the easy virtue of the Maid of Orléans and could even more easily make fun of the Maid of Tonnerre.[2]

I will restrict myself here to giving you the high points of my difficult interview and of the circumference of my long skirt, which lack the grace of novelty. What once happened can happen again in order to convert today's Church, which has become that of the doubting Thomas.[3] However, my story is nothing more than that of the flowering of traditional chivalry dressed up in the modern style of worthy French women who prefer eating black bread in an encampment to white bread in a convent. Therefore, I tell you today that at the time I was staying[f] in Paris on the rue d'Anjou in the house that once belonged to Diane de Poitiers. It was October 21, 1777, the feast day of Saint Ursula, virgin and martyr—the day our honorable Christophe de Beaumont, the great shepherd of our souls in Paris, chose me out of the ardent zeal of his consuming piety, eager to have me suffer purgatory in this life, because nothing impure can inherit the kingdom of heaven. Thus I was not surprised[f] by anything, knowing that our almighty saint could truthfully say to God: *Zelus domus tuo comedit me* [My zeal for your house consumes me].

Mademoiselle Bertin arrived at my door at seven o'clock in the morning in her fine carriage, accompanied by two of her aides-de-camp wearing grenadier-style straw hats, whose brims were turned up with hat pins and adorned with rose-colored ribbons.

Entering my bedroom, she spoke to me with self-assurance: "My honorable Captain and wise Demoiselle d'Eon, your fate is no longer a mystery. It is not possible to prove your virtue more publicly than it was at the English King's Bench in London and in the court of the King of France at Versailles. It is now only a matter of adorning your virtue with the decorum required by law. Here is the trousseau that the King commanded, that the Queen has designated for you, and that I made for you, and about which you were informed[f] by the Court. According to the order brought to you by Monsieur de Varville, a major in the King's Personal Guards, who remains in his carriage at your door with two of his soldiers as guards, if you leave the building in men's clothing, you will be arrested[f] and taken[f] to a convent. Please then, do voluntarily what will be done to you forcibly. Isn't it better for you to be dressed by me, who has the honor of dressing the Queen, than by some witch in a convent?"

"Certainly," I said, "there is no comparison. Therefore, Mademoiselle Bertin, I ask you to go down and tell Major de Varville that I give him my word of honor that, if he will return at two o'clock this afternoon for lunch with Monsieur and Madame Falconnet, Mademoiselle Bertin, and Mademoiselle d'Eon, he will be an eyewitness to my submission to the law and my obedience to the King's will."

The Major gladly accepted my proposal. I then said to Mademoiselle Bertin: "You will now have to dress me in the Queen's gowns, which you brought along in keeping with the decorum appropriate to my age and my status."

Straightaway a peace agreement was reached between the warring parties of the nether regions on the field of glory and virtue.[4] I do not at this point want to take my indulgent reader with me into the steaming hot, cleansing bath, which was to transform my skin, burnt by the sun of the various climates of Europe, into smooth velvet, as gentle to the touch as white satin. Now without any other preamble I will say that my first toilette at the hands of the chaste Mademoiselle Bertin and her modest aides-de-camp only took all of four hours and ten minutes! You can imagine my torment and my need for patience!

Mademoiselle Bertin, with her piercing Court eyes, did not take long to become aware of my impatience. To console me, she said: "My honorable Captain, don't be so surly. On the day when you are introduced[f] to the King and Queen, you will be very lucky if I don't have you awoken at four in the morning in order to be ready[f] by one in the afternoon."

"Alas," I said to her. "You don't understand how I feel. If I had the bad luck to have a bulge in the wrong place, you would straightaway cause me to have a miscarriage out of pure fear."

Mademoiselle Bertin said: "Do not worry; we are well aware that you [were] an independent, but not libertine, dragoon. Before your presentation to the King, I will have the time to accustom you to the patience required by your toilette. Soon it will become as natural[f] for you as it is for your exalted patroness Marie Antoinette."

"Alas," I said, "if I had as many virtues and good qualities, and as much beauty as she does, I would have never left behind my skirt and headdress."

At this point, I am forced in spite of myself to postpone the rest of my audience with Mademoiselle Bertin until the next chapter. Otherwise, I will not be able to finish getting dressed and have dinner with Major de Varville, and he will not have enough time to return tonight to Fontainebleau, where the Court is now staying and where he must immediately tell the Minister of the King's Household that I have completed my sacrifice and that I have drunk to the dregs from the chalice of my Mother of the Seven Sorrows.[5]

I had hardly uttered the last words to Mademoiselle Bertin when Major de Varville, true to his word, returned at exactly two o'clock. Imagine his surprise to see Mademoiselle d'Eon so thoroughly outfitted[f] as a woman! I said to him: "Monsieur, if you find me so magnificently dressed, blame the Queen's generosity and the treachery of the beautiful, confounded dress, which Mademoiselle Bertin brought for me and which reveals all that until now I have kept secret with so much care. *O tempora, o mores!* [Oh the times! Oh the customs!] I already detect a revolution taking place in my lower regions; already I foresee that the fire of a civil and uncivil war is going to spread to the four corners of our globe. Under the laudable pretext of wanting to put things in order, we usually make a mess of everything. For us a beautiful disorder gives the impression of art. Why do men want to be more knowledgeable than nature? Did Horace not tell us: *Si naturam expellas furcâ, tamen usque recurret!* [If you chase nature out the door, she'll come in by the window].

How difficult it is to pick oneself up again, once one has been driven down by the weight of a bad habit. I see now how useful it is to visit or frequent respectable people. One's welfare is often tied to such connections. It's not impossible but it is very rare that a maiden can find the Lord when she is among the dragoons, where one usually finds only the fury of war, prejudice, stubbornness, self-interest, and the love of human glory. From the moment passion gets the upper hand, there is no longer any reason, or common sense, or intelligence. False ambition and deceptive politics take their place. But a converted maiden always finds Jesus Christ in a Christian house. She begins to recognize him there by the works of grace and charity and she receives the precious gift of faith there. As for me, I am still such a novice in my new role that I still see only unrest and confusion."

Monsieur de Varville wanted to persuade me that I had gained considerably in the exchange. This was in vain. I told him: "My dear Major, that's enough flattery. I cannot hide what the law and common practice force me to display. That is my torment. Leave the nature of the beast as it is. Whether it be good or evil, I cannot change it."

Although Monsieur and Madame Falconnet's dinner was rather good, it was also quite sad for me. Why? Because the women joined the men in praising everything that increased my unrest and everything that made the sin of my youth, my military passion, worse.

Mademoiselle Bertin scolded me for not eating. I told her: "How could I possibly eat? You have killed my brother the dragoon. That leaves me with a heavy heart. My body is like my spirit: it doesn't like being tied down or entwined. I have eaten a food with which you are acquainted but which you do not yet know well. That food is doing the will of the King to fulfill the Law."

The Major spoke: "I am here to bear witness to the truth. You have done everything well and in good order. It is time for coffee. I hardly have enough time to get to Fontainebleau tonight to report to Monsieur Amelot, Secrétaire d'Etat de la Maison du Roi, who will have reason to be satisfied by my truthful testimony about all that I have seen and heard, for he is very interested in the happiness of Mademoiselle d'Eon, whom he, his wife, and his mother-in-law have known since his childhood, as well as his father, his mother, and his uncles."

I then said: "Since this is so, Major, I ask you to convey to Monsieur Amelot for me that I no longer need a father, or a mother, or another god-parent, male or female, or outfits, or uniforms, or weapons, or horses, or sabers, or military, political, or diplomatic tactics to become a Christian maiden. I have lost everything. But in God I have found all that I was look-ing for from the Arctic Circle to the Antarctic Circle, which I covered five times. I was dead[f] and here I am resuscitated[f] to return to life. Too greedy are those for whom God is not enough."

Having been surprised, the Major replied to me: "Never in all the orders of the day or the night from my generals have I received an order like the one you give me. I will not forget one word. Mademoiselle, I wish you a happy life in your perfect state. You have certainly earned it by your profound wisdom."

I ended with these words: "Do you not know that according to the Gospels the true wise person is mad in the eyes of the world and that, nevertheless, this whole present life is only one evil day? Happy is the soul who uses it for the sake of eternal life. I claim victory over the world's fatal preoccupation with the opinion of others. This is a considerable triumph over the common enemy of the salvation of the Christian republic without need of *lettres de cachet* under the great or the small seal."[6]

⚜

Chapter VIII

Selections from the great interview between Mademoiselle Bertin and Mademoiselle d'Eon in Paris on October 21, 1777

Mademoiselle Bertin. I have come very early in the morning to spare you trouble and embarrassment. But what else can I do? You must either go through this or through the gates of a convent.

Mademoiselle d'Eon. It is easy to do otherwise. Just leave me as[f] I am. I have lived for forty-eight years this way. I cannot live all that much longer. I am impatiently awaiting the great change that will transform us all, making all of us eternally equal.

Mademoiselle Bertin. The Court in its patience will never have the endurance to wait that long. Remember that it was a deliberate error on the part of your father, your mother, and yourself that resulted in Mademoiselle d'Eon's wearing men's clothing and a military uniform. But since that time things have changed considerably, and today by order of King and the law, the bad boy must become a good girl.

Mademoiselle d'Eon. If I was a boy by mistake, one could inadvertently allow me to continue to be one. While you are correct about the substance of the matter, I am not wrong about the form.

Mademoiselle Bertin. That is not possible now. Your trial created too much of a stir.

Mademoiselle d'Eon. I am a reliable bugler in my squadron. I am not frightened by noise. The Court's behavior, by its very decency, has wound up being indecent. I would have thought that the King would have been willing to allow me to wear the uniform of a former dragoon captain, Knight of Saint Louis, and plenipotentiary minister, since he was kind enough to allow me to wear the cross of the royal and military order of Saint Louis on my dress. Do you see how everything at court is so arbitrary? There one could say every day: *Contraria contrariis opponuntur* [A contrary opposes other contraries].

Mademoiselle Bertin. I concede that every day we see in the streets of Paris a tall young woman in the uniform of a dragoon publicly giving lessons on the use of arms. But remember that this girl was a mere dragoon and that she had no other way to earn a living. To do so, she had written permission to dress as a dragoon from the lieutenant general of the Paris police. But the Court would never grant such permission for a young woman from a good family who had been in France and in the foreign courts as Mademoiselle d'Eon has been.

Mademoiselle d'Eon. In a well-regulated country, the law must not allow preferential treatment to anyone.

Mademoiselle Bertin. You can go to Versailles to argue with the Chancellor of France, your former schoolmate. But with Mademoiselle Bertin, it can serve no purpose to argue. Do not take this matter so far as to have a falling out with the King's ministers or the royal Treasury. Remember, Mademoiselle, that in France a maiden who obeys the law and the King must wear her dress and her petticoat, whether to remain in this world or to spend her time in the convent.

Mademoiselle d'Eon. Your advice is wise and prudent. I would rather follow you into the royal Treasury than into the convent.

Mademoiselle Bertin. My honorable captain, don't think that you are dishonored[m] by having been found to be a woman. The discomfiture is temporary, and the glory will be with you forever. But let us not waste uselessly the precious time needed to begin and end your outfitting before the return of Major Varville.

Mademoiselle d'Eon. I see that Mademoiselle Bertin is correct about all that she says and does and that a lady-in-waiting to the Queen is thus wiser in her comportment and in her begetting than all the children of the Enlightenment and all the captains of the army.

Without delaying further and having followed the instructions of Mademoiselle Bertin, the Dragoon was, in a short period of time, divested of his serpent's skin and transformed into an angel of light. Her head became as lustrous as the sun. Her whole outlook on things changed as much as did her own face. No trace of the dragoon remained in her.

Mademoiselle Bertin thought she was consoling me by saying: "The Queen doesn't despise bravery in a well-born maiden. But out of duty she prefers to find in her decency, honor, and virtue. If Louis XV armed you as a Knight of French soldiers, Louis XVI arms you as a chevalière of French women. And the Queen crowns your wisdom by commanding me to bring to you this new armor, which must accompany your coiffure and your demeanor so that you may become the leading general of all the honorable women of France. The time has come for us to be edified and not scandalized by Mademoiselle d'Eon's conduct. Why don't you offer up your uniform as a sacrifice at Notre Dame de Paris or in your holy anger throw it out the window in order to stand witness before the people of Israel, the Parisians, the Scribes, and the Pharisees that you are now following the letter of the law that Moses gave us in his commandments."

While Mademoiselle Bertin had me get into the bath to be washed, soaped, and scrubbed down by her companions, I told her: "Proceed as quickly as possible; do not waste time with the preparations so that I too may keep part of my own dignity as it is joined with yours and that of your seamstresses. Virtuous Bertin, honest messenger from the chamber of the Queen, I fully realize that the hour is at hand for me to follow the directive of the law and the King. As a victim, I am offered[f] up in sacrifice since you do me harm in order to do me good. All women are going to point at me, and all the maidens are going to thumb their noses at me when they see me dressed[f] in style and done up[f] like a doll or at the very least like a Vestal Virgin who is led to the marriage altar."[1]

Mademoiselle Bertin. Put aside your concerns about what others will say. Must what the mad say prevent us from being wise?

Mademoiselle d'Eon. Alas, at court everything is beautiful. To please the court, does a former captain have to become a pretty boy [*demoiseau*]?

Mademoiselle Bertin. Yes, absolutely, when the so-called "boy" is discovered to be in fact a girl by the systems of justice both in England and in France.

Mademoiselle d'Eon. Speaking of justice, is Mademoiselle Bertin, the
Queen's servant, also the enforcer of justice?

Mademoiselle Bertin was stung. "Don't be angry," I told her, "I simply
wanted you to acknowledge, for you are just in all matters, that I cannot fit
into the dress you brought me."

Mademoiselle Bertin remained disconcerted for a moment. But she
soon regained her composure and said to me: "If you are a patient girl, the
dress that I made for you in the name of justice will soon be taken out to fit
you. And I predict for you that the certainty of happiness will come from
the alleged abyss of your unhappiness."

Then, looking pleased with herself, she said to me: "I am glad about
having stripped you of your armor and your dragoon skin in order to arm
you from head to toe with your dress and finery. In you I have found the
power to possess the benefit of simple tonsure without a papal dispensation.[2] Give thanks to God. You can assuredly double your chances of attain-
ing eternal life, for which all of us search amidst this life's sorrows, troubles,
and suffering. Tomorrow you will suffer less, and the following day you will
not suffer at all. In a little while, you will enjoy the relaxation and the joy
that are the natural prerogatives of a Catholic girl who loyally follows the
breviary of Rome and of Paris, which was annotated, revised, and made
available to the Daughters of Holy Mary and the Queen's women. You are
not yet canonized[f], but soon you will be beatified[f] when your upcoming
marriage is canonically approved.[3] Better this for you than a cannon shot."

Mademoiselle d'Eon. You can even say that regarding a hail of cannon shots.
    . . . But when I reflect on my past and present states, I will never have
    the courage to go out in public dressed as you have me. You have illu-
    minated and brightened me up so much that I dare not look at myself
    in the mirror that you brought me.
Mademoiselle Bertin. A room is not lit up in order to hide it or to keep it
    in the dark, but rather it is placed beneath a chandelier so that those
    who enter can see the light and be edified by your conversion.
Mademoiselle d'Eon. I know that there is nothing hidden that should not
    be revealed or anything secret that cannot be known. Therefore, I will

not seek my own willpower but that of the King who sent you here to Mademoiselle d'Eon to change what is bad into something good. Since he obliges me to choose the best way, it will not be taken away from me. What is worth choosing is worth maintaining. When you came to me, I thought you were bringing me death. Now I go to you in order to be alive, because I am no longer chasing after the false vainglory of the dragoons, but after the solid glory of maidens of peace. I am no longer looking for my own glory. There is another who is seeking it for me and is judging it. This other is the most Christian King following the opinion of his Council and his apostolic Sanhedrin, who grants me glory so that I myself might experience that God's will is perfect, the will of the law is just, the King's will is good, and that of the Queen pleasant, decent, and proper, because the Son of Man came to save what was lost.[4]

After this conversation, I quickly left the room and hurried to my bedroom, where I wept bitterly. Mademoiselle Bertin closely followed me and uselessly proposed both a drink and smelling salts in order to console me. I stopped crying only when my tears naturally dried up. Mademoiselle Bertin, as a crafty member of the Court, took advantage of my weakness by saying: "You are certainly not unaware of the joy experienced by the public in Paris when they heard sung the verses about the Heroine from Tonnerre, which were recently printed and are being sung throughout France."

That was the only thing that calmed me in my distress, for when a heart is not entirely dedicated to God it is partly attached to this world. Only vanity can console such an individual because this world prefers human glory to the divine.

Mademoiselle Bertin. Mademoiselle, I want to discuss with you how best to arrange your presentation to the King, the Queen, and the Court so that it may be most successful.

Mademoiselle d'Eon. Mademoiselle Bertin, here is the best campaign strategy that you could present to the general of the dragoons for overcoming the demon at the Court of the most Christian King. The plan is great and noble. But how are you going to implement it if you do not first teach me your virtues? If I sold all my possessions in order to acquire them, I would think that I had made a good bargain, and my loss would be a gain.

I omit Mademoiselle Bertin's answer because it is too strongly redolent of the Court's Muse, and the very sight of the Muse causes me to faint. I will simply say that, during my first novitiate in the château that once belonged to Diane de Poitiers, one winter night while reading by candlelight in front of the fireplace, my lace and gauze bonnet suddenly caught fire and some of my hair was burned on the right side. This apparently unfortunate accident proved to be very advantageous for me. It gave Mademoiselle Bertin the time to give me practice in my toilette while the Court was returning from Fontainebleau to Versailles. A few days after the Court's return, Mademoiselle Bertin received the order to bring me to Versailles in her carriage. I was arrayed[f] like a victim being led to the marriage altar.

Six days later I was presented to the King and the Queen, which I won't discuss here because it was extremely flattering for me and for your friend Mademoiselle Bertin.[5] I would only mention that Madame the Comtesse de Maurepas was convinced by the advice of the Comte de Vergennes to have me housed in Versailles as a boarder in the house of Madame Genet, whose husband was my compatriot, my friend, the head of an office reporting to the Comte de Vergennes, and an interpreter of foreign languages for the King. At Versailles he had, like Saint Philip the Evangelist in Caesarea, four wise and knowledgeable daughters who prophesized. Two of them were ladies favored by the Queen because they spoke good German in addition to Latin and French. This was rare among the well-to-do and the common folk in Versailles, where one knows everything except how to speak good French.[6]

Madame de Maurepas, a strict and wise director, having adopted the strategy of the honest Comte de Vergennes, had no trouble getting it approved by her husband, the First Minister, who had given over to the discretion of his respectable and chaste spouse the entire responsibility for my new instruction.

In the home of the Genet women, I soon made rapid progress. I was the first[f] to be surprised[f] by my own victorious defeat, *ab obice major* [out of a major impediment]. In fact my ties to the freedom of my slavery in Versailles became famous in Paris, London, and everywhere.

What does it matter that I was tormented[f] in every conceivable way, since it all turned out well for me and I was not embarrassed in any matter as I tried day and night to resemble my virtuous Duchesse in every way. Honest and timid Bertin, pleasant messenger of the Queen, in your pink fingers iron becomes brass, and brass becomes gold when it is subject to the crucible of your wisdom. But you know that in Paris, as in Versailles, ladies besiege me on all sides with their tiresome questions. Without waiting for my reply, they give me gratis their opinions, whether good or bad. All of them had unreasonable arguments, not one argued *ad hominem*. I didn't get[m] off cheaply in such an uneven match. In the end, they saw me as their equal[f].

In spite of oneself one must become talkative[f] when one is with the pleasant flock of maidens and women who are just as busy[m] with making small talk as with dressing up. If you, Madame, find my discourse somewhat long, I will respond that getting dressed took even longer. Impatiently I said to Mademoiselle Bertin: "If this is what it's going to be like, it is not advantageous to be a woman."

Without the slightest movement, she answered: "When one is born a girl, how can it be otherwise? One must nevertheless wear the clothes and the finery of a woman or retire with the dead in the dark reaches of a convent."

I answered: "You have said it well. But teach me exactly how to have the strength of a maiden without her weaknesses, her virtues without her vices."

She said to me: "With the grace of God, there is no need to despair. Do your best and keep going. You do not yet know the power of the hidden virtue attached to your dress. It is a talisman that converts Jew and Moslem and that, out of a hero, makes a heroine."

Out of sorts, I answered: "Say rather a zero, heron, an ermine, a stone marten, a dove, a mallard, or a courtesan."[7]

Mademoiselle Bertin asked: "How could such a thought enter the head of the chaste Mademoiselle d'Eon?"

"Anything can come into my head when I see that the chaste wife of the prime minister, during my first night since my return to Paris, has taken from me all my clothing, my uniforms, my sabers, my weapons, all my books, and even my faithful valet, LaGrénade, whom my mother appointed to take care of me in war and in peace, and in the place of whom the prime minister's wife gives me a large lady's maid named Geneviève Maillot, whom I don't know from Adam or Eve."

Mademoiselle Bertin immediately replied: "I know her well. It was I who suggested her. She works for me in my dress shop. No one is better qualified to dress you and to instruct you in the ways of your new life, to which you have been called[f] by nature, law, and the King."

In reply, I remained mute. Everything has changed for me. Like Solomon, I saw that only the sun was stable and that only God was immortal and that a Christian girl's virtue can be completely safe only in the Congregation of the Daughters of Holy Mary. I had never before found myself[m] at such a fair as the Court. Until then I had always seen myself as the intractable Dragon who guarded the gardens of the Hesperides.[8] My new lady's maid, Geneviève Maillot, was a great help to me in bandaging up my claws every morning and evening so that I might have paws of velvet.

I said to Mademoiselle Bertin, who privately reproached me for having worn men's clothing since my youth: "I do not want, nor am I able to go into any detail about this matter. Do you not know that, from my youth, I was not my own master, but rather belonged to my father and mother, and then to the Prince de Conti and to the King? I cannot change what has been done." As I said these words, they stuck in my throat.

Mademoiselle Bertin then said: "Why are you crying, when you are a believer? You have to submit to Providence and remain silent. Obedience to God, the King, and the law are worth more than sacrifice."

Since it was already eleven o'clock at night, I wanted to keep her only for a moment to speak to her in front of those who were still there, chaste messengers from the chamber of our august Queen: "I ask your approval of my *Trabee* for the day when I am to be presented to our good King.[9] I know that your zeal is farsighted and concerned with the honor of my triumph in society. Your zeal sought to overcome the indomitable captain of the dragoons, and he allowed himself to be defeated by an old maid who must glorify God in very way she can according to her status and the grace accorded her. Happy is she who comes and who gives herself to Him in any manner whatsoever, for the glory of this world passes in a flash.

"A reputation to uphold is a dangerous trap for those who have little love of God. But hating one's own life for the love of God is to love God in truth and, according to God, for all eternity. The weaknesses of the strong, which only last for a moment, serve to console and strengthen the weak. Following the example of Our Lord, they must adore the wishes and the designs of God and submit all natural urges to them. The best means of enjoying a peaceful heart is to seek only the glory of God both in this life and in death. It is the fruit of a holy life to be able to take this attitude in unforeseen circumstances.

"The unbelievers with their troubles and hardships must finally leave it up to God to choose for them what He judges to be the best for the glory of His name. That is what one must do in moments of sickness, when one is near death's door, and in all difficult situations in which one's soul is troubled. The best means of having one's prayers always answered is to ask only for God's will, and what is more, only for God's glory. It is so rare to recognize the voice of God amid the tumult of the world! To seek glory through ignominy, to die to attain immortality: this is a road that we don't want to follow. But when the Lord of the world has shown us the way through His example, who would refuse to follow Him? Let us continually turn to Him who said: 'Without me you can do nothing, and nobody can come to me without being invited by the Father.'[10] We must not hold dear anything that can be taken away by humankind if we want to receive what God alone can give us. If God takes care to inflict trials and tribulations upon His elect, He is even more attentive about increasing in their hearts the joys and the interior consolations that cannot be expressed and that only the elect can feel."

That was all I could respond to Mademoiselle Bertin's questions, whether they were hers alone or from on high. I answered them in a satisfactory manner according to my system of moderation, so appropriate to my position and to the disposition that heaven has inspired in me, and not that of the dragoon, which I drove out of my clothes and away from the wardrobe that the honorable messenger of the Queen had brought me. Thus I can say without flattery that Mademoiselle Bertin is the best of the women who can be found at the Court, in the city, in Picardy, in France, and in this world.[11] My dear Mademoiselle Bertin, it will soon be midnight, return to rejoin your forty Virtues as if it were midday.[12]

⸙⸙⸙

Chapter IX

The hurried departure of Mademoiselle Bertin from Paris to
Fontainebleau on my account, on October 22, 1777

On the day after the investiture in my low ecclesiastical status, Mademoiselle Bertin publicly betrayed me in the great stairway of the Court. Without telling me, and I don't know why, she took a carriage and hurried off to Fontainebleau, where the King was staying at the time. She lost no time telling the Queen that by stripping me of my dragoon uniform, she could see clearly that I was as much a fine girl as I was a brave captain. She said that she had some experience in the matter and had not been so long at Court for nothing. Thus it was with complete confidence that she had had me don the cornette, the dress, the skirt, and all the stigmata of our sex.

I can now say without vanity, Madame, to all pious women: *digna sum intrare in vestro digno corpore* [I am deserving to enter into your worthy body]. There is no doubt that it would have been preferable, for my happiness in this world and my salvation in the one to come, had my investiture taken place forty years earlier, because the dragoon disease is so deeply rooted in me that I greatly fear that our saintly Madame Louise will unite with our holy Archbishop, the good Marquis de l'Hôpital, and his pious spouse to have me put away in a hospital for the incurable.[1] Since my sickness is inexplicable, only the great *Archiâtre* of the celestial court can heal me and earn my inexpressible gratitude because I am indisputably the oldest *cornette* in the two dragoon regiments of the King's army.[2] I have served and fought with the regiments of Picardy, Champagne, Normandy, and Navarre, which are the oldest military units in these historic provinces. While I earned the Cross of Saint Louis through the sweat of my brow, I earned the Cross of the Daughters of Holy Mary through the sweat of my blood.

If I put on skirts despite my body's rejecting them, I am no less obliged to live among my new companions like an angel. It is not the body but the spirit that comforts an angel. Since I have been working[f] to transform my body, I have regained my health, and my body definitely seems to be renewed. Do not believe, as do the pagans and the Mohammedans, that an unmarried woman is a body without a soul, because since I have begun to wear a skirt, my soul is filled every day with the virtues of faith, hope, and charity. Already the Queen's ladies-in-waiting have more than paid me back for the loss of my doublet. I realize that, in high society, envy follows virtue just as a shadow follows a body. But a shadow soon disappears when the sun of virtue is exactly overhead.

Therefore, if the captain of the dragoons were to come to me today full of ardent zeal and say "I believe," without a word I would calmly show him my faith through my works, because I am no longer like that girl who examines her face and appearance in a mirror and who, after examining herself a hundred times, goes off and forgets what she was and what she is. Is it not a body without eyes and without a soul who is not alive? Thus is not faith without works a precious bar of gold that has not yet been pressed into the coins of Our Lord, from whom we acquired the regal law of freedom? Can a single fountain spew out both salt water and fresh water from the same source? Thus I would be guilty of voluntary sin today if, knowing how to do good, I did evil. To be religious, without any transgression against God, one must keep oneself pure from this century's corruption and live and die in this pure state.

In my regiment I sought only the rough and tumble. But in my convent I find only remedies and healing. Thus by a natural tendency I find it impossible to reconcile Mademoiselle d'Eon with her brother, the dragoon captain. The brother is imperfect, the sister perfect. How can one reconcile between the imperfect and the perfect? This is impossible both mentally and physically. One can but reiterate the saying: *contraria contrariis opposantur* [a contrary opposes other contraries]. The sister must therefore do her best to become perfect in this life just as her mother and grandmother are perfect in heaven. That is why order, peace, and the most perfect tranquility reign in the sister's present situation. The law willingly pays tribute to virtue. This is also why I beseech Providence, which has until now helped[m] me so powerfully, to lead me out victorious from a labyrinth more dangerous than that of Crete and to renew my strength to bear the weight of the new dignity placed on my shoulders, not because of my own merit but by the authority of the law and the King, to keep me perfect[f] within the order of society.[3]

My personal consecration by our holy Archbishop of Paris, the great shepherd of our souls, imbued my heart with the most profound sentiment of respect and fear and gives me the hope that I may one day fulfill the holy commitment of my vow to reach the perfection of the virtues of a Christian woman, virtues that must now constitute her whole glory. But every good donation and every perfect gift comes down from on high. I can receive these only by the grace of the Father of mercy, who gives the light of wisdom to all those who ask for it with fervor, perseverance, the tears of repentance, and the sighs of hope. Faith, hope, and charity are the three virtues by which we hope to possess God, and we may obtain the means needed to attain this goal only through the goodness and the merits of Jesus Christ, our great master and lord who through His death gave us life.

⚜

Chapter X

My first visit in a white dress to the saintly Christophe de Beaumont at his archbishopric seat in Paris, in October 1777

The Good Shepherd hears and recognizes the voice of his sheep.

When I, for the first time in my long white dress, was ushered into the apartments of the saintly Christophe de Beaumont, he said to me: "Your prompt obedience to the commands of the law and the King proves to me that our Lord's grace has touched your heart. Your transformation from evil to good will be both advantageous and glorious for you before God and mankind. Always have faith in God, as did Sarah, who did not allow herself to be shaken by fear. Who will do you wrong if you only think of doing good? If you bear something for the sake of justice, you are blessed[f], for it is better that you suffer while doing good, if such is the will of God, than in doing evil."

"Alas," I told him, "I don't know what I have done against God, who has not given me the heart of a woman. Today I certainly feel that it is more advantageous for me to be a good girl than to be a bad boy. But if I had not had a passion for weapons and the cavalry, I would not have become[m] a captain in the dragoon regiment of your good nephew the Marquis de Beaumont d'Autichamp, and I would have never earned the esteem and friendship of your other nephew, the Marquis de Lostange, who is also among the bravest of men. I would have never become[m] a captain of the volunteers of the army, an aide-de-camp for the Comte and the Maréchal de Broglie. I would have never been a Knight of Saint Louis or a plenipotentiary minister for France in England. But by dint of fighting on foot and on horseback, and by working day and night, I became[m], like the Comte de Broglie, courageous[m] and skilled[m] with a pen in both the secret and public service of Louis XV, in accordance with his will, oversight, and his good pleasure.

"Circumstances change one's nature. Today I am but a poor maiden following the path of ladies at Court and in the Queen's palace at Versailles, where I am going to live very soon, for better or for worse. Such is my present and future situation that I value it as much as a ticket for the royal lottery. It was your prayers, your care, and your exhortations that placed the light before my eyes and a lamp at my feet to lead me on the narrow path of Christian virtue.

"But how can I, with chains around my neck and hands and shackles on my feet, walk from my slavery into freedom to accomplish the royal law in keeping with Scripture?

"With God's permission, a stroke of grace from on high, like a cannon ball from below, overwhelmed me in front of the entrance to Notre Dame de Paris, just as Saul, known as Paul, was overwhelmed at the entrance to Damascus. Suddenly a light from heaven shone brightly like lightning all around him. For me, Christophe de Beaumont was an envoy from God who, like a second Ananias, made the scales covering my eyes fall away.[1] I was instantly filled[m] with the Holy Spirit who gave me the strength to live again as I had beforehand. This was done to show me how much I would have to suffer to attain the state of perfection of a maiden converted to God for her salvation and for the salvation of others, others who may have been scandalized by the men's clothing and the dragoon uniform I wore for so long. For weakness is more common than strength when one walks in the fear of the Lord.

"I have not seen dragoons do more evil in my presence than women do. Both groups eat with their mouths; they all live according to their faith so that they may die and be resurrected in Jesus Christ. They invoke as their father he who, without concern for people's appearance, judges us according to the works of each one during the time of our worldly sojourn in this vale of tears. Monseigneur, I hope that, with your powerful help, I will be able to become a good woman judged according to what she does. I know that faith without works is a dead faith. But we also know, according to Saint Paul, that all things work together for the good of those who love God, that is, those who are called to saintliness according to the divine decree (Rom. 8:22 [For we know that all creation groans and travails in pain until now]). Blessed be the great shepherd of souls, who made me live anew with a deep trust in Jesus Christ in order to attain the incorruptible inheritance that cannot be sullied or blackened and that seems to await me provided that God increase and preserve my faith through the prayers and care of our holy archbishop and the rare example of Madame Louise de France."

Our good Archbishop, rubbing his head and his face, then said to me: "The works of grace are as admirable as those of nature, and the least of the works of nature are more perfect that those of art. We know the worker by the quality of his works. But for this one must find a simplicity of mind united with the strength of faith in order to devote oneself ceaselessly to the work of one's salvation. I don't want to apply these words to Mademoiselle d'Eon: *multe littere te decipiunt; melior est rusticus quam superbus philosophus* [you were wrong to read so much; the rustic is more virtuous than the philosopher]. But I will say that the simplicity and the pure faith of Mary Magdalen saved her and that the learning and pride of the Queen of Sheba was responsible for her downfall. Rather than despairing about one's salvation, one must always hope for it by humbling oneself and by asking for it from God through prayer and the goodness of Our Lord, knowing that it is better for you to suffer for the sake of good than for that of evil.

"Therefore, resist all temptations through the strength of your faith, knowing that the same sufferings are experienced by your sisters in monasteries throughout the world. Thus these sufferings are your common bond. May the God of grace, who will call you to His eternal glory through Jesus Christ after you have suffered for a brief period of time, strengthen you, fortify you, perfect you, and render you unshakeable."

I replied with only these few words: "Monseigneur, I am feeling very bad about remaining on earth to see always the same things, the same weaknesses, and the same miseries."

"It doesn't matter, it doesn't matter," said the Archbishop sharply. "Each of us must remain at his post like an army sentinel until it pleases God to relieve us by calling us to Him."

The rest seems useless to report in that it deteriorated into a polite and friendly conversation about my conduct in the regiment of his nephew, the Marquis d'Autichamp, and my wartime detachments under the command of his other nephew, the Marquis de Lostanges, the Maréchal of the King's Encampments and Armies. To tell you what I did would be to report my wartime follies. *Sat sapienti* ["Sufficient for a wise man," Plautus, *Persia*, 4, 7:19]. I prefer to take a few moments to speak to you about the power of Our Lord's grace in my heart, about the authority of the law and the King over my body, and how great an influence on my mind were the favors of the Queen, of our blessed Madame Louise de France, and of our saintly Christophe de Beaumont, the great shepherd of our souls in Paris.

May my privilege of being a maiden from Tonnerre, in peace and in war, not be a source of jealousy for anyone, since it was registered against my wishes in the ministries of Justice in England and France, and since I paid dearly in matters of appearances and legal procedures in the Church and in Parlement. Having seen and personally examined all the documents not at issue in the trial, but available within the dossier and the legal brief of the said trial and appended to it, my mother, my sister, and my family prayerfully — partly out of sadness, partly out of joy — concluded that it was more advantageous for me and for my salvation in this life and in the next to be a good girl in a convent than a bad boy among the high and mighty: woe is life, even the most well ordered and the most honest life, if you examine it without mercy, my God! Every good donation and every perfect gift comes from on high, and depends upon the God of Light, without whom there is no repentance, nor variation, nor hint of change. Let us thus be pleasing to God when all that God wants pleases us. Woe upon the brazen soul who, while straying from you, oh God, hopes to find something better than You!

So as not to make this chapter any longer, I will dispense with my short meetings with the *épistémonarques* of our holy Archbishop.[2] I limited myself[f] to telling them: "The Holy Scriptures are based upon revelation.

And my transformation from evil to good is based upon the authority of the law and the King, as much in England, as in France, as in Europe. If it is not man's place to inquire into the judgments of kings, how can one sound the depths of God's judgments? Everything is good for the Elect, everything works together to support their faith and their salvation when God so chooses. He often permits their downfall in order to inspire salutary fear in the more saintly, in order to render more humble, more vigilant, and more penitent those who fall, in order to edify the community of men and women in the Church, and in order to console and to encourage the greatest sinners to return to the Church."

⋘◑◐⋙

Chapter XI

Addressed to Madame la Duchesse de Montmorenci-Bouteville

No Cross, No Crown

Synopsis of this chapter: The established principle, the corollary, the conclusion, the countertruth, the demonstration, and the examples

God is the first principle of all things, by which everything is produced and everything moves. The first and the most evident truths can be known only by reason and reasoning. That is what links conclusions with propositions, with things of the same nature, the same quality, in such a way that arguments are interdependent. When a principle is valid, the proof is indisputable. Without a principle of reasoning, one can find neither God, nor morality, nor religion. The principles of honor can come only from a moral code, and the principles of conscience only from religion.

When one has good principles, one has soon found through reason and reasoning one's God, one's moral code, and one's religion. One must live in an exemplary fashion, or be punished in an exemplary way, for examples lead to virtue more effectively than do precepts. Truths confound the impious but do not convert them. Miracles do not make saints since the greatest of them all, Saint John the Baptist, did not perform any miracles.

For example, one sees Abraham ready to sacrifice his only son to God because he knew that obedience to God is worth more than his loss. One sees Sarah obey her husband Abraham, calling him her master and her lord. You are her daughters by doing good and by not allowing yourselves to be shaken by any fear.

The countertruth is *contraria contrariis opposantur* [a contrary opposes other contraries].[1] That is the case when what one says is to be understood as meaning the contrary of what the spoken words convey. For example, saying playfully that our good chevalier Bayard was cowardly, or that the Sullys, the Colberts, the Walpoles, and the Pitts, father and son, were pitiful politicians is stating countertruths. There are people who praise and blame only with countertruths.

Demonstration is the clear, convincing, and indisputable proof of a proposition, such as that for example that Our Lord gave to his disciples. It is also an overwhelming response, like the one Jesus Christ gave to the Scribes, the Pharisees, and other hypocritical doctors of the law who were thereby forced to remain still, mute, and *aquia* [like an eagle on its promontory] in their silence.

According to these points of truth, established on principles of certainty, I see, Madame, as in a concave mirror of virtue and patience, that all the happiness or misfortune that has been visited upon me or that I have encountered since my youth happened to me only with the permission of Providence, and that this Providence is the supreme intelligence that directs all things. It is certain that one must abandon oneself to God. But one must not expect so much from Providence that one does nothing to help oneself. It is certain that no sparrow falls from the sky or from a tree, nor a hair from our head, without God's permission. Man proposes, God disposes. It is certain that Saul, burning with hatred, anger, and emotion against the Christians, left Jerusalem with letters from the high priest to bring them to the synagogues of Damascus, so that if he found any men or women of this sect he would have tied them up and brought them to Jerusalem. However, it happened that while walking and nearing Damascus a light suddenly poured down from heaven all around him like a bolt of lightning. He fell to the ground, was blinded, enlightened, and converted by a stroke from on high, that is, from God and from Jesus Christ. That is why the Lord said to Ananias, a faithful servant of God: "Go immediately and find Saul because he is for me a chosen instrument to carry my name to the Gentiles, to the kings, and to the children of Israel. And I will soon show him how much he will have to suffer in my name."[2]

Even though Saul was a violent persecutor and enemy of Jesus Christ, he became the most ardent, the most eloquent, the most skillful, and the most powerful defender of Christians. At once, he began to preach in the synagogues that Jesus Christ was the son of God, and all who heard him were completely carried away and said to each other: "Isn't this the man who in Jerusalem persecuted those who invoked His name and the man who came here for the purpose of bringing them, bound and tied, to the high priests?"[3]

But Saul, without fear, only became stronger and stronger and confounded the Jews and the doctors who were in Damascus, proving to them and demonstrating by means of the Prophets and the Scriptures that Jesus was the true Christ and that they were not to wait for another. After that the Jews conspired to have him killed. But Saul, protected by God, was saved from all their traps, plots, and ambushes. In truth, Madame, I now recognize that God has no interest in people's appearance, but that anyone, whatever his nationality or his social condition, who fears Him and who is committed to justice is pleasing to Him. Thus what God has purified let us not consider to be soiled.

It is certain that it was through a special act of Providence that the Grand Maréchal Ligonier gave a beautiful, young Arabian stallion to my courageous and honorable friend Tynte, a former colonel in the Regiment of the English King's Guards. It is certain that through another act of Providence Mr. Tynte gave me this horse. It is certain that this apparently beautiful horse was subject to a periodic inflammation of the eyes, but when we became aware of it, it was unfortunately too late for me. It is certain that I rode this horse on my way back from Bur-Hill, the country manor of my friend Mr. Tynte, while returning to London;[4] that I was surprised[m] near the Asylum by an unexpected storm in the month of March, which combined rain, hail, and a blustering wind; that to get out of the storm I stuck my horse with both spurs; that he ran like a deer pursued by hunting dogs. Although I was careful to hold him on a tight, short rein and to lean over the horse's neck in accordance with English style, nevertheless because the road had become slippery from the rain, the hail, and the wind, and my horse was partly blind without my knowing it, the two front legs of the horse gave way at the same time, on the downward slope of Westminster Bridge. The sudden shock of the horse's fall propelled me into the air over the horse's head. The horse, even more stupid than its rider, fell over my body and seriously wounded me. Mr. Nicolas Coutant and his wife, who were in my service at the time and who are today well placed in the home of the honorable Lord Walsingham, know that I am not lying. That was the beginning of my misfortune, whose consequences have been cruel for me in many ways. In order to be treated[f] I was obliged to have recourse to doctors, whom I paid dearly to ensure their silence.[5] They kept silent for a long time. But when a trial was finally held about my sex, the so-called apothecary male midwives had hardly been summoned to appear before the royal court of the King's Bench when these terrified individuals made out affidavits that were then recorded and printed for my trial, which took place, by the grace of God, on July 2, 1777. It would be improper to my womanhood to go into detail here about their statements.

Our famous Linguet, a lawyer in the Parlement de Paris, was a witness to the defense and to the outcome of the trial. He reported everything in his political *Annales,* published in London at that time.[6] The truthfulness of this historian is a trustworthy guarantee regarding the truth of the facts he reports. For it is said in the Bible: "The testimony of two honorable persons is the truth."[7] And at my trial there were more than two thousand, five hundred witnesses from England and every other nation in Westminster Hall.

I could not escape my misfortune, and it never rains but it pours. To avoid it I did not ask for any special favor from the court of the English King's Bench but only for justice. But when I saw that God permitted this high court to declare me[m] to be a maiden intact, I said that all this comes from the grace of God. *Fiat justitia ru[t]at coelum, impavidam ferient ruinae!* ["Let justice be done, let the heavens fall, let ruins hit those who are fearless," Horace, *Odes,* 3.38]. If the crumbling heavens fell in pieces, the impact of its ruins would not terrify me. Who can prevent me from living and dying in the grace of God who anticipated my needs in his choice of my destiny?

Here, Madame, I will tell you that when the Comte and the Maréchal de Broglie did their best to prevent their former aide-de-camp from being stripped of his men's clothes, the Ministers of the King replied: "We have one law and according to this law, even if your aide-de-camp had become a general, we would be obliged to have him wear a dress since she is a woman." When I saw the firm resolve of the King and his chief minister Comte de Maurepas, I wrote to Comte de Broglie: "Neither you nor your illustrious brother the Maréchal should worry any more about overturning the will of the King and his First Minister, since you can see that men's clothing is inconsistent with my status as a woman and that it is very awkward to be badly dressed and dressed against one's nature." Then without hesitating, I spoke aloud: "Here I am, Lord, ready to do your will. I accept it, and your law is in the innermost part of my heart. I have come to terms with it like a good captain. I despise acting in anticipation of rumor and the opinions of others."

The pronoun *one* is stupid.[8] One cannot give birth when one would like. Did not the misfortune that befell the learned Popess Joan during her fine procession at St. Peter's in Rome occur all of a sudden like thunderbolts from the Vatican to the great scandal of the whole Church and of all the honorable devout women who were witness to the fine miracle that took place because of an improperly situated bulge? A deaconess or a popess should never take into her service an important vicar because Saint Paul says: "Let the woman or the widow engaged in the service of God not be less than sixty years old; may she have only one husband, who can testify to her having done good works such as having suckled her own children" (1 Tim. 5:9). Despite what others will say about me, the Lord will give me the courage to live in the spirit of his Cross and the humiliations He endured.

I did what I said I did. Hardly had I succumbed to the power of society when God came to my aid and the Lord lifted me[m] up and gave me the strength not to turn red upon seeing my name erased from the catalogue of men and inscribed on the list of women; and moreover, I saw with my own eyes, without crying, the captain of the dragoons inducted into the religious order of the Daughters of Holy Mary and into the company of the Queen's ladies-in-waiting.

I only tell you of my initial reticence and my final discomfort in changing my status from red to white in order that you might take note of and admire the power of the righteousness of the Most High and in order that you give praise to the power of His mercy and grace. God sometimes postpones healing the weaknesses of His men and women servants so that their recovery is revealed with even more force at a particular, important moment to demonstrate the realization of His decree about the Elect. I am now going to bury the body of my sin in the convent, in silence, and in withdrawal. It is better to be alone than in bad company. Happy are those saintly souls who allowed themselves from childhood to be placed in the tomb of a holy monastery to avoid all sin, all ambition, and all the vanity of the world. I was only able to withdraw my stake from the game late; but finally I did leave the type of military and political life that I was leading in order to wait in the calm of my small room for the peace that God reserves for faithful souls.

My Past and Present Positions

As long as I was wearing men's clothing and a uniform and doing political work in the Russian and English courts, as long as I was bearing a large part of the weight for the secret correspondence of Louis XV, the deceased Prince de Conti, and the Comte de Broglie, I did not have a moment of rest. I was constantly upset and anxious, afraid[f] of my double and triple secret being discovered. I was the only one aware of my deplorable state. Since the time when the law and the King awarded me the dress I am wearing, I have left behind every military and political matter. I am taking pleasure in the peace that surrounds me, and I sleep as securely at night as in broad daylight.

I have been instructed[f] in all the areas of wisdom of the Daughters of Holy Mary and the Queen's ladies-in-waiting, who are powerless in effecting harm but very powerful in speech, actions, and good works. It is only with them that I have found peace and tranquility. With them I enjoy, not full freedom, but the atmosphere of freedom, which is refreshing and salutary. I am no longer exposed[f] to the frequent earthquakes to which the Court at Versailles reacted by rising up like a great plain of mushrooms irrigated only by the blood and the marrow of the people. It is at court that I suffered so many severe blows at the whim of an ignorant minister and an idiot ambassador, close friends of each other for thirty years wherever they went: *Adinus, Adinum fricat* [Asses frequent each other]. Lord, do not accuse them of sin because they did not know what they were doing; they thought they could fish in troubled waters, but Louis XV was an adept fisherman and a fearless hunter of stags, wild animals, and ministers. This good King, as well as his unfortunate successor, have amply repaired the injustices done to me. They have both provided me with good public as well as secret pensions drawn from the royal treasury. But suddenly a revolution sprang up in my beloved country like a raging tornado, and my treasurer and the royal treasury went to the devil.[9] My greatest fear and my greatest illness when I was wearing pants was loose strife, that is, commonly called *souci-d'eau, percebosse,* or *chassebosse.*[10] But all fear has subsided since I became[f] a wet hen from Numidia and a lady-in-waiting in the Versailles menagerie.[11]

My transformation produced the expected result of the improvement in the revenue from my simple tonsure benefice. It also produced a natural coalition between me and the Daughters of Holy Mary.

During my illness in London, after the fall from my horse, I sinned only by being too cautious and paying the doctors to keep my secret. Since I began wearing my dress again, I have sinned only by being too elaborate in my attire, but since Mademoiselle Bertin was in charge of my wardrobe, my hair, and my jewelry, and since the King was so generous as to pay the expenses, I cannot be accused of any sin, any foolish expense, neither of vanity nor lust during my sojourn and my performance on the great stages of Versailles and Paris. I certainly did not derive any profit.

Conclusion

Who am I to stand in the way of God, the law, and the King? Was I not publicly judged[f], declared[f], shown[f] to be a girl by a legal decision at the Bench of the King of England and that of France and condemned[f] to wear once again my first dress of innocence? Is not the hand of God responsible for all things? Thus I responded to God, the law, and the King by my humble obedience.

My good fortune is not worthy of envy because no one is envious of doing the will of God and of the law. Nevertheless each person can become happy in his or her condition. Our happiness always depends on our own good actions. Good fortune, according to the pagans, was a capricious goddess who was responsible for both happiness and misery, all successes and all failures.

According to Christianity, our good fortune, that is our happiness, comes only from God through the merits of Jesus Christ who gave us life by his death. The fortune of the pagans could be stopped only when she was grabbed by the hair or when a nail was driven into the wheel. Our Christian fortune can be secured only by focusing our heart on the sufferings and the Cross of our Lord: no cross, no crown. Unfortunately, all the fortune in the world is a mortal enemy of Jesus Christ and of virtue.

The sequence of misery and happiness in my life is the result of my affliction and my philosophical and Christian consolation in my old age and in this vale of tears and misery where there are as many different sentiments as there are heads. *"Tot capita tot sensus: Quisque habet animi sensum Patres conscripti"* [So many heads, so many feelings: each one of the Senators has his own way of thinking] said Cicero in the Roman Senate.

Yes, I would say from experience that there are on this fertile and ungrateful earth as many blind as one-eyed people, as many hunchbacks as cripples, as many good as evil minds, as many excellent as perverse hearts, as many saved as lost souls. It is a very bizarre army this assembly of human beings, this compact between Whites and Blacks. The honest, knowledgeable, and very virtuous Wilberforce, with a courage worthy of Cato Censorius, has been working on this in vain for twelve years in the midst of the Senate that has the most integrity and is the most learned in all of Europe, that is, in the world. We all fear what others will think about us, and no one fears God who is the only one who is good, just, and to be feared. Why? Because the God of heaven is distant from our spirit and because the devil of the world is close to our heart.

Nevertheless, Madame, I want you to know that all the things that have happened or been foisted upon me unexpectedly in my life have served only for my greater advancement, not at Court but in the perfection of the divine city, which makes me see myself as a cosmopolitan woman of this terrestrial globe. Thus the departure of the captain from the dragoons and the volunteers of the army of the Maréchal de Broglie and his entry into the pure company of the Daughters of Holy Mary and into the honest company of the Queen's ladies-in-waiting, as well as his ties in the convent and his detention at Versailles have become famous in England, in France, and everywhere, so that his captivity freed her.

I am not ashamed of it because I know in whom I have believed, and I am persuaded that He has the power to have me keep my faith and my dress of innocence until the day of His apparition, having called me[m] to Him through a holy vocation, not because of my works, but through His chosen intention. My fall caused my misery, and my misery caused my happiness, depending on one's way of seeing things, because Father Malebranche, for example, saw everything in God, Saint Paul saw everything in Jesus Christ, and I see only stupidity in this world.

It is certain that our Lord did not consider it beneath Him to assume a human nature in the breast of a virgin in order to save humankind. It is certain that He had me leave the army like a lost lamb to have me enter into the company of the Daughters of Holy Mary, because He did not allow me^m to be mixed up any longer with the billy goats, the wolves, the dragons, and the rattlesnakes of the Court. He wanted to have me live with the pure virgins of Holy Mary, and He will deign to keep me pure^f and sinless and on that day will have me enjoy with these women the glory He prepared for His chosen ones in the kingdom of His Father.

I therefore judge myself to be happy^f now, and I am joyful^f to have been made^f worthy of suffering embarrassment because of the weakness of my sex and the strength of my faith. This gives me the enthusiasm to praise God and to give thanks to the Lord. Therefore without foolish and presumptuous confidence, I will say: "By the grace of God, I am who I am. And His favor has not been in vain: I have traveled, I have negotiated, I have worked, I have been in combat more than most of those who are still tempted by the desire to oppose me. Have they ever fulfilled as many roles or carried out as many delicate, difficult, and dangerous missions? Each time it was not me but the grace of God in me. And I am in no way different^f from those who seem to be somebody."

God is not concerned with the exterior appearance of people. Those who are held in esteem have given me nothing new except this old dress of innocence. Those who wanted to joust against me did not know my^f face. They had heard it said: "He who was once in combat with the dragoons and the volunteers in the army is now in combat with the congregation of the Daughters of Holy Mary and the company of the Queen's ladies-in-waiting in keeping with their good works." However, my present strength comes only from my weakness. Meanwhile, men and women separately and together in the same spirit and with similar words glorify God because of me. That's why I am careful to try not to put any stumbling block or scandal before my brother or sister. He who serves Jesus Christ in these things is pleasing in God's sight. Let us seek that which leads to peace and that is edifying to us all. Let us think of all those things that are honorable and venerable, just and likeable, of good reputation, where there is virtue or praise to be earned, and seek to do such things ourselves. Those of us who are strong must thus bear the infirmities of the weak and not merely please ourselves because Our Lord did not come on this earth to please Himself but to suffer.

May Our Lord God of patience and consolation give us the grace to feel all the same way in accordance with Jesus Christ. Our suffering will end tomorrow. Our misery is only the dream of one night. A thousand years in the eyes of God are but a minute. The past, the present, and the future are always present in His Spirit. And the inheritance He has promised us in the kingdom of His Father will be without the slightest variation or change since it will be eternal.

Everything is good for the Chosen ones, everything works together to support their faith and their salvation when God wills it so. He often allows their downfall so as to inspire a salutary fear in more pious individuals, to make those who fall more humble and more vigilant, to edify their fellows and the entire Church through their penance, and to console and encourage the greatest sinners to have recourse to the Church.

Despite my mortal sickness amidst the dragoons and the light infantry and among the politicians of Europe, who had even less power than the Black Hussars of the King of Prussia, than the Pandours of the Queen of Hungary, than the Cossacks, the Callimouks, the Koubous, the Bachkins, and the Karakapak Tartars of the Emperor of Russia, I found[m] myself healed[f] amidst the Daughters of Holy Mary and the Queen's good ladies-in-waiting. I returned[m] to my home in Tonnerre glorifying God aloud with my mother, my sister, and my whole family. All the residents of the town and all the lords of the surrounding châteaux discussed me in this way: it is the same person, it is not the same person. The whole town celebrated this event that took place before their very eyes. By means of retroactive, previous, concomitant, and subsequent grace, I reestablished, like the wife of Aurelian, the affairs of my home. The local women, unable to go back that far in history, compared my transformation to the retreat of the Duchesse de la Vallière to the Carmelite convent in Paris. Like Saint Theresa, she wished fervently to die in order to live with God by the grace of Jesus Christ, who is the only one who looks for the stray lamb and who is the only one who saves what was lost.

I know that all this will work toward my salvation through your prayers and through the continuous help, not of the spirit of the Court or of the world but of the Lord, according to my present expectations and hopes, and that I will not be misguided in any matter. Rather I have every assurance that Jesus Christ will be now, as He has always been, glorified in my body, whether through my life or my death, because Jesus Christ is my life, and in dying I win.

None of us lives for himself, and none of us dies for himself. Whether we live or we die, we always belong to the Lord, as it is for that reason that He lived, died, and was resurrected—so that he could have dominion as much over the dead as over the living.

In Praise of the Convent and Virginity

Quam bonum fratres habitare in unum, quam secundum servres, manere in templo Domini [Just as it is good to live together as brothers, so it is nourishing to remain servants in the Temple of the Lord].

More than twenty-eight years ago by order of the law and the King, in England as in France, I was obliged to leave my regiment and men's clothing in order to enter the convent and to wear a dress.[12] The advantage of being a virgin must not be criticized, for Our Lord told us: "Nothing impure can enter the home of my Father, nothing sullied can inherit the Kingdom of Heaven."

Since I have been living with the Daughters of Holy Mary and the Queen's ladies-in-waiting, all their virtues have entered me as if I were their natural habitat; and no one can ever again make them leave. At present I am living in profound peace; and my joy is so great that I praise God in three languages so that a greater number of people may partake of the happiness of the angels in this life while awaiting the crown of ordinary martyrs. *Nunc Genofeva d'Eon est nomen meum; quam suave et dulce est laetitia mea!* [My name is now Geneviève d'Eon; how delightful and how sweet is my joy].

In the convent my mind being conducted in a spirit suitable to my station, as [I] had formerly and justly acquired it and with their moral[s] and manners ameliorated and may give a wrong bias either to taste or customs as usual, and very respectable references will be given. My station in

[the] monastery give[s] me some character of female achievement in sanctity suitable to my new dignity.[13] It is good for a faithful maiden to be so intertwined and immersed in the solace of the virtues of His existence that she can no longer leave it. It is pleasant for a Christian maiden to remain in a convent with her sisters and companions. They pray together, they work together, and they act with the unity of a common will and a common spirit to give glory to God, to build up the Church, and to edify their neighbors by dint of their charity and their good works.

A legitimate vocation and a holy and edifying life are what is most powerful to disarm the calumny of the world. When one is holy by one's status or vocation, one must also be holy by one's mores. One's life, actions, and works must correspond to one's public declarations. A Christian woman, a nun, must be motivated even in her most common actions by the spirit of Christianity and religion. When she sees that the world does not agree with her and that all is closed to the truth, she must escape from the hands of the enemies of truth so as to serve truth in retreat and in prayer while awaiting the fulfillment of God's plans.

It is in vain that a maiden prides herself on being a Christian if she does not perform the acts of a Christian. It will not be the name, or faith alone, or a good work that will make her known as a daughter of God. It will be the works, the sum total of her actions, her whole life: it is thus that one is either a Christian woman or a woman of the world. Whoever wants to know whether he belongs to Jesus Christ must see if his life is Christian and carefully examine if it conforms to the Gospels.

Lord, can one have even a little faith and not choose to do everything and accept everything for your love? *Nunc omnia in christo qui me corroborat!* [All are now in Christ who strengthens me]. Strengthen, oh my God, what you have done within me. Since I have the freedom to enter with confidence the monastery of the Daughters of Holy Mary, my glorious and august patron saint, the monastery of the maidens of the House of Saint Cyr, and the Abbey of the Ladies of Haute Bruyère between Versailles and St. Hubert, and am following this new and vibrant path that the Virgin laid out for me by allowing me to take the veil, I will approach her temple without fear, with a sincere heart, and perfect faith.[14]

Oh Virgin whom the Heavens admire, fill my heart with your faith, set it ablaze with the fire of your love. Make me sigh tirelessly after my Savior

Who died for me; and may, in my suffering soul, His ever-present holy death nourish my soul and my faith. *O virgo virginum pretara, mihi jam non est amara me terram plangere, fac ut tuum portem sortem, fac me in christi cruce inebriari* [Oh excellent virgin of virgins, it is not unpleasant for me now to beat the ground; make this your due part and make me intoxicated over the cross of Christ]. Now is the day God made for me, here is the place that He chose for my faith. Thus, so that we might give a good example to those on the outside and that we not be blameworthy, let us live our lives in the transports of joy. Let us render grace unto the Lord because He is good, because His mercy is endless, and because He will allow his men and women servants to die in peace in His holy temple, for Jesus Christ was given over to death for our sins and He was resurrected for our eternal justification. My God, grant me some rest to take new strength in Jesus Christ.

PART II

Other Autobiographical Writings and Fragments

Mademoiselle d'Eon's Second Visit to
our Holy Christophe de Beaumont, Archbishop of
Paris, in 1777

"I am very glad to see you again, Mademoiselle. All the good things that I heard about you from my nephew the Marquis de Beaumont d'Autichamp, your former colonel, and my other nephew the Marquis de Lostange, your former general in Germany and during wartime, seem incredible for a girl."

"Your Eminence, when God so wills, the arm of Saint Geneviève, my patron saint, can be as strong as Joan of Arc's. Miracles are only for those who have true faith. The nonbelievers who believe in nothing do nothing. They are always afraid of making a mistake. They are right because they do not believe in God. A nonbeliever is like an undecipherable code for all Christians. Even the rabbis do not understand such a person. I will consult Rabbi Maimonides on this subject."

"Mademoiselle, do you understand Hebrew?"

"Your Eminence, I know it well enough to condemn myself to a Jew and to save myself to a Christian disciple of Jesus Christ and Saint Paul."

"Mademoiselle, I congratulate you. You are more learned[f] than I am."

"Your Eminence, I am gifted at languages, but you have the gifts of good works, miracles, and a charity that accompanies all your acts."

"Mademoiselle, tell me what I can do for you."

"Your Eminence, pray for me. I know that the Lord listens to you and answers your prayers because you ask Him only for what is just and reasonable. I do not need anything. The Queen has Mademoiselle Bertin dress me. The King has given me a pension of twelve thousand pounds from the royal treasury in order that I do no wrong. I am so busy[f] doing good that my head spins. Yet I perform the duties and functions of a Christian woman rather poorly. Perfectionism can drive out the good."

"Mademoiselle, you are correct. Whoever seeks to progress too quickly in a career with which he is not well acquainted often breaks his neck. I observe, with satisfaction, that there is nothing more to correct in your dress and your conduct. Here you are appropriately dressed[f] according to your station. It will be difficult[f] for you now to revolt against the spur and the goad of your gender."

"Your Eminence, 'Happy are they whose sins are hidden. The law intervened in my case with the result that my offense was abundant; but where there is an abundance of sin, there is an overabundance of grace' (Rom. 4:7). How difficult it is to know and to heal pride, since God allows the abundance of sin so that the proud one may be humbled by his falls, that he may confess his sins, seek a doctor, and be healed!"

Then our saintly Archbishop said: "Mademoiselle, who can refuse his love to the Lord, who only wants to reign in our hearts to make us holy in this life and happy in the next?"

I will not report the end of this visit here because it contains only reciprocal expressions of civility and praise. Alas! Who in this world is insensitive to the love of praise?

⟐

Selected Correspondence between d'Eon and His Mother

Excerpt from the letter from Madame d'Eon to Mademoiselle d'Eon in Paris, Tonnerre, October 28, 1777

What consolation for a Christian mother to have her prayers finally heard by God for the salvation of a daughter possessed by worldly concerns and military prowess! Why are you so distressed? Because the courts took from you the man's clothing that you wore against the law. In that act recognize the beneficent hand of Providence. This apparent harshness prepares you for extraordinary favors. God tests those upon whom He wishes to bestow special graces. Soon you will come to love your condition, and you will agree that a dress is the only appropriate clothing for a woman. You have never been afraid of good behavior. Why then are you afraid to commit to it? The white dress is the symbol of purity for she who wears it in church, at court, or in the town by order of our most Christian King. People talk. Let them speak the gibberish of fools. Should they prevent you from being well behaved? The King has preserved your privilege of wearing the Cross and the Red Ribbon of the Royal and Military Order of Saint Louis. This proves that you were courageous in your madness. He has not only preserved but even increased your pension from the royal treasury. In addition, he generously sent you a wardrobe of dresses to allow you to pass honorably from the company of the dragoons to that of the Daughters of Holy Mary, and then to that of the ladies-in-waiting to the Queen. This alone should be enough to grant you tranquil sleep at the very heart of peace.

Tell those who envy you: do the same thing and you will have as much as I have.

Each of us must be content in this world to remain in our place and not desire any other beyond the will of Providence. Everything that pleases God should please us. Leave it at that, my very dear and good daughter Geneviève, and lead your sheep not to the royal treasury but to the lush pastures of your celestial homeland. Whether it is windy or rains or hails or thunders, there one has nothing to fear!

*Excerpt from Mademoiselle d'Eon's response to her mother in
Tonnere, Paris, November 3, 1777*

I received your letter dated 28 October.

I cannot calculate how many thanks I owe to Providence, the King, the Queen, and my good mother Saint Monica, who prayed to God day and night that her bad boy might be converted into a good girl. There must be so few who ask for this favor! Already I begin to foresee the good effects of your prayers and that God has made everything for the best! Sometimes God's inspirations are mistaken for illusions. God's light makes us distinguish clearly between the two when justice is pronounced and the King commands. The ways of God are little understood, and often what He does for our own good terrifies us; but when our Lord speaks and we know how to hear Him, His truth appears, and everyone is reassured.

I must not seek to be the only one[f] to profit from Jesus Christ, His truth, and His gifts. Others must be invited to partake, to spread the sweet smell of His name, to help the weak in any way we can, in order to repair the scandal I created. These are some of the duties of a newly converted woman. Happy is the sick woman who does not grow tired of looking for the true doctor through faith and trust accompanied by good works! It is the heart that must be washed. It is one's inner self that must be examined when one has been out in the world.

You must not think me to be entirely purified[f] simply because the Queen has generously given me beautiful white dresses and because I can wear them with confidence in her chapel, in her court, in the town, and in the countryside. I have yet to be able to wear them purified before God. Sacrifices, fasts, mortifications, alms, and humiliations are good works in themselves; but it is a body without a soul when the heart is not changed, reformed, sacrificed, and sanctified by the spirit of God, the only source of innocence and purity!

The white dress is nothing? Since there are ten thousand seamstresses, haberdashers, and milliners in Paris and in London who make them from morning to night; are they whiter because of that? I do not know. A dragoon comes from afar, when he comes from the land of sin so distant from God, to be purified and sanctified in the congregation of the Daughters of Holy Mary—as if in a camp—entrenched and enclosed by all the Christian virtues and defended by the canons of the Gallican Church, which has its trenches that no one can cross without having the necessary good qualities.

Since the Lord, through His grace and through a miracle, had me recover in court my first dress of innocence, I will never again be seen chasing after the pleasures of this world. I will faithfully follow the will of my divine master by entering the temple of Mary soon, where nothing impure can enter, for this temple is as rich as heaven for it contains a virgin mother of the savior of the world. There I will have ample time to look at myself in the mirror glowing ablaze with all Christian virtues so that I might, like Mary, relate all my actions to the glory of God. Under her powerful protection I will obtain the extraordinary favor of salvation by swimming off to the haven of grace amidst the cruel storms of this flood of corruption. I place all my hopes in her compassion during my internal and external sufferings.

Mary was so holy and so perfect, says Saint Ambrose, that her life can serve as an example for everyone (Ambrose: *Book 2 of the Virgins*). I will follow the advice she gives in the Gospel: Do everything that my son tells you to do (John 2:5). It is a great source of confidence for us to see that the first miracle of our Lord occurred through the intercession of the Virgin who is our mother: "It was the first of Jesus's miracles; it occurred at Cana in Galilee and through it He made His glory known, and His disciples believed in Him" (John 2:11).

Lord, you know what my soul is by itself. It is weaker than water. Give me the wine of your grace, which will be all my strength, this wine that makes virgins fruitful with good works. After the bad water was changed into good wine, no conversion can appear unbelievable. Nothing is impossible for Him who every year changes water into wine on the vine and who, from prayers alone, creates children for Abraham.

All must live for Him who died for all; all must come back to life for Him who is resurrected for us. Everything is new, but only for him who has a new heart. As long as one is attached to this life and to the world, one should not believe oneself to be a new creature.

What is more fitting than to dedicate one's life to Him who redeemed it through His death? To be a new creature one has to lead a life freed from the senses, far from all carnal sights, and impervious to temporal interests. One must have a taste for only heavenly things and love only for God. For there is no glory but in Him; and no one is justified except by a new life and a faith in Jesus Christ. Whoever builds on any other foundation builds on hay, straw, and mud. Happy is the Church that has as many choices as it has children through charity, for it is written: Rejoice, you who are sterile, who had no children; shout for joy, you who did not become mothers, because she who is abandoned has more children than she who has a husband. Whoever loves the Church as its mother cannot see its fruitfulness without trembling with joy. What an abundance of consolation for those who receive by God's mercy the confidence that they are the children of God according to the promise and the immutable decree of divine favor!

"We are not children of a servant, but of a free woman, and Jesus Christ granted us this freedom" (Gal. 4:31).

◆❀❀◆

Selection from the Letter of the Chevalière d'Eon to Madame the Duchesse de Montmorenci-Bouteville, Versailles, May 1778

If God be for us, who can be against us? (Rom. 8:30)

Section I

Most dear, virtuous, and courageous Duchesse, who can ride a horse, go down into a ravine, hunt, shoot a rifle or a pistol as well as I can, you merely lack the experience of charging an enemy of the King and the nation in company formation or in line on a fine day of battle. Alas! I have done all that, and I am no better off[m] for it.

Our unbending holy mother Church who hates bloodshed has forbidden her dear daughter Geneviève d'Eon any activity that presents mortal danger to ourselves or our neighbor. As a result, I was obliged[f] to retreat by donning a dress and entering a cloistered order. That is hard to swallow for a former dragoon captain.

But what a consolation for those who are marked as God's faithful while they suffer in their worldly existence, to have God on their side and to have no other enemies than His! Even if all the powerful people at court, in the town, on earth, and in hell are against us, that is nothing so long as our interests are linked to God's, and our cause is His. Nothing makes us realize more that God is on our side than the transformation He worked within us in order to separate us from the dragoons of the volunteer army and the diplomatic service, that is from the devil and the body of sin, at no matter what the cost, in order that we may become a member of the Congregation of the Daughters of Holy Mary and a lady-in-waiting to the most Christian Queen. What more valuable proof of God's and the King's kindness toward us can there be! I squandered all the grace I received at birth. I can no longer receive grace except through Jesus Christ in a new birth. His love for the faithful is eternal, unchanging, and invincible. Nothing in this life can take away from him those whom He loves eternally. He who has overcome death and Hell could easily save us from the evils of this life; but it is more glorious for Him, and more useful for us, to triumph over these evils through his grace by suffering them.

How admirable and how impossible to understand are the ways of God! What separates the outcasts from Jesus Christ is the way He has chosen to unite Himself more closely with his faithful. It is a significant accomplishment to triumph over all the evils of this life; but it is even greater to triumph over sin and over ourselves through Him who loved us. This is what the grace of Jesus Christ effects within us, to make us triumph over sin until the end. Cupidity makes poor use of the best things; charity makes good use of the worst things by being attached to God alone and by only loving Him and Jesus Christ, whether He punishes or consoles, whether He tries us or blesses us.

Section II

The gift of the stipend that was bestowed on me as well as on Madame the Duchesse consists only of the complete freedom to come and go in the convent of the Daughters of Holy Mary, in the house of the young women of Saint Cyr, in the abbey of the Ladies of Hautes-Bruyères, and in the court of the Queen's ladies-in-waiting.[1]

Although my estate is one of simple tonsure without the charge of or discharge from canon laws, from the laws of souls and the laws of conscience, that did not exempt me[m] from obedience to the rules in the common places within the cloister such as the refectory, the dormitory, and the warming rooms.[2] I consider the power of my dress to be like that of charity, which brings along with it all the other virtues through concomitant grace. Everything is so well ordered there that God showered his blessings on these holy and blessed cloisters.

I[f] am able to partake of these many gifts only because of my status as an adult woman, beneficiary and in possession of my mother's rights, which cannot be declared obtainable by any dragoon or military volunteer, any man in the court, the town and country, or the countryside. The Pope himself with all of his celestial and earthly power cannot give anyone a dispensation that would allow him to possess my inheritance. Although it is only a simple tonsure, it is legitimate, as decided upon by Church council, and according to legal and royal precedents as much in England as in France, or any other place, inasmuch as I was born[f] under the sign of the Virgin, as was the Popess Joan.[3] An inheritance passes automatically to the nearest relative in every country ruled by Roman jurisprudence and common law.

As in the matter of estate, the definition of the *possessoire* is made by the royal judge and the definition of *petitoire* by the ecclesiastic judge.[4] I have passed through the hands or rather the paws and the claws of these two courts, and the King's High Council has decreed that the *possessoire* and *petitoire* go to Charlotte-Geneviève-Louise-Auguste-André-Timothée d'Eon de Beaumont. Who can prevent me from being the legitimate heir of my mother through inheritance, a status granted to me by the offices of the comte of Tonnerre, my native land, verified by the president of Sens, under whose control Tonnerre falls for civil cases, and Auxerre for criminal cases, and that was granted to me in the royal provosty of Versailles, my current residence, then registered at the Châtelet in Paris, approved by Parliament, and ratified by the Chancellery under the nose of my major and minor enemies? Whatever their size, roundness, fatness, or height, my enemies do not frighten me. If God be for us, who can be against us? I do not worry more about my enemies with black beards than those with red beards. I still have enough strength and ability to shave off their beards when I please, without saber or razor, no matter what kind — be it the beard of a billy goat, a nanny goat, a monk, a fox, or Jupiter.

However in my dress and in the convent I have lost my freedom, and although I am not fickle, I am obliged[f] to bless my bondage. In exchanging the old leather trousers for a blue satin dress, I acquired the virtue of a Christian woman. I enjoy the repose that constitutes the peace of this life. Supreme happiness was my destiny, since it resided within me. But I was so blind that while looking at it, I could not see it. *Ignoscenda quidem si fata ignoscare possunt* [This must be forgiven especially if the fates are able to forgive it]. I shun all these insinuating tones, these passing fancies, this glum welcome, these tricks, this blackness, these acts of treachery, this poison, these injustices, and this darkness with which the current fashion has molded the hearts of the great sinners at the court of the best of kings, whom we can criticize only for having too much patience and kindness.

Now I have only to consult the mirror of the long-lasting virtue of the chaste Comtesse de Maurepas in order to go up to the chapel of the château and down to the city without the assistance of the young Marquis de Sotenville. In this temple dedicated to prayer, I have no need of a breviary because everything is sung to music and in choral harmony, which enchant both the spirit and the heart. Seeing the King and the Queen sustains my faithful resolve in the midst of my sorrows. I must obey. I do so without complaining. Obedience has become my most prized finery. I am content with my status for fear of encountering worse. Of two evils, one must choose the lesser to avoid having a fever in the heat of May. If I was cold upon our departure from the city of Einberth, I was hot upon leaving Hoxter at the surprise attack of the château of Cassade and the aqueduct of Cassel, which parenthetically is an amazing construction and one of the most beautiful in the world. I was even hotter at the battle of Attrop, and the one at Osterwik, the battle of Philinhaussen, at the defense of the wealthy abbey of the Benedictines at Willebadessen, which is five miles from Paderborne, upon my entrance into the cloister of the Daughters of Holy Mary at Chaillot and in the citadel of the château of Dijon, which can be entered only with a *lettre de cachet* from the King himself.

All these entrances, all these exits, all these comings and goings from the south to the north, and from the north to the south did not change my situation at all since I must now keep still and am not even permitted a game of skittles while wearing a cornet and skirt. So as a wise captain and knowledgeable aide-de-camp I packed up my sack and skittles [and] retired to the convent.[5]

In my new position, I have only my sewing needle to lead the rank and file. The only masterpiece left for me to accomplish is my mother's masterpiece. The nuns in the convent have often asked me: "What harm did you inflict in war?" I answered them: "Be careful, you are unwittingly touching upon a very delicate subject for a courageous soldier. I did my best to do good while doing the harm required by my former profession. I note that if in peace one kills a man, everyone says 'what a monster!' But if in war a general hacks ten thousand innocent soldiers to pieces, everyone seeing him pass by cries out 'there goes our hero!' Why this difference? It is because when you are in battle you have to strike while the iron is hot. Our hero, while doing harm, accomplished a good act, which led to peace."

Section III

We cannot force our passions to be awakened or extinguished. We believe we have overcome them when they merely shift their focus. We are not the masters of our physical existence; but we are the masters of our moral life. God gives to each the body that it pleases Him to give, and each one is appropriate to its recipient. Everything comes from God. He must be praised for everything. By the grace of God I am what I am. And His grace toward me has not been in vain. I studied, worked, and fought as much as my brothers in arms and much more than my sisters; in any event it was not I but the grace of God within me. In all the positions I have held in war and in peacetime, I was bold[f] and paid for it personally. And I am no different[f] from those who seem to be very important, no matter what they used to be, since God pays no heed to the external appearance of persons, because those who are well esteemed at court, in the town, or in the Church have given me nothing new.

"Are we not all children of God through our faith in Jesus Christ?" (Gal. 3:2).

Let us live then the life of children of God, or let us stop usurping that title. God makes known when it pleases Him that He is the master of the heart. He alone can change us, He alone must be glorified by the change we have undergone, for He has made us overcome the prejudices of birth and habit. Since the Fall, nature is a servant girl who can give birth only to carnal children and sinners. Nature's path is already decided; but God has allowed for the works of grace. Christian freedom does not consist in living independently, or in doing whatever one wants to do, but in renouncing one's freedom by subjecting it to the will of God, His law, and those to whom God has made us subject.

He who has discovered his own weakness through the experience of failure has no problem recognizing that he owes everything to grace. One's calling, choice of work, progress, perfecting one's work, all this comes from God, from whom everything emanates, by whom everything is accomplished, and in whom everything is fulfilled. What was believed by the first Christians must also be believed by the last ones. We work in vain to be successful in this earthly life. The end of all things will soon come: it will be the final overthrow of all human plans and the final desolation for all the conquerors of the world.

The shortness of life is a common principle of the message of Jesus Christ and that of Epicurus. But their conclusions are completely opposed! The Epicurian says: "Think only of drinking and eating, since tomorrow we will die." Why not say, rather, with the Christian: "Let us stay awake, fast, pray, and do penance, since we may have only one day left to live." Even if we were to live as long as Methuselah, we should give thanks to God every day, since heaven, earth, sea, and everything they contain exist only by His order and with His permission, for a thousand years for God are less than a minute for man. All time, past and future, are present before His eyes.

Whoever does not believe in another life beyond this one does not believe in God. Whoever believes and yet remains in sin is already dead for eternity. Faith commands us to rely on God. The difficulty with faith is not so much believing what God tells us as believing what we can neither conceive of nor explain. Why? Because we are only weak mortals and God is all powerful and immortal. When Louis XIV had a minister who did not do what he was told to do, the King exiled him. When a powerful noble questioned the King's authority, the King sent him to the Bastille. What a cruel exile to be deprived of the presence of God forever! And God's Bastille is Hell! What will happen to the great Duchesse de Monfalcon, who says that she would prefer to be damned alongside people of her own class than saved with maids and lackeys?

Impurity among the privileged is a more dangerous example than among the disadvantaged. This most contagious, most persistent, and most shameful vice makes people suffer more than all the other vices. It has the same effect on the soul as the plague has on the body. The purity of the Gospel can not abide adulteration. Our Christian condition makes us holy. Let us be holy as well in our lives. The purity and unchangeable character of the Gospel constitute a holy unity. Let us not fear taking it too far when we follow Jesus Christ and his Apostles. As I see it, the Gospel of Jesus Christ is still virtually crucified between two thieves: between, on the one hand, the Jews who make it more difficult by adding to it the insufferable weight of the law and, on the other hand, the bad Christians who want to make it easier by lightening the welcome yoke of the Cross. Nature defends itself against the former; grace must make us terrified of the latter. Whoever believes he can bring together the opposing interests of Jesus Christ and the world knows neither the world nor Jesus Christ, for Saint Paul tells us: "If I yet pleased men, I should not be the servant of Jesus Christ" (Gal. 1:10). The doctrine of the Gospel is entirely divine. The Apostles are only the agents and the conduit; God alone is the source, and Jesus Christ is the doctor and the great teacher. It is neither an invention of the human mind nor the fruit of study and philosophy but a gift of God through Jesus Christ. It is only for Him to know and to teach how He wants to be served by humanity.

Happy is he whom retirement has made a stranger to the world, and who makes known his conversion without showing his face! God shows when it pleases Him that He is the master of the heart. He alone can change us, He alone must be glorified by our transformation. One instant can make the difference in a whole life, and we think about it so little! The spirit of God in our hearts is the fulfillment of the mission of the Son of God. An inheritance is only for children, and one is only a child through love. Can we remember that we are Christians and yet at the same time focus like a Jew on the wealth of this life or like a courtesan on the pleasures of this world? Let us choose either this world or heaven. Time is for sowing, and eternity is for reaping.

Section IV

The word of God consists not of words but of virtues. The outcome must be the acts of good works. This is why I woke from my lethargic sleep when I reflected upon these words of the Bible: "Grace has been given to each of us according to the measure of the gift of Jesus Christ" (Eph. 4:7). The diversity of grace and gifts in the Church of Christ contributes to its unity. It is not merit that determines the distribution but the will of God and the designs Jesus Christ has on each member of His Church to use each one as it pleases Him. The duty and the best interest of everyone is to be happy with his portion, not to rise above it, to allow oneself to work hard, to receive without vanity, and to transmit without envy what is given by our leader, and our leader is the only son of God.

Teach me, Lord, to make use of what is given to me in a manner worthy of you. May my heart be among the happy captives whom you will pull along with you to heaven! May your gifts make me give myself to you.

The more we humble ourselves, the more we will be victorious over sin, the dragon, death, and the Devil. Until when will the saints yearn for you? The devil has only as much power over us as we allow him. Souls belong to God. His spirit conserves them in His safekeeping and prevents the devil from entering therein. Our reconciliation with God is the principle and the goal of the mission and the embassy on earth of the only Son of God.

The truth of His divine doctrine taught me to cast off the old man I used to be in my first life, who became corrupt by following the illusion of my imagination (Eph. 4:22; Col. 2:8). It was this truth that taught me to renew myself from within my soul and to clothe myself as a new man, who is created according to God in true justice and holiness (Rom. 6:4; Eph. 4:24; Col. 3:12).

Lord, who have virtually cast off your very self in order to be reclothed with us, it is for you to strip us of ourselves and to reclothe us with yourself, your justice, and your perfect holiness. Happy are they who on that day when the children of God are entirely freed from the slavery of sin and of corruption, will have preserved the seal of grace in its entirety!

Let us often compare what we were on our own with what we are through the mercy of God and the merits of Jesus Christ. A Christian who does not use the light of faith to walk forward on the road to heaven is a traveler who sleeps during the day and who will be caught by the darkness of night. Thus I awoke^m from my lethargic sleep when I carefully read the following passages from Scripture, which speak to me clearly: "Wake up, you who are sleeping, and raise yourself up from the dead, and Jesus Christ will light your way" (Isa. 26:21, 60:1; Eph. 5:14). According to what is said in Hosea: "I will call my people, they who were not my people; and my beloved, she who was not my beloved" (Hos. 2:24; 1 Pet. 4:10; Num. 9:25).[6]

Thus Isaiah exclaimed while speaking about Israel: "Even if the number of the children of Israel were equal to that of the grains of sand on the seashore, there will still be only a small number saved. For God in His justice will cut short, consume, and reduce His people. The Lord will effect a great reduction in this world" (Isa. 10:22; Rom. 9:27). The same Isaiah said earlier: "If the Lord of hosts had not saved several of our race, we would have become like Sodom and Gomorrah" (Isa. 1:9; Rom. 29).

What will we then say, if not that the Gentiles who were not searching for justice embraced justice, a justice that comes from faith; and that the

Israelites, by contrast, who sought the law of justice, did not attain the law of justice. And why? Because they did not seek it through faith, but rather they sought it as if justice could be obtained through the works of law. For they collided with the stumbling block, about which it is written: "In Zion I am going to place him who is the stumbling block, the stone of scandal; and all those who believe in him will not be confused" (Isa. 8:14, 28: 16; 1 Pet. 2:7; Rom. 9:33).

Saint Paul writes in his epistle to the Corinthians: "Repay my love with love. I speak to you as my children; reach out to me with your heart" (2 Cor. 6:13). "Do not attach yourselves to the same yoke as the infidels, for what union can exist between justice and iniquity? What commerce can there be between light and darkness? What kind of agreement between Jesus Christ and Belial? What society between the infidels and the faithful? What relationship between the church of God and idols?" (Lev. 26:12; 1 Cor. 3:16–17, 6:19). For you are the living temple of God as God Himself said: "I will live in them and I will walk there; I will be their God, and they will be my people" (James 2:11).

"That is why you must leave the world of these men, says the Lord. Separate yourselves from them and do not touch what is impure. And I will welcome you. I will be your father, and you will be my sons and daughters, says the almighty Lord" (Jer. 31:9).

Oh, happy is he who can say that God is truly the God of his heart, that He walks there, that He resides there, that He lives there, that He operates there, and that He reigns there! He who prefers to be the slave of his passions and of this century's covetous desires rather than the child and the heir of God merits being abandoned to the disorder of his heart. Since the Almighty vouches for what sovereign truth promises, what are we waiting for, after such a promise, to give ourselves to God? Is this not enough for a heart as narrow as ours? Do we hope to find something better than Him among His creatures? But, Lord, is it not the very nature of your light to enlighten the blind; to go after the lazy one who turns away in order not to see the light, to awaken him who is asleep because he has forgotten God and his own salvation, and to open his eyes; to revive the dead and hardened heart, which hates the light; to give him eyes to see the light and the will to love it? There is no doubt that your very light informs and prepares the heart that it wants to inhabit. May then this divine light of your grace shine in my heart, may it operate there, and may it dissipate my illusions, my military passions, and my diplomatic shadows.

Christian prudence is advice from the Gospels, which consists in seeking and studying the will of God in all matters, studying science so that His will may be known, and virtue so that it may be practiced. It teaches to endure everything with patience and to prepare for the days of salvation by divorcing ourselves from everything that does not lead to them; to abandon everything in order to save everything, if needs be, through a desire to give back to Him all the good we receive from Him, which we do through Him, and which we possess only in His name.

To make our sacrifice truly worthy of God, the praise of our behavior must be united with that of our tongue and the suffering of our heart. The self-annihilation and the servitude to which Jesus Christ reduced Himself constitute the highest praise He gave His father. Whoever imitates Him best in his humility, subjugation, and dependence is he who praises Him even more (2 Cor. 5:5).

Section V

That is why, virtuous Duchesse, I left the circles of the dragoons, courtesans, and diplomatic demons. I purified[f] myself of every stain of body and spirit by completing my sanctification in the fear of God, so that Satan would not have the upper hand with the dragoons of the most Christian King. We are not unaware of his machinations, his traps, and his ambushes; for the plenipotentiary minister of hell, my adversary, circles around me like a roaring lion who searches for a place to devour his prey.

This is why, commanded by the law and the King, advised by our saintly Madame Louise de France and by our saintly Christophe de Beaumont, a great shepherd of our souls in Paris, I beat[f] a retreat to the convent of the Daughters of Holy Mary as if to an inaccessible, unassailable, and impregnable citadel, for it is defended by all the canons [pun on *cannons*] of faith, hope, and charity and by the whole musketry of good works and Christian virtues.

"If therefore someone belongs to Jesus Christ, may he be a new creature. The things of the past have passed away, behold all things have become new, and all comes from God, who reconciled us with Him through Jesus Christ" (2 Cor. 5:17; Isa. 43:19; Apoc. 22:5).

Quod longa peccavit dies, ama! expiet dolor! [Because he sinned for a long period, love. Suffering will expiate it].

"Now God has formed us for this; He has also given us the spirit as a pledge; for we walk in faith and not by sight" (2 Cor. 5:5).

"Unless a man be born again, he cannot see the kingdom of God" (John 3:3).

All is new but only for Him who has a new heart. He who has not dressed himself in the sufferings of Jesus Christ and His justice cannot dress Himself in His glory. Let us strive through good works to make ourselves a garment that we may wear in front of Him. Submission to God allows us to bear our present life, and the desire to be with God makes us desire the life to come. It is this struggle of spirit against spirit and flesh against flesh that makes the saints wail. A Christian who does not perceive his own exile has never known or loved his country; a Christian's country, however, is the kingdom of God Himself. This judge is just and enlightened, his judgment inevitable, the hour uncertain, His ruling without appeal, and no one thinks about these things.

What could be more just than to dedicate one's life to Him who saved it for us all by His death? Few people can elevate themselves and lose themselves in God through meditation on the highest truths. It is easier for a financier, a banker, a broker, or a city merchant to speculate successfully in trade with China and Indochina and to sell short and long the public funds of a bank or of the East India Company than it is to attend our Lord's banquet in the heavenly Mansion House, where God will welcome only virtuous, upright, and pure hearts crowned with works of faith, hope, and charity.

"But the Lord is that spirit, and wherever the Lord's spirit is, there too is freedom. Therefore we all contemplate, as if in a mirror, the glory of the Lord face to face. We are thereby transformed in the same image, from glory to glory, as if through the spirit of the Lord" (2 Cor. 3:17, 4:7–17).

It is true that we carry this treasure in earthen vessels that are as fragile as glass, porcelain, and clay. But we do so that it may be clear that the excellence of this force comes from God and not from us. All these light afflictions, which are only temporary, produce in us the eternal weight of an infinitely excellent glory. For we no longer look at visible things but invisible ones, the visible being only temporary while the invisible are eternal.

Let us not fear losing our freedom by handing it over to this sovereign spirit so that he may do with it as He pleases. Our will is His work; He knows its impulses. He knows how to handle it and how to make it work without taking away any of the power that He gave it over itself. But what will it be like when we see the light within light itself and when our darkness is transformed into this light of Jesus Christ, which comes from God Himself. One misunderstands God's designs if one imagines that secular brilliance and special talents are the means selected by God to advance the great work of the Gospels' truth. God wants to do everything out of nothing so that man does not take credit for anything but rather glorifies Him for everything. That is the major and perpetual design of God in all the operations of grace. Let us work with great humility, faithfulness, but also with confidence and gratitude, and let us leave it to God. Let us keep our freedom of spirit and a heartfelt joy during the most severe tests, let us keep our courage and invincible determination, a lively faith in the guidance and the providence of God, who sees and ordains everything. And let us have perfect confidence in His aid in whatever depths we may find ourselves. Nothing gives us more right to the life of Jesus Christ than to lose our own life. Yet His goodness toward us is that of a father. His generosity is so divine that from the height of the Cross He cries to us: I died for you, live only for me.

There are several conditions and several different kinds of grace in God's Church, but faith is one and the same throughout and in everyone. It is a great grace for a Christian to live on faith and a rare faithfulness to speak, to write, and to act only by the impulse of faith. To suffer and die for faith is the highest and most perfect grace and faithfulness. One loses one's life only for a moment, but one gains eternal life in God and Jesus Christ. The winnowing basket of persecution will separate us from one another; but what joy to find ourselves one day all together before God and Jesus Christ, perfectly reunited there for eternity! Let us live for this hope; nothing will destroy us, and everything will bring us consolation.

The destruction of a domestic enemy, such as our rebellious body, is a great step toward victory. What does it matter how this wall of mud, which prevents the perfect renewal of our soul and which impedes its vision of its God, is destroyed? This is what must constitute a Christian's joy and raise up his spirits in sickness, old age, pain, acts of penance, torture, and even in facing the approach of death itself.

Section VI

Every day beneath the Cross and always joyful. This is a paradox that only the grace of Jesus Christ can make us understand and practice. On the one hand, he who always hungers for justice, always prays. On the other hand, he who loves God and his neighbor always prays. One always prays when one always does the will of God, whether by suffering or by acting for Him. One is always happy with God and praises Him for everything when one searches only for His will in everything. Opposing the designs and the works that serve to edify one's neighbor truly extinguishes the Holy Spirit. Having doubts about everything is impiety and ignorance; not having any doubts at all is vanity and superstition.

One must not judge faith, but one must judge everything according to the rules of faith, whether they be miracles, revelations, prophecies, unusual effects, or extraordinary practices. Where peace is not found, holiness cannot exist. We feel perfect peace when the movements of the body are subservient to the soul, the passions of the soul to reason, and the light of reason to God who is the true light and the eternal truth. One great means to be always faithful to God is to have forever present in our mind the future arrival of our Lord, which is as certain as the sunrise in the morning; for Jesus Christ is the sun of God's justice. He who looks for a path other than Jesus Christ, who is the new path and the only one that leads directly to heaven, is similar to Admiral Polacre, who wanted to sail from one pole to the other without a compass and without knowing about the North Star, or else he is similar to the man who sees his real face in the mirror and who, after having reflected upon what he saw, goes away and quickly forgets what he has seen.

Pure religion toward our God involves keeping oneself unblemished in order to appear before our Lord. Far from us the leaven of Scribes, Pharisees, and Sadducees who, while making themselves slaves of the law, believe that they have no need for faith. The old law is only a rough draft, a shadow of the Gospel. It is the law of the weak, of the inexperienced, and of slaves and leads only by means of the fear of worldly evils and the hope of carnal rewards. The Gospel is perfection, the law of the strong, the perfect, and the children, it makes known the true good and the true evil. It is only the practice of the Gospel that liberates the heart from the enslavement of sin, the malediction, the law, and death. They who practice it contemplate it profoundly, consult it as their yardstick, and have it always before their eyes as their model.

One assumes the name of Christian in vain if one's piety is only external, superficial, and flashy, instead of making the name of Christian pleasing to God through an interior religion, exempt from superstition and vanity, a faith that loves and practices everything that is true charity and hates and avoids all forms of cupidity. One can have no more certain evidence of a religion that seeks and adores only God, and of a faith that desires only eternal good, than to take no part in the present world and to help those from whom we can expect nothing.

"The old law was therefore our teacher that brought us to Christ so that we might be justified by faith. But once we have faith we are no longer subject to the teacher since we are all children of God through faith in Jesus Christ, for all of us who have been baptized have been dressed in Jesus Christ, where there is no Jew or Greek, no slave, no free person, no male, and no female, but we are all one in Jesus Christ. Now if we belong to Jesus Christ, we are therefore the descendants of Abraham and his heirs by virtue of the promise" (Gal. 3:24).

An admirable promise, which contains the entire secret of the covenant of God with man, the key to the old and new Scriptures. It is Jesus Christ who is the race promised to Abraham and the inheritor of the spiritual promises. We ourselves become this race and this heir by becoming its members; and we take on rights concerning the goal and the means by becoming one with Christ. Let us be continually in a state of thanksgiving, having in mind these truths, which are so consoling.

The Law keeps the arm in check by means of fear until the heart is changed by love. Faith, as well as Christianity, is for all the ages. The New Testament was covered by the Old Testament, as if by a veil; the Old one is unveiled by the New. Whoever does not find Jesus Christ in the Old Testament will not understand the New Testament. The shame surrounding our first birth is covered by the justice of Jesus Christ, with which we are clothed by our second birth. If we are now all clothed with Jesus Christ, may others see in us nothing but Jesus Christ, that is, his charity, his humility, his sweetness, his purity, his modesty, his patience, and all that constitutes the holiness of his morals.

The new law gives us a new birth, which teaches us that one must die and rise up from the dead in body and spirit to follow our glorious and immortal leader. The obstacles made by men are God's means of acting. Let us leave it to God and let us follow His leadership. The glory of the Cross is alone worthy of a Christian in this world because it is the means by which Our Lord chose to be glorified Himself.

The spirit of God causes all things to be well used. He is the one who must be invoked on every occasion so that He may transform our evil into good. Death wins, but he who has lived only for Jesus Christ recovers his life in Jesus Christ through death. I do not obliterate the grace of God for "if justice is accomplished through law, then Jesus died in vain" (Gal. 2:21).

He who gives himself over to fear, which is the effect of law, is only a vile Jewish slave who fears a beating in this world. He thereby excludes the necessity of love, the fruit of grace. Does he not render grace unnecessary and useless as much as he who attributes everything to the law? May our God of hope fill us with every joy, every peace and consolation of faith, that we may thereby be filled with hope through the enjoyment of the Holy Spirit, who proceeds from the Father and the Son who is our enlightener, consoler, and sanctifier.

Let us love in our weaknesses only that which reflects the glory of the grace of God and that which reflects our humiliation in our own eyes; let us moan about the rest.

Section VII

Virtuous Duchesse, since I was obliged by law and by the King to abandon men's clothing and forced[f] to clothe myself in my first dress of innocence in order to have the freedom to enter holy places, which is the new and living path that was traced for me by the opening of the grill and the veil of the virgins of Holy Mary, I entered[m] my new condition with humble obedience and with a sincere conviction and complete faith that I would not be embarrassed[f] in any way, for my heart was purified and my body washed with clean water. Thus I hold to my declaration of hope without wavering, for He who made me promises is faithful so that I might accomplish all the good works of faith, hope, and charity for the instruction of my neighbor and the edification of the Church while repairing the scandal I created by wearing men's clothing in peace and in war the uniform of the dragoons, who are lions, or rather mad, wild demons. For if I sinned willingly after having learned the truth, there would no longer be any way to repent for my sin. And if I restored what was destroyed in me, I would show myself to be rebellious and unfaithful to the commandment of the law and the King, which has given me nothing new in either England or in France. I truly earned this dress I wear, by the sweat of my unwilling body.

If I set little value on my person in the army, I was never reckless with my body either. I always treated my body harshly in order to eliminate any desire it might have to rebel against me. As long as I was engaged in warfare as a dragoon with the volunteers of the army, I never got[m] in a bed whether in winter or in summer without undressing. I always slept on straw with my bearskin, while my boots and helmet were on my left and my sword on my right. I placed all my hope in God and all my strength in my ability to use bladed weapons. Gunpowder is good only for those who like to fight from afar. A military girl likes to fight hand to hand. Thanks to God, the law, and the King, I no longer fight either hand to hand or from a distance, since I have begun to wear a dress and have adopted a new body at the Convent of the Virgins of Holy Mary, which I consider to be an elite reserve unit for fighting, dying, and resurrecting in glory, despite the envy that follows virtue as a shadow follows a body in midday or under a full moon. In any event, I have remained[m] where Providence placed[m] me, finding myself[m] to be in harmony with, and of the same kind of disposition, affections, and inclinations, as these good nuns. I found[m] myself strengthened from one day to the next by the virtue of these holy sisters, for whom their convent is like an impregnable citadel. Therein I responded to divine inspiration for my salvation.

As a captive member of the Congregation of the Daughters of Holy Mary, I was in a single day linked[f] with your glory and your destiny. I was thus forever included in the interests of the common cause of all women in the past, the present, and the future. Your greatest privilege is to have more virtues than I do. Your greatest advantage is to have been dedicated to active service for thirty-five years. But time and practice will give me the same advantage. I am not paid[m] by the month as are the King's soldiers, but I am paid[m] quarterly by the royal treasury. Whatever the pain and embarrassment of my situation, it is still a great advantage to have recovered all my former rights, which I thought I had lost because of the passage of time

(Acts 1).[7] I see that what is evil among men is still good in the eyes of God. In Him there is no lapse of time nor any prescription for what is good.

Due to the sudden fall of my young Arabian steed, who became afraid and overly spirited on the Westminster Bridge during a storm with rain, hail, lightning, and thunder, and because of a great number of horses and carriages that were hurrying off to seek shelter in town and my prodding with my two spurs to get his attention and arouse his courage, unfortunately my terrified horse suddenly lost his footing while crossing the bridge. This terrible fall threw me over the horse's head a considerable distance onto the cobblestones, which were scattered about in order to be used to repair this beautiful bridge. I received a serious wound, which bled profusely at the battle scene and in my bed. Without my permission I was attended to by doctors, for I wanted to die of shame and despair about this accident, whose consequences for me were so enormous that the law, in England as well as in France, effected my conversion from a bad boy to a good girl.

It was in this fashion that Saint Paul, by an invisible hand, by the triumphant thunderbolt of grace, was struck down and converted on the Baradi Bridge that leads to Damascus, where, impassioned by blind courage, he wanted to tear apart the young Church of Christ. Instead he came away the most zealous, most competent, and most intrepid defender of His divine doctrine (Isa. 4; Acts 19).[8]

Since my fine conversion, with daily patience I overcome evil with good. This good is now necessary so that I may return to the natural order of society, which constitutes a legitimate right, while respecting the law, which is the guardian of public and individual order and which gives me the perfect peace that I now enjoy. Everything tells me that I will play an active, broad, and glorious role in the general execution of a Christian woman's functions, duties, and occupations, which are so appropriate to the dignity of her new character.

Thus as I work with the nuns who are my companions, they see that I have not received God's grace in vain. For He Himself said: "I answered you at an opportune time, I helped you on the day of salvation" (Isa. 49:8). Behold the moment of opportunity, behold the day of salvation.

Now I am careful to avoid any possible hint of scandal in anything at all so that my transformation not be criticized by the ignorant or by detractors. I look for those things that lead to peace and that are mutually edifying so that the character of my new dignity not be dishonored. By acting in all things as my fellow nuns do, I am trying to make myself commendable for my great patience with work, with calamities, with reduced circumstances, extreme affliction, vigils, fasting, prayers, charity, by the word of truth and by the power of God. I trust only Him; with Him I remain both in life and in death.

What does it matter how we appear in the eyes of men provided that we live in God's eyes and in His heart of hearts? In the midst of the greatest dangers and of inevitable perils, I always placed my hope in Him who afflicts His own in order to punish them and not to destroy them. He allows the world to try them, but He reserves for Himself the right to determine the moment of sacrifice.

Providence is a good mother, full of love and wisdom, and faith places all assets in the hands of the one who leaves everything for God. One has everything when one has Him, and one loses nothing when one loses what should perish. One is wealthy and powerful when one places one's hopes only in God.

Lord, deign to make it a matter of your glory to have me submit to your law and to make my flesh serve the Spirit. Mortal men cannot be easily convinced that glory must be born of humiliation, abundance of poverty, and eternal joy of a temporary sadness. Life is a brief moment on which hangs a happy or an unhappy resurrection. Who thinks about this issue, or rather, who thinks enough about it? Let us change our hearts if we want to change our bodies. The struggle is for life, but life is short. The victory is only for life in heaven, but it will be an eternal one!

Section VIII

I did not receive the spirit of slavery from the Jews, or from the courtiers of Herod's palace so as to live in fear. I fear only God, the law, and the King. I fear only the ministers who do not know how to read or write or how to pay those who write for them. I fear only special ambassadors who ordinarily poison their colleagues at the table after having invited them in as friendly a way *propio pugno* as I have shown publicly in court.[9]

But God is so good and so powerful that he draws out the good from the dark maliciousness of powerful men and has them loudly condemned in the court by the grand jury in the county of Middlesex, which is the most important province of England because the beautiful city of London is there, just as the fair sex lives in the middle of the capital.

In this country people are judged without the slightest regard for outward appearances. One respects only God's law and the national constitution. Here the axiom of common law is: *Ruat caelum, fiat justitia! Sancta sanctis foris canes* [Let heaven fall and justice be done. Get out of the holy of holies, you dog].

Faith makes me bear equally the good and the bad, which comes to me from on high or from below. To be patient in misfortune is enough for a Stoic philosopher. To bear misfortune with love is the mark of a true Christian. To take glory from misfortune is a divine grace. To take all our joy from suffering with Jesus Christ is the *chef d'oeuvre* of faith and the triumph of grace. Despite the number of our sins, let us trust Jesus Christ. His grace is more powerful for saving than sin is for destruction.

"For the law arrived so that our trespasses would abound; but where sin abounded, there grace abounded even more" (Rom. 5:20).

What heart can hold back its joy and its gratitude here? Who can refuse his love to the Savior of the world, who wants to reign in our hearts only to make us holy in this life and happy in the next? God is our origin and Jesus Christ our goal; we want to live only for God in Jesus Christ.

Human servitude creates only miserable people; servitude to God makes only saints in the scope of time and kings in eternity. Christian grace is a grace of combat. One is mistaken if he expects to become holy without doing violence to himself. But such violence will arm us, knights of faith, with hope and charity, prayer, vigilance, patience, obedience, and the courage to persevere. It is up to you, Lord, to give us the weapons, the knowledge, and the grace to use them. It is from you that we hope to receive them.

One cannot be a child and heir to God and co-heir to Jesus Christ if one does not participate in your suffering. This is a necessary condition of the new covenant. The price is borne by the flesh, but does it not often cost one more to be damned? May human wisdom be silent and learn to submit to a wisdom it cannot understand because it is God Himself. Far from complaining, let us worship the goodness of God, who saves those He could have destroyed. Jesus Christ knows His sheep; but if He does not search for and attract them to Him, they will never go to Him. Lord, I am this wayward and hidden sheep that you sought among the dragoons, the volunteers of the army, the roaring lions, and among the diplomatic beasts of wayward politics in Europe, Asia, Africa, America, and frozen in Siberia. God often thinks of the lost souls who do not think of Him. But this is a grace that He does not extend to all. Oh abyss of God's judgments! We recognize that we owe your gifts to your liberal spirit and that your gifts are really graces of your generosity and mercy. May we not be discouraged by the uncertainty of our fate. We cannot perish as long as we are attached to Jesus Christ through a lively faith in the power of grace. One loves only a ghost when one loves the observance of the law without seeing in it Jesus Christ who is the fullness, the goal, and the fulfillment of faith.

"For all those who will believe in Him will not be confounded" (Isa. 28:16).

"And all those who invoke the name of the Lord will be saved" (Joel 2:33; Acts 2:21).

Without obedience, knowledge will condemn us. The very word of Jesus Christ strikes the eardrum in vain if it does not open the ear of the heart. Do we believe that God is speaking to us when the truth is announced? Our life must vouch for our faith. God is jealous of His chosen ones. He searches for them, He attracts them to Him, and then He hides them from the world, and often from the saints themselves. Who would not admire, Lord, the hidden resources of your wisdom? One must not judge anyone, but rather fear and hope, worship and give oneself up to God with trust, serve Him while uniting ourselves in our hearts with those who are His, without being known by anyone else except Him.

Lord, you who saw Nathaniel hidden under the fig tree before Philip called him (John 1:48), you who knew me ten thousand years before the birth of my mother, I dare to ask you the triple grace of being among the small number of those whom you set aside by decree, whom you hide from other men, and whom you keep for yourself. When God chooses us and looks for us to have Himself sought, we inevitably find Him.

I wander[f] like a sheep lost somewhere between the south and the north. Look for me, my God, and draw me to you. Do not allow me to fall once again into the hands of Jews and Arabs, abductors, thieves, assassins, and poisoners, since you are my savior who saved[m] me from the hands of the Bohemians, Pandurs, Talpachians, Kara-Kallpakk Tartars, and Abyssinians, who are as cunning as asps, snakes, and scorpions. Change into good, Lord, all the evil that you see in the diplomatic corps and make it serve your glory. You have the power to do it.

The judgments of God are hidden from men so that the holiest ones tremble under His hand, depend upon Him, and are glorified only in Him. Whoever claims to have found the outcome of God's hidden designs and prides himself in teaching us through reasoning the secret of God's conduct will not teach us anything else except his vanity and his own presumption. Who gave Him something first that he expects a reward?

Protect me, Lord, from all these illusions of human pride. I have nothing of myself to give you in return for your mercy except an infinite collection of troubles. You could not be conquered by all the heartfelt malice of your enemies. You alone can fill my heart with the light of truth and the sweetness of your charity. Your victory will become mine if you deign to apply the virtue of its power to me. I dedicate myself to God in order to glorify Him in any way that pleases Him; for everything comes from Him, everything is done through Him, and everything exists in Him. May glory be given unto Him as it was in the beginning, as it is now, and as it will be eternally. Oh future centuries in exchange for the present world! Oh eternity for a single moment! Oh endless rest for a fleeting labor, for the sacrifice of a corruptible, miserable, and criminal life! Happy oblivion of terrestrial objects, which make room for eternity in the heart of a Christian!

Remember, dear Duchesse, that early part of my youth, which I lost in peace, in war, and in politics. Remember the most recent period of my life, when, after having been enlightened[f], I endured this great struggle with suffering such that my ties in the convent became famous in the courtrooms of London, Paris, and everywhere else. Now if I must boast about something, I will boast of my sorrows, my afflictions, and my suffering. But I will also and endlessly boast of the strength of the virtue that my venerable Duchesse had me find in the weakness of our condition, by herself giving me the best daily example at court, in the town, and in the countryside. This virtue has now become my consolation, for I know that it will result in my salvation through your prayers, through good works, and the constant help of the spirit of Jesus Christ. Waiting as I am, I will not be confounded[f] by anything, but I have every assurance that Jesus Christ will now be, as He has always been, glorified in my body, whether by my life or by my death. For the Lord is my life, and dying is to my gain.

If I write such a long letter to my virtuous Duchesse, it is because I realize that my heart is overflowing like an overabundant spring when I am in your presence and because it is too late to make it shorter. This long letter is not written to improve my position with her, since she has known me since her youth and since it is she who speaks highly of me to all of her illustrious family. Your acts of charity toward me have long made it clear that you are the charitable letter of Jesus Christ carried by the virtuous spouse of the Duc de Montmorenci, the first Christian baron and prince of the holy empire. The empire of the first Christian baron can exist only in the empire of heaven and, until that moment, in the sensitive and beholden heart.

— Of your very humble, devoted servant[f]
and your faithful female companion,
[signed] The Chevalière d'Eon

꧁ ꧂

Letter from Mademoiselle d'Eon to Madame the Duchesse de Montmorenci-Bouteville, London, June 15, 1789

Dear most honorable and most honored Duchesse,

There is no doubt that the search for justice, piety, faith, and charity earns great rewards and that patience and a gentle heart bring spiritual satisfaction in this life as well.

Ambition, pride, and the love of wealth are at the root of the seven deadly sins and of all evils. What would ambition and wealth do for me? I cannot climb any higher than to heaven nor descend any lower than this earth, which will cover the rich and the poor equally.

God gave me intelligence, the King sustenance, the Queen her protection; all this should be enough for a miserable creature who has no hunger other than for the word of God or any other thirst than for the truth.

I seized the chance for eternal life to which I was called[f] before the creation of the world, and for which I roundly professed my faith in front of a crowd of witnesses in England and in France, and for which I hope to make my confession in front of the army of angels prostrating themselves at the foot of the throne of the Most High when He appears with the Lord to judge the living and the dead. It is then that all the powerful and all the evil will believe, will lament, and will say to the mountains fallen upon us: "Hide the multitude of our sins and the abyss of our iniquity." But what purpose will this remorse, this belated repentance, serve? They will all be pushed into the Black Sea and will perish in the Strait of Marmara.[1] The few who survive will be judged in the Jehoshophat Valley and will feel the blade of the two-edged sword of the word of God, for without bloodshed there is no forgiveness of sins.

"Jesus Christ, having offered himself by his bloody death a single time to wash away the sins of many, will appear a second time without any trace of sin for the salvation of those who await him. For by the oblation of his body he consecrated forever those who are sanctified." (Heb. 9:28, 10:10, 10:14).

"And to this the Holy Spirit also bears witness after saying: 'This is the covenant I will make with them; from that moment on, I will engrave my laws upon their hearts and I will write them upon their minds; and I will no longer remember their sins or their iniquities.' But where there is forgiveness of sins, there is no need for redemptive offerings for sin" (Heb. 10:15).[2]

I will keep the profession of my hope without wavering because He who made the promises to us is faithful. If we then willingly sin, after having received knowledge of the truth, there is no longer any sacrifice for these sins. All that is left is the horrible wait for judgment and a burning ardor that must devour the adversaries of salvation.

I recall the time when, after having been judged[f] and enlightened[f] by the King's Bench, I endured in France a great battle of suffering because the boy unfit for his regiment was transformed into a girl appropriate for the convent. I will not mention my patience, for it was immeasurable. But knowing in my heart that I had in heaven a far better possession, which will never perish, I summoned up[m] the steadfastness of Sarah in her faith and the patience of Job in his misfortune and his hope. I will therefore not allow my trust to waver, a trust that is destined to receive such a great reward. I still need much patience so that, after fulfilling the will of God, I may become worthy of receiving the results of the promise. The righteous will survive on their faith, says the Lord. Soon, He who is supposed to come will come, and He will not delay. But as for me, I am careful not to subtract myself from the yoke of Wisdom that was imposed[f] on me by the law and the King and by the judgment of the saintly Christophe de Beaumont, a great shepherd of our souls in Paris. It would mean my condemnation and my perdition. But I am resolute in my faith as I professed it for the salvation of my soul and the edification of my neighbor. The mantle of Christian charity covers a multitude of sins, as in the past the brilliance of the purple robe of the Gentiles, Greeks, and Romans covered a multitude of murders and iniquities.

Because of her faith Sarah received the ability to conceive, and she had a son at an age when she could no longer normally have one because she was convinced that He who had promised this son to her was true to His word. That is why from a single man who was already weak and old were born descendants as numerous as the stars in the sky and the grains of sand on the shore, which no one can count. Since the time when I was surrounded[f] by an army of witnesses in Russia, Poland, Prussia, Germany, France, and England as I cast off every burden and sin, especially that which easily overtakes me, I have followed day and night the path that has been selected for me. Concerning Jesus Christ, the leader and redeemer of faith, He, in the name of the joy for which He was destined, had disdained and suffered the humiliation of the cross, He who was just for the unjust and is now seated at the right of the Throne of God.

This is why I reflect carefully about He who endured such a contradiction on the part of sinners who all rose up against Him: it will help me not to be dejected by my momentary sufferings. I fought[m] with my very blood for my King and my country, but for God I have not yet fought to the death against sin. That is why, by seizing the kingdom that cannot be shaken (Heb. 13:21), I retain the grace that allows me to serve God in peace and tranquility and to be pleasing to Him with respect and a holy fear in my continual exercise of good works. It is with this goal that I left[f] the dragoon camp and joined Jesus Christ in bearing his opprobrium, so that now, as a recluse[f] in my convent, I can say with confidence: the Lord is my help; I will not fear anything that man could do to me.

I was stripped of male clothing and my uniform, I was dressed[f] in my first dress of innocence and placed[f] among the Daughters of Holy Mary and the Queen's women only that I might experience a new life and not live the old with a letter of promotion to the war office and the King's certificate sanctioning my service to my rank in the twenty-four regiments of the dragoons commanded by Colonel Beelzebub, head of the dragoons.

Therefore do not be surprised by the great change that has taken place in me. It was only in order to be changed [m] that I was transformed [m] from black to white. I was given absolution for the past only that I might pass from imperfection to future perfection. This is a great and noble goal! But how can one reach this goal without prior, concomitant, and subsequent grace from on high? "For the law intervened so that the offense might be abundant. But where sin even more was abundant, sin reigned in order to bring death; so too grace reigned through justice to give us life. What profit did this bring me? Things about which I am ashamed now that I have been freed [f] from sin and subjugated [f] to God. I have my reward in sanctification and as my goal the life of the Angels, for the wages of sin are death, but the gift of God is eternal life through Jesus Christ." [3]

This is why I do everything today with the decorum and manners of a young woman who is well brought up and disciplined, since this is her rational obligation. I do not commend myself to you yet once again, Madame, but I give you the opportunity to be proud of me; I do so so that you have the means to close the mouths of those who put their faith in appearances and not in the heart.

"For if I am out of my mind, I am so for the glory of God: if I am sane, I am so for you" (2 Cor. 5:13). For it is you who helped me a great deal in strengthening my calling and in helping me overcome evil with good for the edification of my neighbor, who was scandalized by my male uniform. How great my efforts must be to become an angel like my pious Duchesse, whose eyes are two torches of light descended from heaven to serve as a guide for sinners on the narrow path of virtue.

You strengthen me with you in Christ. You are the one who has given me the first understanding of wisdom and of the Holy Spirit, which is in our hearts and which must be profoundly engraved in the hearts of all maidens and all women who live, not for men or for the world but only for God and Jesus Christ. We therefore contemplate: "as in a mirror, the glory of the Lord with his face uncovered; we are transformed into the same image from glory to glory, as if by the spirit of God that moves us. That is why we no longer live for ourselves but for Him who loved, died, and was resurrected for us" (2 Cor. 3:18).

"If therefore someone is in Jesus Christ, may he be a new creature. Everything old has passed away. See, everything has become new! All this comes from God, who reconciled us with Him through Jesus Christ our unique savior" (2 Cor. 5:17).[4]

I do not regret all that I have suffered in order to bring about in me such a necessary change. I was saddened only for a while. I now rejoice that I was sad for the sake of God. For sadness for the sake of God produces a salutary repentance that one never regrets, while the sadness of the cloister is like the joy of the world, it leads to death.

Now I wear my whalebone corset more comfortably than my former breastplate, and my dress as readily as male clothing, my woman's cape as easily as my man's coat. It is only my cornet that I do not wear as willingly as my helmet and my hairstyle that I do not do with as much good humor as I rode a horse, *qui quatrupante pede, qualit ungula campum* [who was galloping with his hooves, seeking the wide open spaces].[5]

But with obedience, patience, and the grace of God, I have overcome everything, I have surmounted all obstacles, and in every way I have shown[m] myself to be pure[f] in taking care of my transformation. Regarding my clothing, I have chosen[m], for the sake of order, uniformity, and economy, the dress of Christian, widowed, and chaste women. I now wear only white or black dresses. I have left it to women of the court to wear the dress and jewels of courtesans and to women of the town to wear the dress of madwomen, who have no other law than the imagination of their whims. Similar to those grasshoppers who have come up from the depths of the abyss, they have spread throughout the earth with a power similar to that of rattlesnakes (Apoc. 9:3).[6]

As for women dressed in long white dresses, they are the ones who have escaped great tribulation and who have washed and whitened their dresses in the blood of the Lamb. That is why they are in front of the Throne of God and serve Him day and night in His Temple: and He who is seated on the Throne will live with them forever. They will no longer be hungry or thirsty. Neither the sun nor any other heat will beat down on them any longer because the Lamb who is at the Throne will have them fed and will lead them to the liveliest waters of the fountains, and God will wipe the tears from their eyes (Apoc. 7:14).[7]

When one has continuously devoted oneself to all kinds of good works, one dies with a good conscience. "Happy are the dead who sleep in the Lord, they are resting from their work and their good works follow them" (Apoc. 14:13). "It is a terrible thing to fall into the hands of God who judges without appeal the living and the dead" (Rom. 10:31).[8]

If I am so changed[f] during my life, I will be even more so after my death. But fear must not terrify the one[f] who must die in the world in order to live eternally in God by the grace of Jesus Christ. "He will transform our sickly, base, and weak body, which is nothing but ashes, dust, and decay, so that it will be like His glorious body by means of this grace by which he can make all things subject to Himself" (Phil. 3:21).

You know as well as I do that Jesus Christ is the same today as He was yesterday and that He will be eternally the same in order to come to the aid of those who have placed all their confidence in him.

I beg our God of peace and mercy, who brought back from the dead the great Shepherd of the Sheep, by the blood of the eternal covenant, to make me successful[f] in all good works that I might do His will and that He may do with me whatever pleases Him through Jesus Christ. May He have eternal triumph like His eternal Father's.

That is why, dear and honorable Duchesse, I wish that my glory and my crown in this world may be steadfast with our Lord as your very humble and devoted servant[f] Charlotte-Geneviève-Louise-Auguste d'Eon de Beaumont, your chevalier[m] in the Church, at court, in the town, in the country, on foot, on horseback, in a coach, in a landau, and in a cabriolet.[9]

You are cruelly wounding my heart by reproaching me for remaining too long in England. You know that I am unhappy anywhere you are absent and that I am comfortable only where you are. But how can I leave London without having finished the main business that brought[m] me here? *Honni soit qui mal y pense* [Shame on those who think badly of it]. I am still owed here more than six thousand pounds sterling, which is equal to more than one hundred and twenty tournois. I will not find such a sum in the tracks of a horse either in Paris or in Tonnerre.[10]

꧁꧂

The Reply from the Duchesse de Montmorenci-Bouteville to Mademoiselle d'Eon in Paris

Since you have been wearing a dress once again, Mademoiselle, your spirit has become as light as our sex, as clear as our muslin, as transparent as our gauze, and as brilliant as the diamonds with which the Queen had your head adorned. If you continue as you have begun, you will become the most beautiful jewel of our society. We will no longer need lights and mirrors in the hall of Versailles, you will be the universal mirror for the court and the town.

Men are becoming jealous of your success. In their envy they say that you have stolen the spirit of the Greeks and the Romans and that you have had yourself dressed in the French style by Mademoiselle Bertin, who makes everything she touches beautiful. For us who in our judgments are a hundred times more fair minded than men, we do you far more justice, and we strongly maintain that Mademoiselle Bertin has the right to take the most beautiful feathers from the birds of Macedonia, Greece, and Italy and from the ancient peoples to adorn our modern beauties and that such a theft is permitted, legitimate, and authorized by the forty Immortals of the French Academy.

If all the dandies were not decorated with the feathers of Pan born on Mount Parnassus, they would be like turkeys on the Grenelle Plain or they would be paddling like goslings off the banks of the Seine. Only Mother Grouchy of the Carmelite convent, only Mother Grey Grouchy of the Château of Versailles could blame Mademoiselle d'Eon and Mademoiselle Bertin for this legitimate larceny.

When it comes to wit and talent, men have no more loyalty than women do in matters of beauty. Everywhere, one finds *a laudator temporis acte* [a eulogist of a bygone time]. Yet nothing was more magnificent than the acts and deeds of Joan of Arc, nicknamed the Maid of Orléans, and the English burned her at the stake with clenched teeth. But they must be forgiven this bloody act committed in a wrathful fit of their *colera morbi* [disease of anger].[1] They have repented, and since then they have become milder and more civilized for the benefit of Geneviève d'Eon, our Maiden of Tonnerre.

> *Sic Homines et urbes nobilitantur,*
> *Sic tempora et honores mutant mores,*
> *Sic oliva vetus Cyneus Couvertus in mulierem,*
> *Quantum fuit mutatus ab illo Hectore!*

> [Thus men and societies are rendered famous,
> Thus time and honors change customs,
> So the olive tree was transformed into the woman Cyneus;
> How much was changed by that Hector!][2]

Have we not seen the invincible Hercules take the distaff of Ompale in order to weave with the maidens? Have we not seen with surprise that Ompale seized Hercules's enormous club to fight the lion in the forest? Hercules was nonetheless admitted to the ranks of the Gods in the Elysian Fields, where he still takes charge on Mount Olympus. What can one say to this but that great and small actions are not incompatible in a hero even though they may seem to be in conflict. *Olim truncus eram, nunc sum Deus* [Once I was a human body, now I am God].[3]

⊰◈◈⊱

Christian Reflections

Written by Mademoiselle d'Eon de Beaumont since the time of her passage from the dragoons and volunteers of the army in Germany to the Congregation of the Daughters of Holy Mary for the salvation of her body and soul in this life and the next. The next world will have not the slightest sign of change, in accordance with the promise of the eternal One, who does not waver, unlike our great cabinet ministers in Versailles, who are as stable as birds on a branch shaken by the four winds of the south and the north, agitated by the black devil of politics and white magic.

Since I left the world, I say with joy: Lord, tell me what you want me to do through your law, since without you what can I do? It is a great consolation amid the miseries that one experiences to feel that no goodwill can come from us but that it is Jesus Christ who creates it within us.

Fortify me, my God, against myself, for I have no more dangerous foe. Lord, be wary of me today because I will betray you tomorrow if you leave me to my own devices.

Christian grace is a grace of combat. We fool ourselves enormously if we expect to become holy without doing violence to ourselves, for our Lord said to his disciples: *Regnum Dei vim patitur, et violenti rapiant illud* [The kingdom of God allows force, and the violent seize it]. It is the glory of our Lord to make us submit to His law and to have us triumph over the world, the dragons/dragoons, and the demons of Hell.

This life is not a time when God gives outward signs to His chosen ones. In a little while we will know what a child of God is. Happy is he who uses this moment to pray to God, to bemoan his captivity, to cry over his sins, and to yearn for the grace of deliverance! Far from complaining, let us admire the goodness of God who saves those He could destroy!

How happy is the lot of women to find in their situation and their duty the incalculable advantage of not having to act outside the convent and having to preach only by love and the practice of silence, humility, obedience, dependence, and through the sweet smell of Christian virtues! There is never any honor in not doing one's duty or in leaving the order, silence, and dependence in which God has placed us. If any haughty woman wants to ignore what she does not want to do, she herself will be ignored and scorned.

It is an advantage rather than a loss to be forgotten[f] or ignored[f] by men; but to be forgotten[f] and ignored[f] by you, Oh my God, who can think of such a thing without being withered with fear? If it is to be damned to not know God, or to be excommunicated to not love Jesus Christ, what must those individuals expect who make a specific lesson of it and who hold a public school, so to speak, of not loving Christ at court and in the town? If they are not as common in the villages, it is because they are afraid to die of hunger, to be burned alive by the good women or stoned by the decent men in the countryside. But have patience; the devil will soon take them to the Jewish Sabbath, where they will be circumcised at the hand of the old witches in the Herodian and Samaritan Sanhedrin, where the hungriest cats of Hell will refuse to touch their old relics embalmed in the quintessence of their crimes.

It is impossible today to find a Demonograph from the pantheon of demons of the Athenians anywhere. We are now familiar only with the Pantheon of Rome, constructed by Agrippa—who had stolen and gripped a large part of the Romans' money to have it built—and which is still standing.[1] Today it is one of the most beautiful temples and is called Santa Maria Rotunda.

The only request that I make repeatedly of heaven is to pray to our God of peace that he might soon crush Satan beneath our feet by the grace of God and Jesus Christ our Lord and Savior. We do not await any other!

I have endured many afflictions, but God tests his elect through tribulations. He does not give his crown to ordinary martyrs.

In order not to be condemned in heaven, one must not judge on earth.

"Humble yourself in the presence of the Lord, and He will raise you up. He who speaks against his brother speaks against the law and judges the law. If you judge the law, you do not observe the law but you set yourself up as the law's judge. There is only one legislator and one judge who can save and who can destroy. But you, who are you to judge the law and your neighbor?" (James 4:10).

Can a sinner who has violated God's law have the insolence to place himself above both the law and God Himself, thus usurping His authority like a highway robber in the dark forest?

God is jealous of His authority. To want to use His authority once it has been forbidden is to put oneself in His place and to insult Him. Only the creator has the authority to judge His creatures from the inside, and no one can judge the heart of the Creator who has made him. Respect is the tribute paid to virtue. There is no more rigorous and more feared tribunal than that of a pure conscience guided by a true belief in God and in Jesus Christ.

I respect all the judges appointed by God and by the Law; but God is the sovereign judge on earth as well as in heaven.

◈◈

Important Document in My Present State

Happy are they whose sins are hidden. (Rom. 4:7)

The time has come to display one's courage, determination, and loyalty in order to reassume the rights of natural freedom, for we are not false claimants but legitimate heirs.

Given the financial difficulties arising from the critical circumstances under which I exist, or rather I groan, my most pressing duty is to behave as I am doing before the eyes of God, the King, the law, and men of faith. In my present situation, I receive daily practical instruction concerning all of the duties of a Christian woman. The Lord's grace will take care of the rest with time, patience, and obedience to the law of God. One is always happy[f] with God, and one praises Him for everything, when one seeks only His will in all things.

I am living everything and loving what is good. I abstain from everything that appears to be at all evil. An appearance of evil can often have a more negative impact on the weak than even the example of evil for the strong. He who does not take care to avoid what can kill the soul of his brother will give himself a mortal blow. Where peace is not found, holiness cannot exist. What is the purpose of instruction if not to make us want the grace to practice what we learn, of desire if not to have us pray, of prayer if not in order to humble, to purify, and to enflame our hearts?

How ephemeral are the consolations of the world to a heart that has the eternal consolation that God loves him for eternity. Firmness in following true doctrine and the practice of goodness are a measure of that consolation of which God alone is the author. It is for Him alone to give consolations that go directly to the heart.

May you be blessed and praised, my God, for having given us such an easy, direct, perfect, and effective path to lead us to you. Given that all ancient moral law is contained in the Gospels in a clearer and more perfect way, Moses, who passed on only the letter of the law, should be silent. Let us listen to Jesus Christ, who, like God, gives grace and spirit. God is happy without us, and it is only to make us happy with Him that He has us know His glory through the Gospels and that He asks our obedience.

Whoever does not want to base his conscience on his faith runs the risk of basing his faith on his conscience. Everything that can be related to God as its principle and its end is good; everything that cannot be related to Him in this manner is evil.

Anyone who leaves Jesus Christ after having chosen Him as a husband cannot have any other except the devil. My new birth has created within me a union of joy and extreme affliction, which I feel every day beneath the Cross and always joyfully. This is a paradox that the Gospel teaches us and that only the grace of Jesus Christ can make us understand and practice. Let him who does not have an abiding need for God and who does not continually feel his own wretchedness cease praying and moaning. One is always happy with God and praises Him for everything when one seeks only His will in all things.

Grace, peace, and rest are the sole object of the Christian soul's desire. The soul is happy that the desire is satisfied provided that the soul knows and does the will of God. Christian life consists entirely in serving God and in waiting for Jesus Christ as a captive awaits his liberator. Let us imitate Him whom we are awaiting if we seek to fall back no longer into the anger from which He has delivered us. How sweet it is to have in one's heart this knowledge that one did not fear men when God was to be served!

It is not a small thing to have to answer to God's plans and not to have in one's heart any opposition to all that goes against our natural inclinations! Public penance for public sins is necessary to set an example. The punishment of the one is useful for the many. One owes the edifying example of humility to those who have been scandalized by one's sin.

Lord, when will your word, which has besieged my heart and made it beat for such a long time, force my heart to surrender to you? Mad is he who, having God for his country, witness, and judge, imagines himself able to avoid His knowledge and His justice. When one wants to serve God, it is prudent to choose a condition in which one cannot be obliged to be a slave to the world. Since Jesus Christ assumed the name, the condition, and the nature of servant, this is seen as an honor and a help for salvation in the eyes of faith. A servant who exploits the goodness to which his master has been inspired by Christianity would deserve to have a Turk, an Iroquois, or an idolater for a master.

How rich we are when we have little, when we desire nothing, and when we are greedy only for the sole good that can fill the heart (Saint Paul's Epistle to Timothy, chap. 7). For we have brought nothing into the world, and it is certain that we cannot take anything with us when we leave. You did not have any possessions yesterday, you will no longer have them tomorrow. What folly to become attached to them today for a brief moment. We should be happy with having enough to eat and something with which to cover ourselves.

One can be poor in spirit in the midst of wealth; one can be rich through cupidity in extreme poverty. The first is sanctified by possession of wealth. The other can damn himself by desiring wealth. This very desire produces sins and crimes. But however horrible the consequences may be, men are not afraid of riches.

Let our faith confront this great truth, since our very faith is at stake. He who seeks earthly goods with such greed can hardly retain his faith in heavenly goods. How deceitful is the trap set for us by the devil for our love of wealth! It is this false good that allows the devil to begin his hell in this world. It is a happy struggle when faith fights for faith itself, when the victory consists in overcoming the world and its cupidities, and when eternal life is the goal, the prize, and the triumph. One must be faithful unto death when Jesus Christ will judge us each individually. This fidelity is quite rare and yet decisive for eternity.

The advent of Jesus Christ is highly desirable for Christians who have kept their baptismal dress free of stain or who have whitened it once again in the water of penance, but it is terrible for sinners. He who forgets that all comes from God makes a god out of his money, and his money is all that matters to him.

Pride and harshness toward the poor create what we call the wealthy of this world. Humility and charity create the wealthy of the time to come. He who builds his foundation on uncertain and perishable wealth will perish with it. He who builds his foundation on a living and immortal God will live His life and will share in His immortality.

It is a double advantage for the wealthy to be able to do good unto others in this life and to enrich themselves for eternity. Two conditions for Christian alms: to do it with a pure heart and by the principle of charity; to do it with humility and by a principle of justice. For the wealthy must look at their surplus as the share of the poor, of which they are only the trustees, and they must share with the poor the common capital.

What do Adam's children seek in temporal wealth if not the pleasure of possessing treasures, having splendid houses, and leading a delightful life? But what does he find in his alms, he who spreads his wealth among the poor, receives them in his house, and saves their lives, if not a treasure of immortal wealth, the foundation for a heavenly and eternal house, and the prize of a divine and happy life?

What is the usual result of the greed for wealth? It is similar to that of a vain curiosity and a philosophy filled with pride and presumption, if not a fatal distraction from faith. That which inflates the spirit, fills it with vanity, and makes it incapable of the humility and the obedience that faith requires can lead only to destruction.

The holiest instructions do not sanctify man if grace does not make him practice them. Let us open our ears to the word announced by men. Let us open our hearts to the grace of God. But who will open it, if not He who opens without anyone being able to close it, and who closes it without anyone being able to open it? Therefore, my Lord, open the heart that you want to fill with your truths and make it love them, retain them carefully, and practice them faithfully in order to receive their just reward in eternity.

⋆❀❀⋆

A Special Request by Mademoiselle d'Eon for a Small Favor from Readers, Authors, and the Members of the Universal Republic of Letters

Set forth in Europe by the press without priests, gunpowder, or cannon, for God gave us the gift of reason, a layman founded the press, a monk gunpowder, and a pope canon law. Ultima ratio regum [The reasoning of kings is final].

If it is difficult for me to explain how good angels live in heaven, it is even more difficult for me to understand how bad writers survive in this world! Nevertheless, I saw how it pleases God, who gives me everything, and how it pleases the Revolution, which gives me nothing.

Without this fine and great Revolution I would have never known poverty, and without this financial difficulty, I would have never dreamed of publishing my letters and memoirs on this lost era and unpredictable future of my miserable life.

Poverty has no rules; it has forced me in my peaceful old age as in my military youth to make a living from death. When it is a matter of physical survival, the hungry stomach is obliged to cry out.

I have always been of the opinion, and I am even convinced, that it is impossible for an author to write the story of his own life. Either his pride, which is an integral part of the human heart, raises him to the heights of vanity, or modesty reduces him to hypocritical humility. I forgive Saint Augustine for having written his confessions to God, but I do not forgive Jean-Jacques [Rousseau] for wasting good paper publishing his general confession to mankind, which did not ask for it. On the contrary, he refused on his deathbed to make his personal confession to the good village priest, who asked him for it, wanting to give him a free passport to find in heaven the wisdom he could not find in this life, although he searched for it on all fours from his youth to his old age.

Regarding my personal confession, I must say that since my life has had neither head nor tail, I do not know where to begin or end.[1] A Vestal Virgin cannot confess as boldly as a philosopher from Geneva [Jean-Jacques Rousseau] or a married woman under the nose of a high priest. Since my beginning was not normal, there was no normal order in what followed. I write as I have lived. In my fine disorder, however, I have taken great care to conduct myself not according to the ordinary rules for girls but according to military discipline, the wisdom of the King's commands, and the prudence of the dragoon amid the lions of the army, the serpents of the court, and the crocodiles of the great city of Paris.

In my work I do not seek to write a novel to please the public. I report only the facts, which I saw with my own eyes. My *bills* are not an apothecary's charges but very much the truth.[2]

Truth, says Dr. Armstrong, is a tenacious witness; it alone suffices to expose lies and deception. If I find myself forced[m] to present authenticated deeds concerning my past life, it is because slander sought to engrave the errors, and truth clamors for the history of my life.

I am sorry[m] that in certain parts of my writings I have been obligated[f] to speak the truth about certain persons. But if my writings are not seasoned or sweetened by reason, by the salt of truth, and by the spice of justice, how will they be able to resist the corruption of this world, which is like a gnawing worm devouring all virtue?

If certain modern philosophers do not approve of my conversion, it is because they do not believe in God, the law, or the King. God forgave me[m], the living law vindicated me[m], and the legal systems in England and in France awarded me[m] full rights to wear a dress. Louis XV and Louis XVI were my[m] patrons, the Queen who is the daughter of the Caesars had me dressed in her court by Mademoiselle Bertin; the very woman who dresses the Queen did not turn up her nose at dressing Mademoiselle d'Eon grandly.

Madame Louise de France, my good and holy patroness, showed me the way to divine virtue. Christophe de Beaumont, Archbishop of Paris, who is saintly by profession, a great shepherd of our armies, and consumed by his zeal for the house of God, wanted to have me live a golden legend despite myself.[3] Wanting me to stride along the narrow path of the Gospel, his ardent charity for his neighbor's salvation prompted him to remove from the sight of the people of Israel the scandal of the man's clothing, which I had worn. The effect of his action was political, moral, and religious. Thus in order not to deviate in my conduct, I must follow in the footsteps of a sacred leader who is as pious as he is enlightened in the celestial principles that have guided him.

This is still today the principal object of my work, as much for my own benefit as for that of the women who serve God, often with sincere hearts and misguided minds. My goal is to make it known that the grace of God was not given to me in vain. I have always admired His greatness and His goodness and how He acts so powerfully in the hearts of those who have always loved Him in good faith. I would like my Christian philosophy, which has nourished me[m] and which has raised my soul toward its creator, to have the same influence upon the souls of my readers who are animated by the same divine sentiments.

I know that my work is not in the order or in the style that I would like. It is not the glory of the historian but that of the Christian that I am seeking. Like Voltaire, I do not have the ability to write history in detail, in theory, or from memory. I write like they work in the department of foreign affairs at Versailles, where they write out letters or draw up reports on each subject individually. This manner of working is more reliable in fact and in politics than in vain literary works, in which truth is sacrificed for the embellishment of painted lies. What is important in a personal history is not necessarily so in a broader history.

My work proceeds in pieces and in snatches, sometimes in war, sometimes in peace, sometimes under the reign of the moon, sometimes under the empire of the sun. Often in my epistolary correspondence, my responses are written hastily because of time restrictions or because of the departures of mail coaches. Once they have left by post, it is no longer in my power to retrieve or to change them.

I have written and answered hastily as it pleased heaven to inspire me during the past century, in the reigns of our last kings. My work was not done to be devoured by an unexpected and voracious revolution. The revolution appeared suddenly like lightning from the Orient to illuminate the Western world.

Even if I had had the virtue of the four virgin daughters of Philip the Evangelist, who all prophesized, if I had had the wisdom of the prophet Agabus, if I had been a seer like Nostradamus and a sorcerer like the diabolical Merlin, I could not have foreseen that the light of a monarchy that shone brilliantly for fifteen centuries would suddenly be put out like the lantern of a Savoyard or that of a peasant from Mont Blanc or Mont Saint Bernard.

Who would have thought that the foundation of such an empire, built as solidly as that of Mont d'Or in Auvergne, which is 180 meters high, would suddenly fall like the Pont du Diable at Mont Saint Gotham?

I see clearly today, as did Saint John, that God is the only truth that will exist forever. Just as public edification has been the only goal of my behavior since my conversion, it remains the goal of my personal work as well. In this respect, my work's greatest merit is to be felt; thus it must be read in the same spirit that inspired me[m].

Whether I am praised or blamed, a woman in every country has the freedom to dress as she pleases and to choose her finery, her makeup, or her writing according to her taste and fantasy, without worrying much about the fashionable styles of Mademoiselle Bertin or the fine rules of Aristotle, Quintilian, Horace, Boileau and Boivin, Boisrobert and Merovert, of critics such as the Abbés Prévot, des Fontaines and Clément, and those of the Jesuits Sertier, Frérou, and Raynal. The Prince of Roman orators said before the assembled Senate: *Quisque habet animi ensum Patres conscripti, tot capita tot sensus!* [Whoever lives has an opinion, conscript Fathers; so many people, so many opinions].

And the Prince of the Apostles told us (2 Cor. 13): When we are weak, we are so for the glory of God; when we recapture our strength, we do so to our own advantage, because the love of Christ embraces us.

The Revolution made me^m so rich that today I do not have the means to buy ink or paper. How then could I buy venal pens in France or in England, where everything is so expensive, where everything is for sale, even including time, day, light, and darkness?

I beseech each journalist, every hack writer, not to dress up my story in his own way.

Do you believe that Mademoiselle d'Eon is a Tacitus, who must give you more to think about than to read? You are fooling yourself most curiously. She is not so stupid. She is not a woman for nothing. She must get dressed and prattle according to the style of the day in Paris, where it takes 24 in folio volumes to say what Tacitus said in four duodecimo pages and where women, when they are well dressed, wear a gauze dress as light as a spider web.[4]

Do you believe that Mademoiselle d'Eon doesn't understand that her work is quite long, but that if she had shortened it, she would have cut off her food supply at the market. She would have lost credit with her moneyless banker and with her apothecary who has no sugar.

I would just as soon suffer childbirth as to be doing this painful work of writing, which I have begun because of the destitution to which the Revolution has reduced me^f. To console me, my publisher, spurred on by English zeal, tells me that he has available a translator to transform my poor French into good English. But I answered him: "Don't you remember that, during the reign of Charles II, Dryden did what the English call a 'translation' of Virgil into Dryden's native tongue? The Bishop of Rochester told Dryden at court that his translation was the best ever, equaling and even surpassing the original. Dryden answered: 'My lord, everything loses something in translation except a Bishop.'"

Whatever can be said for or against translation, I personally am acquainted with the value of wise and enlightened censors. I know that the most precious moments for them are those they dedicate to protecting innocence without concern for the newness or the antiquity of what they are reviewing. I brought this matter to the attention of the famous Kaestner, a professor whom I met at the University of Göttingen when our upright, courageous, and honest Général Comte de Haux occupied it with his troops in 1761.[5] Since that time Mr. Kaestner has come to London in 1787 and, as he was the personal friend of my great friend William Serran of the Royal Society, both of them became close friends to me. I wanted to pay Kaestner this little tribute of gratitude, as well as my honest Aristarques, who showed me esteem and friendship at the venerable, scientific Oxford University.[6]

My spiritual memoir will also serve to remind the many professors still living among us, whom I met in Germany, Moravia, Bohemia, Hungary, Poland, Lithuania, and Russia, of me. I will not be sorry[m] if they learn and discover everything: that I am no longer a disciple of this world since my wonderful conversion, which separated me[f] completely from the body of the dragoons and from the sin of my uniform and which finally stripped away the old man in order to make of me a totally new being before Our Lord, in the eyes of men, in front of the Queen's ladies-in-waiting as well as the Daughters of Holy Mary, and in the hopes of the fortune reserved for me in heaven. The knowledge of that fortune has filled me[m] with complete wisdom and spiritual intelligence so that I might bring to fruition every good action and so that I might behave as befits a Christian woman not only before the world but also before the Lord, since during my novitiate I was washed[f], probed[f], tested[f], corrected[f], corroborated[f], strengthened[f], and rooted[f] in every way, which I endured, in complete patience and spiritual tranquility, the Lord having erased my obligations, which consisted of military orders, orders contrary to my spirit, and which He completely abolished and replaced with my new obligation to live and die in the essential purity of my innocent dress, no longer thinking of those things here below but only about those on high.

I therefore give thanks to Him who delivered me[m] from the power of darkness, who freely forgave my offenses and who made me holy[f], unblemished and blameless so that I might share in the inheritance of the saints and the virgins in the light of His glory, that for which I strive by endeavoring, using the power of His grace, which works mightily within me, not to follow the pathways of the world but those of my faith and my hope in Jesus Christ, who is the doctor of the doctors of the most famous universities in the Christian world, for the entire scope of the Scriptures and of divinity resides in Him. And it is in Him alone that all good doctrine is realized.

It is in Him that I live and, like another Saint Theresa, I long to die. While awaiting this great godsend, my life is hidden with Jesus Christ in God, in whom there is no Gentile, no Greek, no Jew, no circumcision, no foreskin, no barbarian, no Scythian, no slave, no free person, but Christ is everything in everybody (Col. 3:11).[7]

I am clothed[f] in the dress of charity, which is the site of my perfection in humility, in grief, in spiritual patience, and I remain there every day so that it may be made manifest to the eyes of my neighbors, who were scandalized by my past life among the dragoons, that I am now fulfilling the will of the Lord, the divine commandment, the decree of the law, and the wish of my mother, because in the spirit of justice I have granted her this affirmation that she always zealously sought, that I might wear my first dress of innocence. She told me privately at least one hundred times that outside of the will of God there was no salvation at all for my virginity.

If one finds fault with my manner of writing, I respond in advance that I am not writing a novel but simply a personal history of my life. The novel needs to give flight to its imagination in order to paint dreams that are based on lies, modeled on fiction, and given a rhythm based on the prestige of style. Personal history does not have any need for external ornaments. Truth is its only finery and its only merit. Simplicity alone is appropriate to it, just as the shawl of modesty befits a virgin.

PART III

Historical Precedents Found by d'Eon

Pious Metamorphoses

The history of the women who disguised their sex in order to consecrate themselves to God and to adopt the monastic life and who have been recognized as saints by the Greek and Latin Church, by Mlle. La Chevalière d'Eon

Sedit qui timuit ne non succederet. Esto!
Qui qui pervenit? Fecit ne virititer?

HOR. EPIST. LIB. EP. 17

Preface

In the midst of my numerous and varied readings, I was struck [f], while secretly disguised myself, by the example of the extraordinary women who, like me, lied by wearing the costume of a sex that was not theirs in order to follow a courageous instinct that led them to march to a different drummer, which they could not have done wearing the costume of their own sex. That I was, as I say, struck by this phenomenon is easy to understand: these were like so many mirrors reflecting my own image.

That because of the force of this impression I began to work to collect the various details of their lives, to write about them with all the care of which I am capable, should seem completely natural. More than once I thought that I was working on my own memoirs, so much do the same positions produce the same situations and arouse the same emotions!

I leave for general history, with which everyone is familiar, the Semiramis, the Joans of Arc, and other well-known heroines whose exploits could have made this study even longer. Those whom I chose to include seem to warrant their selection by the very fact that they are less well known.

Praise and public esteem are marvelously elastic. One can rise to great heights when one relies on them. But an individual who does great things makes extraordinary sacrifices when he fears praise and refuses the world's esteem. This individual thereby demonstrates incalculable strength, since he or she draws all his strength from within or, if you will, from the force of grace that the individual could merit only through an interior concentration of which the masses cannot conceive and that will always amaze reflective souls and demand their admiration. The sources for my information are also more reliable than any other testimony. Most of the ascetic writers from whose works I have drawn what follows recount what they saw, sometimes what their fathers told them, but always the sources are either eyewitnesses or only slightly removed in time from the events they have passed on to us. It is highly reasonable to believe that they would not have exposed themselves to being proved wrong by altering the essential facts in their writings. And in fact almost all of them focused on essential facts; very rarely did they go into extensive detail.

I hope that I will be forgiven for including in this collection the much-talked-about Popess Joan. Not content to merely question her existence, the erudite Protestant Blondel went so far as to classify her as a fictional character. The learned essays of M. Spanheim put her back on the list of pontiffs from which Blondel had erased her, as had most of the dictionaries compiled by Roman Catholic authors, whom this extraordinary episode disturbs immensely. Rationalizations and consternation do not obliterate a fact. Despréaux said it well: "What is true is sometimes not plausible." I would add that in these kinds of situations in which the implausible is not pushed to the point of absurdity, it is perhaps an additional proof of historic truth. First, the bizarre is not invented; one recounts it because it happened. Next, scandal is always fabricated by one's enemies, and were we to assume that the popess was invented, the Vatican has always inspired such universal respect that one cannot conceive of an author so daring as to create such an extravagant fable, if it were but a fable. In fact, in any discussion about this matter no one now believes that the truth or falsity of this episode has anything to do with the honor of the Holy See. Accepting or not accepting that Joan was pope is therefore simply one of those unimportant opinions that each individual is free to hold as he wishes.

Another subject whose inclusion I have no intention of apologizing for is that of the Comte de Comminges, which I have placed at the end of this book: this passage, filled with sensitivity and grace, is a model of its kind.[1] A woman's pen was no doubt necessary to express such lively and yet delicate emotions, to convey the subtle contrast between divine love and human love. From this ensues the simultaneously alluring and terrible position that gives this inimitable work its charm. But it was also necessary that this woman, like the witty Madame de Tancin, know the torture of seclusion, that she feel the grip of the monastic chain, and that she bear the yoke of religious observances and austerity.

All passions slacken and lose their energy in society. It is in retirement from society, it is within the walls of a convent that they become energized and heightened. And it is in that state that their depiction draws us in, interests us, and touches us deeply. Therefore, woe be to the arid spirit, the dry heart, and the cold soul who will not be grateful to me for exposing him to this charming writing, if he is not yet acquainted with it, or for giving him the opportunity to reread it, if he has already read it. I repeat, therefore, that far from begging for mercy for having had the idea to reproduce these texts, I am convinced that if my project or its realization were to find any censors, this work would suffice to silence them and to win universal approval.

Story of Popess Joan

Charlemagne had just conquered the Saxons. These ferocious people, who were so often rebellious and so often defeated, finally submitted to his laws but still rejected his religion. The emperor, who could not believe that his conquest was complete as long as his new subjects had not recanted their errors, encouraged the emigration of several learned individuals, who went from France, and even from England, to Germany to preach Christianity there.

One of these preachers, who had with him a woman abducted, they say, from her family, was forced to stop in Ingelheim near Mayence to give his companion the time to give birth to a daughter. This is the heroine of our story. When the mother recovered, their household settled in Mayence.

The father, a man well versed in all the known sciences of his time, raised his daughter there with the utmost care. He oriented her toward study and made it his duty to cultivate the surprising aptitude of this precocious genius, who from her earliest childhood gave evidence of all one might expect from her as she grew older.

Historians are divided about her Christian name. Some call her Agnes, others Gerberte, Jutte, etc. But the majority are in agreement that it was Joan. Those who are surprised at not finding her family name in the histories no doubt do not know that at this time surnames were not used. Men who had distinguished themselves by their talents and who wanted to be more easily recognized added to their given names that of their country. This no doubt explains why several scholars refer to her as Jean l'Anglais [the English], for she was of English extraction.

Nature, who was generous to her, lavished her with all her favors. I have mentioned her spirit. If I wanted to describe her face according to what others have said about her, I would be accused of creating a fictional heroine. This would be an easy accusation, because she is credited with adventures typical of a fictional character.

It is claimed that at twelve years old she inspired a strong passion in a young monk from the Abbey of Fulde. It is said that he induced her to share this passion, that he convinced her to run away from her family, to disguise her sex, and take vows to enter the monastery to which he belonged.

It is said that finding themselves under scrutiny and fearing no doubt that their pleasures would be disturbed, they left the monastery and went to England, his native country, where they continued to live together, loving each other and instructing each other with equal fervor.

Joan's lover had become, they say, a man of great merit. As the student of such a teacher, it was natural that she make great progress herself. As her fondness for the arts and humanities matched his inclinations, study was for her a taste grafted on a passion, so to speak.

At this point historians no longer agree. Some say that in England she lost her cherished teacher, who died in her arms despite her tenderness and devoted care, and that in her despair she renounced all pleasures in order to focus entirely on expanding and perfecting her knowledge. In fact, Joan had no other option. The most powerful consoler is work and effort. Books keep our minds busy and alter our thinking in a hundred different ways. They pour on the wounds of the soul a soothing balm, which eases the pain and soon begins to heal them. Other writers, on the contrary, maintain that she traveled with him all over France, Italy, and Greece disguised as a man. One of them even has her receiving the degree of master of arts and the doctor's hood in Paris. And they all agree that Athens was the end point of their travels.

It is true that Athens was no longer the Athens celebrated for its abundant intellectual life in every field, but one would still encounter scholarly people there as well as an academy that still maintained something of its former luster. Joan and her friend made a dramatic impression there. They did not attend the public academies for long before they were given a distinguished reception. Joan especially attracted a wide audience. She had a gracious manner and a very endearing face. In her soft-spoken voice there was great persuasive eloquence. She spoke with so much charm, expressed herself with such clarity, and stated her opinion in such a modest way that everyone came away enchanted by her conversation. Well versed in the humanities and arts, history, philosophy, and theology, she had made herself conversant with the best selections from the sacred and profane authors such that one was no less struck by her memory than delighted by her elocution. Adored secretly and admired publicly, such was the fate of our heroine. But it is the nature of happiness that it does not last. The majority of writers agree that it was in Athens that the companion of her pleasures, the principal author and witness of her success, died.

From that moment on, the advantages she enjoyed in this city disappeared from sight. Her stay there soon became unbearable. It was in vain that efforts were made to console or distract her. She could not bear the places that reminded her of precious moments of the past and that therefore continually heightened the pain of her grief. She went to Rome.

For the gifted, this capital of the Christian world was still the most brilliant of theaters. Joan, a short while after her arrival, invited the scholars of this city to hear her defend theses on the most difficult questions in the arts and sciences. This became a competition among the learned men that her reputation, which had preceded her, attracted to the gathering. Used to this kind of exercise, our scholar showed herself to be superior to what anyone expected of her. She answered all questions, overcame all difficulties, and left her audience ecstatic about the accuracy of her judgment, the vast breadth of her knowledge, and the variety, the number, and the choice of her expressions.

In Rome at that time there was a school called the Greek School, which was renowned for its students and professors. It was honored to have among its former professors the Doctor of Grace, the torch of the African Church, the great Augustine, who had previously taught rhetoric there. Our Joan became the head of this school, whose reputation she augmented by association with her own. An extraordinary number of people attended her courses. Students came to hear her from the most remote places. The various lectures she gave in different circumstances earned her an acclaim that was all the more flattering in that it was unanimous. She did not limit her courses to the liberal arts according to traditional practice; she included the study of the other sciences. The clarity of her ideas and the subtlety of her explanations earned her auditors and disciples in all her classes among prelates, priests, and even scholars, who consulted her as their leader and considered her decisions as oracles.

It is plausible that at this time she entered into holy orders. The custom of shaving one's beard, which was then becoming common practice everywhere in the West, was perfect for helping her hide her sex. Moreover, as she was naturally reserved, she lived in complete seclusion. Charitable toward the poor, careful to fulfill all her religious obligations, austere in her moral standards, her virtues soon inspired as many zealous partisans as her talents had enthusiasts.

At this time Leo IV was pope. He died. The procedures used for the election of a pope in those days were different. The clergy were in the running; and even the laity, whose approval was sought, had some influence. It was not irrelevant that the pope was or was not to the liking of the Romans. After the cardinals spent fifteen days without agreeing on a successor to Leo, the people came out for the priest John. Thus they called out her name and demanded her elevation with loud cries. The clergy, joined with the people and the cardinals, recognizing that it would be impossible to appoint a more worthy person to the highest of human positions, elected her unanimously, to the acclamation of both the masses in Rome and the reputable citizens of this queen of cities.

This election, according to the most plausible chronological calculations, took place in the year 854 at the end of the month of August.

Joan, wearing the triple tiara and seated on Saint Peter's chair, did not find herself out of place in this high position. She took the name of John VIII, dedicated churches, ordained priests, consecrated bishops and abbots, and celebrated holy Mass with the pomp and ceremony typical of the Roman Catholic Church. Scholars wrote to consult her and to obtain books, which were rare in those days. With Saint Ambrose as her model,

she composed various prefaces to Masses, which have since been banned
but which were still known in the middle of the fifteenth century. We learn
this from Martin Franc, the official historian of the Holy See, Provost and
Canon of Lausanne, and secretary to Amadeus VIII, elected Pope Felix V
in 1439. In his *Champion of Ladies*, a text in verse that he wrote as a reply
to the *Roman de la Rose*, he speaks about Popess Joan in these terms:[2]

> I know that she was learned in the humanities,
> That for her learning, she was named
> Popess and Priestess of Priests.
> Oh, how well she studied.
> Oh, so much praise there was
> For this woman disguised as a man
> She denied her own nature
> To become Pope of Rome.

And then he added:

> Still you can be shown
> Many a preface that she dictated
> Set out well and in a saintly fashion
> Where she never hesitated in her faith.

A sixteenth-century writer, André Tiraqueau, in one of his rhapso-
dies (which were then called *productions*) credits her with a book on necro-
mancy, but the attribution of this unknown book does not warrant any
more credence than the very science it is said to have discussed.[3]

It appears that Joan was able to hold court with a dignity that attracted the respect of her powerful contemporaries. Æthelwulf, the King
of England, had his youngest son make the trip to Rome during the era of
Pope Leo. Finally rid of his worries about the Danes because of his victory
over them at Ockley, Æthelwulf himself undertook this same voyage and
brought the young prince back to Joan with him. This was Alfred, who later
became one of the greatest kings of England. We may conjecture that he
received from the sovereign pontiff several important lessons, instructing
him in the difficult art of ruling and in leading to happiness men who, while
searching endlessly for happiness, always flee from it. In order for these men
to be happy, they needed to be taught how to be so.[4]

As for Æthelwulf, to gauge the respect and the veneration that the Holy Father inspired in him, it will suffice to recount what the King did for the Roman Catholic Church upon his return to his kingdom. The Rome-scot, or Peter's Pence, was collected only in Wessex and in Mercia; he extended it throughout his whole kingdom.[5] In addition, he humbled himself further by sending to Rome annually three hundred pieces of silver, two hundred of which were for candles in the churches of Saint Peter and Saint Paul, and one hundred of which were for the personal needs of the Pontiff. Such a tribute proves better than the most extravagant praise the influence that Joan had on those who dealt with her.

Troubled by wars and internal conflicts during the weak reign of Charles the Bald and already affected by barbarian incursions, France was completely preoccupied by its present unrest and the sad future that its situation foretold. France had no ties with the Holy See.

In Germany, Lothair was aging. He was overcome by disgust with the world and its demands. He abdicated in order to become a monk in the Abbey of Prym. His son Louis II succeeded him. He came to Rome and received from Joan his scepter and crown along with the apostolic blessing. It was said that the new emperor, impressed by the great qualities of the Pope and by his simultaneously noble and gracious welcome, indicated his satisfaction in such expressive and flattering terms that Joan, in return, as a sign of her esteem, extended to him an exemption to the collection laws of Gratian.[6]

The period of her pontificate was not always marked by fortunate events for humanity. There was a flood of the Tiber, there were earthquakes. According to Petrarch: "Blood rained on the city of Brefseneu (Brixien). In France there were clouds of monstrous grasshoppers with six legs, six wings, and extremely strong teeth, which devoured all the greenery they could find in the places where they came down. A raging wind pushed them toward the English Channel, where almost all of them drowned. But their bodies, thrown back onto the shore, rotted there and infected the air to such an extent that large numbers of people died in the area. The grasshoppers thus caused a plague in the very place where they had initially caused a famine."

Let us return to Joan. Some writers claim that her morals changed with her fortunes, that the benefits of sovereignty, luxury, and all the pleasures that came with her position corrupted her soul; that she had a lover, whom she made happy, and that, because they were carried away by their passion, she became pregnant. This last point is perhaps the only accurate fact in all the adventures attributed to her. A young girl, overcome by a violent desire for knowledge and for the celebrity that learning offered, disguises herself as a man from her youth on. She pursues her career with all the ardor of a passionate heart. She succeeds and manages to attract everyone's attention. All this is natural. There is no room in her life for love or for numerous pilgrimages, which would have used up a large part of her life on the road.

This is all the more plausible in that early historians speak little of such activities. Where then have modern historians found all the details they use to enliven the story of this extraordinary woman? Note especially that the latest scholars appear to be the best informed about the sexual anecdotes regarding her, that is, about what is most hidden in people's lives. Her great merit earns her the tiara. In her household, the mystery of her gender is uncovered, an event that could be the result of any number of circumstances; in which case she is then inevitably at the mercy of whoever knows her secret. Perhaps that person took advantage of the situation. He took from her what she would not have consented to give him. Why do scholars not interpret her pregnancy to be the result of being taken by surprise, of violence? It appears, at least because of the catastrophe that revealed her identity to all of the Roman people, that she was not familiar either with libertinism or with the resources it could provide for debauchery. This would seem to refute what has been said about her intrigue and her long relationship with the alleged monk from Fulda, who is called her lover and even her husband but whom no scholar names.

Whether she was forced or seduced, Joan was pregnant and nonetheless fulfilled all her papal duties. It is said that, one day while the consistory was in session, a possessed man was brought in to her. She exorcised him. Among other questions, she asked the devil when he would leave the body of the wretched man he was tormenting. The answer was as follows:

Oh, Pope! Father of fathers,
Tell us about when you will become a mother;
In turn, I will tell you
When I will leave this body.[7]

This little story is too obviously a fiction for it not to have any variants. Accordingly, one chronicle from Germany reports it in another way. The devil, according to this version, appeared to Joan and said to her: "Pope, Father of Fathers, childbirth will prove that you are only a popess. Then I will take you away in body and soul and you will be with me forever." This horrifying threat, according to the chronicle, filled Joan with a salutary terror. She recognized her sin, wept sincerely, and sought forgiveness through penance. God, moved by her repentance, sent her an angel, who gave her the choice of eternal punishment or public confession. She chose the latter.

But let us leave aside all these episodes in order to continue the story. Rogatian Day arrived.[8] Joan, who was in an advanced stage of pregnancy and dressed in her pontifical regalia, rode her horse, accompanied by the clergy who made up the procession and preceded and followed by a countless number of the devout and the curious. She led this procession according to traditional practice from Saint Peter's in the Vatican to the Church of Saint John in the Lateran. Having reached a street between the Church of Saint Clement and the Coliseum, the pains of childbirth overcame her. Cries that she could not hold back and signs of suffering on her face caused the procession to halt. She was brought down from her horse, and hardly had she reached the ground than she gave birth to a male child in full view of the crowd, which surrounded her and filled the windows, the balconies, and the terraces. It would no doubt be difficult to express the amazement such an unexpected event generated or the murmur and the uproar that followed it. An enormous throng of people crowded around the deplorable Joan, and no one bothered to help her. A deep sense of shame increased the perilousness of her condition, so much so that she died at that very place along with her child.[9] They were both buried without honors on the very spot where the tragic event occurred.

Boccaccio claims that she did not die but was driven out of Rome and went about complaining that "she had become a wretched, weak female."[10] A certain Abraham Zachut, a Jew, advanced the same version, adding that her child was killed. But these two authorities are insufficient to stand up against the unanimous account of other scholars, who agree that she did not survive the scandal of childbirth, a position too plausible not to be true.

This childbirth and the circumstances in which it took place appear to me to be strong arguments in favor of the innocence of the unfortunate popess. How likely is it, in fact, if her pregnancy were the result of a continued unchaste relation, that her accomplice, even supposing that she was completely ignorant of what could result, would not have warned her, alerted her, about what was happening? So close to the end of her pregnancy, did not the change in her waistline give her enough of an excuse to claim to be indisposed or ill? Can we even imagine that he would have allowed her to expose herself so imprudently to an almost inevitable catastrophe? I must therefore return to my conjecture of a bold man who, having penetrated her disguise, chose to take advantage of the situation. Joan, betrayed by his strength or, if you will, by nature, succumbs, then banishes the guilty man, and remains alone a victim of the consequences of a single fateful moment. She is in that case far less criminal than unfortunate and far more to be pitied than blamed.

Several valiant scholars of the Roman Catholic religion have considered a woman occupying the Holy See as a terrible blot on that office. They groan and bemoan this occurrence. Leaving aside the position of the canons who forbid women to practice the holy ministry, I do not share their opinion. Women have reigned with distinction. Does not a crown carry with it a large part of the honors of the tiara? A woman's hand did not demean David's scepter. Why do we believe that she would disgrace the keys of Saint Peter?

I do not go so far as to adopt the cynical opinion of Abbé Lenglet, who in his book about the practices of the Romans seems to regret that women were excluded from the papacy.[11] At the same time, I cannot keep myself from including a passage he cites by a Protestant writer, the well-known Jurieu, whose pen, soaked in venom when he talks about Catholics, cannot be seen as suspect in this case: "I do not find that we (he is speaking on behalf of the members of his party) are very interested in proving the truth of this story about Popess Joan. If indeed the papal See was surprised by having named a woman pope when they thought they were naming a man, and if this woman then gave birth in a solemn procession, as it is told, this would not constitute a great disgrace in my opinion. And the advantage we would obtain from it is not worth the trouble of our having a great trial over it. I even find that the way that this story is told gives the Holy See more credit than it deserves. We are told that this Popess had studied a great deal, that she was learned, clever, and eloquent, that her fine talents made her much admired in Rome, and that she was elected by popular consensus, although she appeared as a young, unknown stranger without a friend and without any support other than her own merit. I say that it does much honor to the Holy See to presume that a young, unknown man can advance solely on the basis of his merit, for we know that since time immemorial the only way to be elected pope is through intrigue" (*In Defense of the Reformation*, vol. II).[12]

Not only did the story of the popess provide the subject for several long and erudite essays in which her existence was alternately affirmed and denied, but also she is the subject of a small poem of ten cantos written in decasyllabic verse by a Monsieur Borde, an academician from Lyon whose rather mediocre works are published in four volumes. In these volumes we find neither the Popess nor *Parapilla*, another free-spirited work by the same author in imitation of Saint Falion. Despite several licentious descriptions and some satirical jabs, the poem about the Popess had only limited success and did not merit any more.

Saint Eugenia, First Century

Virgin, then monk, then superior and abbot of the monks of Tabenne, succeeding Saint Pacoma and Saint Theodore, and finally martyr in Rome

Saint Eugenia, the daughter of the Roman nobles Philip and Claudia, was born during the reign of the Emperors Commodius and Severius.[13] Her father, having been named governor of Egypt, brought her, along with his wife and his two sons Avitus and Servius, to take up his position of leadership in Egypt. It was there that Eugenia, drawn by curiosity to several Christian meetings, and having heard songs claiming that the pagan gods were demons, made up her mind to adopt this religion in which one took pride in worshiping a single God. Reading Saint Paul's Epistles, which some Christians had given her, made her conversion complete. Although her wealth was commensurate with her birth, she renounced marriage. She hardly even appeared in public, and when she went out she covered part of her face. *Ne satiaret aspectum, vel quia sic decebat* [Lest anyone enjoy her face, and in this way she behaved properly]. To hide more successfully and to avoid the abuse of her parents, she disguised her sex with men's clothing and went to the monastery of Saint Theodore, the abbot of the Cenobites, that Saint Pacoma had founded. She was welcomed by Helen Eucque of Heliopolis. Eugenia learned the Bible while practicing the virtues of penance and Christian humility. She reached such a high level of perfection that she succeeded Theodore.

Melanthia, the wife of a senator and sick with quartan malaria, came to see Eugenia to be cured of this illness and fell madly in love with her, but she did not succeed in corrupting Eugenia. Her criminal passion disturbed Eugenia's peace and solitude. Like the wife of Potiphar in the case of Joseph, taking advantage of her husband's gullibility, Melanthia made her husband act unjustly and cruelly toward the saintly Abbot Eugenia. Carried away by violence and passion, Melanthia accused Eugenia of attempted seduction before the governor of the province. In this distressing situation, which was scandalous for the new Christians and especially for the monks of Tabenne, for whom she was both the superior and leader, Eugenia was obliged to appear before her father, the governor, who had long believed his daughter dead or lost. What a surprise for him and for everyone else when our saintly abbot revealed herself to be the governor's own daughter, whom he had sought so long in vain! Melanthia died of sorrow and shame, and her husband the senator went mad from despair and anger toward his wife.

Saint Eugenia, obliged to give up her disguise and the leadership of the Cenobites in the monastery and in the wilderness of Tabenne, converted her entire family. Widely known, she was led as if in triumph to her country, where she was the object as much of curiosity as of admiration. The father, having become a Christian, left his governing role to return to Rome. His daughter, having convinced many people there, including several of high birth, to convert to Jesus Christ, received the crown of martyrdom on December 28, 108, along with her father.

Saint Eugenia, Third and Fourth Centuries

Virgin and general of the Carmelite White Friars, succeeding Father P. Fronton

Father or rather Mother Saint Eugenia was a virgin from Alexandria, different from the Saint Eugenia whom we discussed above.[14] After working to convert two eunuchs, her servants, she had them join her in her plan to take leave of the world and her father's home. They consented, and on the pretext of traveling to see the world, she ran off disguised in men's clothing with the two eunuchs, Protus and Hyacinthe. In this outfit she went to see Father P. Hélène, the prior of the Cenobites of Alexandria and later the rector-general of the Carmelite White Friars.[15] She threw herself at his feet and asked permission for herself and her two companions to wear the holy habit.

The friars, who saw a young man with a fair and delicate complexion (for Eugenia had disguised her sex), raised some objections about accepting him, for fear that he could not endure the austerities of the Rule. They yielded, however, to his perseverance and importunity.

Brother Eugenia soon became an example to the whole monastery. His penance in no way changed his honest, civil, and considerate ways; and it won over the hearts of all, while rewarding him with the love and the pleasures of the monastery. After three years of monastic life, Father Hélène died. At the request and entreaty of all the friars, Eugenia was chosen to be prior of the monastery in Alexandria. After the death of Fronton, the third general of the Carmelite Order, Eugenia was elected to his position by unanimous acclamation, aided by the inspiration of the Holy Spirit. Do not be surprised, reader, that a woman was placed at the head of the monastery of the prophet Elijah because, as Saint Jerome says, it was the law of the Scriptures and the sacred Testament of God that women would take the place of men. These are divine decrees. This choice was, therefore, a celestial intervention, a work of the right hand of the Most High, and one of the secrets locked away in the treasures of Divine Providence.

Eugenia formed excellent disciples under her leadership. Her two eunuchs, Fathers Protus and Hyacinthe, died as priors of Carmel. It was to her glory to have guided the two priests Ammonius, one of whom was a Carmelite prior, and Father Seleucus, who later became a martyr. She sent to Tabenne as their new superior Father P. Ammonius, known as Saint Ammon of Tabenne.[16] She saw as many as fifteen hundred Carmelites living in this monastery as Canobites and almost fifteen hundred monks brought together in the wilderness. She led them in a manner worthy of their vocation and along the narrowest of paths of penance. Their clothing inspired a love of silence and retreat: their faces were always covered by their hoods, which they pulled down so as to not be seen by anyone and to not generate curiosity. They took their meals in such reverential silence and with so little attention for their brothers that they were not heard moving about, and not one of them could say how or whether their closest neighbor had eaten, although they were always together. The life of each one was as unknown to the others, as if they all had lived in separate cells. Each monk, as he wished, hid his self-mortification under the veil of humility, and nothing gave access to smugness and pride.

Eugenia and Ammon had no difficulty watching over such a docile flock. They often took care to instruct their monks with lectures appropriate for such withdrawn souls, or they taught them that which might further purify their virtue. One can see in the governance of this monastery and this wilderness what the prudence of the general and the abbot who directed them must have been, because by keeping their religious thus both together and apart, they inspired fervor through example. By allowing them the freedom to hide their self-mortification from each other, they freed them from vainglory.

Saint Eugenia's solicitude extended to nuns as well as to friars. She did not miss a single opportunity to provide them with new places for access to prayer. The empress Helen founded on Calvary a fine convent for women. Mother Mary was its first abbess. After her there followed Mothers Syncletic, Mattone, Sara, and Nona, all women of the highest nobility in the order.

The leadership of such a worthy general was gracious and gentle. Her style of governing had nothing hard or repugnant about it. Everyone obeyed her with joy: but it was a respectful and tender love such as a well-born son has for his father. Everyone was anxious to open his heart to her, to reveal to her his interior troubles, and to admit his temptations. All enjoyed an ineffable pleasure in these outpourings of the heart, felt comforted in their sorrows, and received infinite consolation from the intimate communications that they had with the reverend Father Eugenia.

When she died, they wanted to wash her body according to tradition: but what a surprise to find only a woman rather than a man! This caused a redoubling of tears and sighs. The whole monastery was stricken with sadness and grief, like a family that has lost its head. Some cried for a sister, others for a brother, some for a mother, others for a father. The friars, and the even more distressed nuns, sought in vain for their father and leader as well as their comforting mother. All were inconsolable over this loss for a long time. In their amazement, the White Friars and the Carmelite nuns from the cloisters of the provinces and the people from the surrounding areas came in large numbers to admire this holy virgin. Each one was anxious to see and touch this chaste body, and all of them wanted to have some relic of her.

Saint Marie, Fourth Century

Penitent, niece of Saint Abraham, who clothed her in the habit of a monk and had her pass as his nephew. She is included in the list of saints of Mount Carmel.

Saint Marie was the daughter of the sister of Saint Abraham, a monk in Mesopotamia. When she was seven years old, she lost her mother. As she was an orphan, she was brought to her uncle's cell so that he might decide his niece's future.

The Saint, without considering profane views, dressed her in the habit of a monk, had a cell built for her next to his, where he had her housed and took care to instruct her, through a small window between the cells, in all the duties of the faith and the practice of the Rule of Carmel, which the other monks in the wilderness followed. Together they prayed and sang praises to God and led a very saintly life. He had her learn by heart the Psalms of David. He explained the Holy Scriptures to her and inspired in her a taste for prayer and penance. For her part, she responded perfectly to her uncle's plans and advanced almost equally in age and in piety. Shut inside her cell, she imitated her uncle's style of life and virtue in every way. She fasted, prayed, and stood vigil as he did, and she worked part of each day making mats as did the other monks in the wilderness. When he believed her to be sufficiently advanced in the path of justice, on which she walked with such fervor, he had distributed to the poor the fortune that her father and mother had left to their daughter. He constantly advised Marie to keep her heart completely unattached to the creatures of the world, aware as he was of the schemes of the Devil, who transforms himself into the Angel of Light.

For her part, the niece begged the uncle to commend her to God in order that He might distance her from all thoughts contrary to chastity and the kind of life she was leading. She had placed her heart in a position of such abnegation regarding the world that God filled it entirely and provided her with a thousand joys that supported her love of self-mortification and silence. She spent twenty years of her life in this strict discipline. After having risen so high, she nevertheless had the misfortune to fall into the abyss. A short distance from the hermitage was a market town full of idolaters, who remained unswayed despite the zeal of the diocesan bishop and the efforts of the numerous missionaries he sent there. This bishop believed that Abraham the monk could do what the others could not do. After having ordained him a priest in his cell, despite Abraham's futile resistance, the bishop made him leave his cell and sent him to preach the Gospel to these barbarians.

The Saint began his mission with fasting and prayers. He chose an old monk from his wilderness to take charge, during his absence, of his niece, whom he passed off as his nephew. Despite his careful admonition to his niece not to reveal her true sex, the clever Devil set a trap for her from which she did not have the force to escape. In a short time, the hypocritical monk, having discovered through confession or other means that the young recluse was of a different sex, visited her often and conversed with her through her window under the pretext of advising her and of benefiting himself from her teachings. Soon he was on familiar terms with Marie and began to inspire in her worldly ways of thinking and made her lose interest in her mystical state by speaking of the sinful passion he felt for her. She resisted for a whole year. But that was not enough, and her first mistake was to say nothing about it to her uncle, who occasionally came to see her and help her bear his absence. Because of the number of conversions that God effected among the infidels through Saint Abraham, the Devil, as a revenge for the losses the Saint had cost him, once again used the old monk to attack the niece's chastity. He even transformed himself into the angel of light and assumed his language, the better to seduce Marie. He finally persuaded her to leave her cell and made her fall into sin. She ran away with the apostate friar. This is how one begins with the spirit and, far too often, finishes with the flesh.

Marie had no sooner committed the sin than she was overwhelmed with repentance. Embarrassed and in despair over the fault she had committed, and without hope for forgiveness, she strayed farther and farther

from the path of duty. She fled the country, changed her clothing, was reduced to serving the evil man to whom she had yielded, and then gave herself over to all kinds of debauchery. With the profits from this despicable
life, she bought herself new clothes and jewelry to better seduce men and
increase her profits. She went to a city where she was not known and took
up residence at an inn, where she continued for two years to live in the same
disorder.

At the very edge of the precipice God took pity on sister Marie. During two consecutive nights, her uncle, Saint Abraham, had a dream in which
he saw a dragon, whose head was covered by a hood, devour a dove. Not
having received any news from his niece or her spiritual advisor for a long
time, he became consumed by worry. He stole away from his mission one
night to knock at his niece's window. Since no one answered him and he
heard no indication of prayer or sleep, he sadly applied his dream to his
niece and her advisor. In despair but in vain he sought information about
what had become of them. For two years he learned nothing and spent all
his time sighing and praying to God to reveal to him where she was. As soon
as he discovered her whereabouts and learned of the deplorable life she was
leading, he had money and a riding outfit brought to him. Although he was
a decrepit old man, the good father Abraham mounted a horse, covered his
head with a large hat so that he would not be recognized, and went off to
find his lost sheep, in order to save her from the mouths of wolves and to
bring her back to the fold. He went straight to the city and the inn where his
niece was residing, had a copious dinner prepared, and told the host to have
brought to his room a young woman who was staying at the inn and whose
beauty was renowned. The host informed Marie, who was always ready to
receive travelers.

When her uncle saw her enter dressed as a courtesan, he was grief-
stricken. He was able, however, to restrain himself and appeared to be open-
minded and light-hearted. He closed the door and took this tender and
lovely nymph in his arms. Then after taking off the large hat that concealed
him, he spoke to her in the tone in which he always addressed her in the
past: "It is I, my child. Well, Marie, do you recognize me? Where are the
signs of your penance? What have you become, my dear girl, since you left
me? What has happened to the murderer who so cruelly assassinated you?"

Marie was so surprised she could neither talk nor lift her eyes. She remained prostrate in the arms of Saint Abraham, who used all the devices of his kindness and his charity to help her in her shame. He eloquently described for her God's mercies and cited the example of several individuals who returned to God's graces after sinful errors like hers. Marie, still dumbfounded and silent, fell to her knees, pouring out a torrent of tears, which her uncle allowed to continue without interruption for a long time. He spent the rest of the night consoling her and persuading her to return to her former cell. Marie finally made up her mind to leave. She asked her uncle what she should do with her money, her clothes, and her jewels. He had her leave them behind, for they were the riches of the devil. Placing her on his horse, he led her on foot to his monastery. Marie, to cleanse herself of her sins, wanted to bury herself alive, as if in a tomb. With this in mind, she had the door and even the window walled in, leaving only a small nailed opening to allow in daylight and the small amount of food that she consumed. She covered herself with a hair shirt and mortified herself continuously, spending days and nights praying, sighing, and asking God for the grace of His forgiveness.

Her uncle lived for yet another ten years, doing the same kind of work as before. Marie, after his death, spent the last five years of her life lamenting her sins. Through a long and difficult penance, she atoned most impressively for the scandal she had caused. She died at the age of forty-five. And God made it known, through the miraculous cures He gave her the power to perform, that He accepted her penance. She has been considered by the elders as the model for true penitents. The Church celebrates her memory on October 29.

Saint Euphrosyne, Fourth Century

Virgin and hermit, took vows under the name of Brother
Smaragde with the White Friars of Carmel, who placed her
among the holy men of their order

Saint Euphrosyne, a virgin from Alexandria, was the only daughter of the Blessed Paphnuce.[17] After receiving a thoroughly Christian education, she was baptized at the age of seven. She had been betrothed by her father to a young nobleman who suited the father's plans for his daughter. She was then eighteen years old, and the marriage was about to take place: but the power of grace over one's heart is limitless!

Euphrosyne had for a long time felt herself to be married to Jesus Christ. She would have no other spouse. Inspired by heaven, she fled from her father's house. Fearing that her parents would not allow her to enter a convent, she put on a man's clothing and went to a monastery on the other side of the Nile, near Alexandria, to find Father Théodose, the abbot of the monastery of the White Friars. There were then three hundred monks. The father of our young saint had often praised these hermits in her presence. She had once gone there with him and commended herself to the prayers of Saint Théodose. Thus she went to see this saint and pretended to be a eunuch named Smaragde, following the advice of a former hermit she had consulted. She pleaded for the habit of the Blessed Virgin Mary of Our Lady of Mont Carmel. The abbot, who mistook Euphrosyne for a eunuch because of her voice, her beardless chin, her beautiful face, and her fine features, welcomed Smaragde with joy. The neophyte was placed under the direction of Father d'Agapet, who was in charge of novices, and soon began winning over the hearts and the affection of the friars. She noticed that some of them were not insensitive to the charms of her eyes, and she feared that this would generate some passionate arousal in the monastery and that some sparks might fall on her own scapular.[18] As a result, the young postulate asked for permission from the abbot to leave the convent and to be shut up in a cell.[19] The abbot gave her permission and had her isolated, because of her beauty. There she spent the rest of her days as a recluse. In this retreat she lived in perpetual silence, spending day and night in prayer and giving fine examples of piety.

Her father, who looked everywhere for his daughter, came from time to time to the monastery to find some consolation for his loss. He often saw Brother Smaragde. Without suspecting anything, the father talked with her several times for his own edification. In speaking with the friar, he always felt deeply moved, and something about her drew him to the priest. But he never recognized Euphrosyne. How could he have imagined that this White Friar was his daughter Euphrosyne? Sister Euphrosyne, worn out by fasting, abstinence, and feeling close to death, was upset that she had worried her father, who did not know what had become of her. She had him come to her and explained her behavior while revealing her identity to him. Her father, with tears in his eyes and a heart full of joy, sorrow, and emotion, went to Abbot Théodose to declare the sex of Friar Smaragde and to tell him that the friar was his daughter Euphrosyne, which surprised the whole community and embarrassed some of the friars who had had too much affection for Friar Smaragde.

The father was so struck by his daughter's courageous resolve that, following her example, he dedicated himself to God in the same monastery and died there a saintly man. Euphrosyne died at the age of 56, having lived for 38 years in this isolation. The Greek Church honors her memory with a public celebration on September 29, and her feast day is very solemn in the East. Roman Catholics and especially White Friars, who have included her among the saints of their order, celebrate her feast day on February 11. Her relics are said to be found in the Abbey of Beaulieu near Compiègne in the dioceses of Soissons, Boulogne, and Trèves. This claim, however, does not seem sufficiently supported.

Sister Hérène, Fourth Century

The Blessed Sister Hérène, Carmelite monk

The convent grille, that fatal reef upon which the purity of religious women is often pitifully shipwrecked, was the reason for Saint Marie's fall.[20] Such a distressing occurrence made the other sisters of the wilderness more cautious. Sister Hérène learned from this fall, and so that she might avoid other opportunities for committing sin she made a decision that was more admirable than repeatable. She disguised her sex completely and hid away in a dreadful wilderness in Egypt. To her detachment from the things of this life, she added reverential silence. She lived for a long time in austere penance, separated from all human contact and eating only grass and roots as animals in the countryside do. She said that fasting was not enough to mortify the body, if one did not work as well. As a consequence, her body was so worn down that she could hardly hold it up, and she no longer felt any sense of rebellion coming from it. Until her death she practiced these rigorous acts of self-denial so above her sex and finally went to receive her reward in heaven. Although she was not canonized, her life is found in the catalogue of Carmelite saints; and the Popes have permitted that her feast day be celebrated.

Blessed Marguerite, Fourth Century

Blessed Marguerite, newly married, became a White Friar Carmelite under the name of Father Pélagius

Blessed Marguerite, through a secret inspiration from heaven, dared to do the same thing as Saint Euphrosyne.[21] During her wedding night she left her husband without giving any explanation. After changing her name as well as her clothing, she took the name of Pelagius and went off to a White Friar monastery. The abbot welcomed Pelagius with open arms, gave her a monk's tonsure, and entrusted her, a short time after she took her vows, with running a convent of Carmelite nuns.

Father Pelagius was accused of having lived in a free-spirited and libertine manner according to the mores of his century.[22] The nuns entrusted to him were apparently not all virgins. Several of them became fallen women. Father Pelagius was suspected of having had contact with them elsewhere than in the confessional. He could have easily justified his innocence and made known the calumny of the accusation. He carried the proof of it on himself, and it was irrefutable. But he preferred to appear guilty in the eyes of men and to submit to the harsh laws of the White Friars against those who cannot control their desires. He was judged in keeping with due process and condemned to prison for the rest of his days in a horrible cell, fed only bread and water, and only in very small quantities.[23] The bread was made only of barley and was placed in the hands of the pitiless monk who was her jailer and who made her bear, in all their rigor, the full range of punishments imposed by the laws of the order. Thus Father Pelagius spent the rest of her days in humiliation and penance. Far from complaining, she accused herself of being a great sinner and constantly asked God for forgiveness. Her innocence at the time of her death was like her sex: an enormous surprise for the community.

Saint Theodora of Alexandria

A female penitent disguised under the name of Theodore,
received as a White Friar Carmelite

The memory of what happened to Friar or rather Sister Eugenia was
still very recent when Saint Theodora, a Greek woman, after having broken
her conjugal vows to her husband, went off, through divine inspiration, to
join the White Friars, as if to a protected port where she would be shel-
tered from the storms after a shipwreck.[24] She was welcomed there under
the name of Theodore. It was common practice during that century and
the following ones for most disgraced women and girls to disguise their sex
and, under the outward appearance of eunuchs, to join the White Friars, as
though their monasteries were houses of refuge for repentant prostitutes.
This situation provoked the fall of several friars, and caused a scandal in
several monasteries.

Sister Alexandrine

The Blessed Sister hides in a tomb in the wilderness of Mount
Carmel under the name of Alexander

Sister Anastasia and Sister Sylvia, the daughter of the nobleman Pufin,
who was prefect of Alexandria, lived together. They believed that it was safer
for them to live in a cloister with virgins like themselves than with men, with
whom one's chastity is always vulnerable to harsh temptation. But Sister
Alexandrine, driven by a strong attraction for a life of retreat, locked herself
up in a tomb under the name of Alexander, where she lived for twelve years
without any communication with anyone, and received food only through
a small hole, without seeing the light of day. Saint Melanie, a Roman lady,
came to visit her and stood in front of this sepulcher; she reported that Alexandrine never wanted to be seen. When Saint Melanie insistently asked her
what made her leave the city of Alexandria and the world to bury herself in
this way, Alexandrine answered that it was to cure a man of the mad passion he felt for her and thus to avoid harming a soul that God had created
in his own image.

When God made it known to her that her hour had come, she placed herself in the position in which she wanted to be seen after death. The person who brought her weekly supply of bread and water arrived at the small window but did not hear her respond as she usually did. She alerted the bishop about it. He arrived there with several members of the clergy. The entrance to the tomb was opened, and she was found dead.

This kind of life was quite normal among the White Friars, although their style of life was not uniform, at least not in the Orient, where several lived alone as hermits as they saw fit. Some of them spent their lives in caves and among the rocks. Saint Nil lived this way. Others lived on top of columns and pyramids, weighed down by large chains fastened to their feet like beasts of burden, always standing and never lying down, and exposed to all the ravages of the weather. Such were the lives of the two Fathers Simeus Stylites, a type of life practiced by the Fakirs of India.

Permission to retire to the wilderness was usually given only to those who been tested over a long period of time in the monasteries and who had demonstrated the solid foundation of their virtue. Sometimes, however, the large number of individuals who came to the monastery to become monks, combined with the small amount of lodging available, necessitated that this permission be granted more easily. Thousands of White Friars lived in a single monastery. The monastery of the Abbot Isaac had a very large number of friars; that of Father Echéon was inhabited by three thousand.[25] We do not know exactly how many there were in the monastery governed by Mother Saint Eugenia. But the holiness of the superior and the austere conduct of the friars lead us to believe that it was no smaller than the others. The monastery governed by Father Eugenia in Syria became famous for the retreat of Saint Marine the virgin, whose memory the Church honors on July 17. Her history and her adventures are too glorious for the Carmelite White Friars not to warrant a separate article on her alone.

Saint Pelagia, Fifth Century

Penitent and hermit, disguised as a man known by the name of Pelagius

Among the large number of beautiful women who shone in the city and on the stage of Antioch, and who captivated the hearts of young men, there was none comparable to the famous actress Pelagia, either in physical charms or in the subtlety of her intelligence. This famous actress lacked nothing, except chastity. *Huic mulieri cuncta alia fuere praeceptet honestum animum* [To this woman all the rest are perceived as a virtuous soul] (Tacitus).

Her mother, one of the most beautiful women of her time, had given her beauty with all its charms. Her speech was pleasant and courteous, and her wit was very lively. She knew how to dress appropriately with an engaging modesty and how to surrender herself to her voluptuous impulses when she so desired. She never worried about her reputation and never distinguished between a lover and a husband. Without enslaving herself to her own inclinations, or to the inclinations of others, she yielded equally to everything she thought would be useful to her. She was famous for her talent and even more so for the excesses of her way of life. Her beauty, her dress, and her immodesty not only attracted the eyes of those who saw her but also involved them little by little in sin. She had thus acquired for herself much wealth and many protectors.

She usually traveled the streets riding on a mule and accompanied by a group of girls and boys. All those who were ruled by the desire for pleasure in the city of Antioch, where she lived, had eyes only for her. One day she was followed by a group of young men anxious to pay court to her. She was magnificently dressed but with an air of softness and voluptuousness. She passed in front of the church of the martyr Saint Julien. Maximian, the patriarch of Antioch, had called a meeting of the provincial bishops to discuss the affairs of their churches. Nonnus, a monk from Tabenne as well as the bishop of Heliopolis, was a member of this group. When he saw her go by with her retinue and dressed as she was in their presence, he could neither tolerate the impudence of this courtesan, nor hold back his tears, nor keep himself from taking his colleagues to task for their indifference. Nonnus stared at Pelagia and said in a trembling voice that he was afraid that this woman, who had taken so much trouble to adorn herself in order to please men, would one day be the downfall of Christians who are themselves so little concerned with pleasing God.

The next day, a Sunday, Pelagia, who had once been a catechism student but had never since that time had the slightest interest in learning anything about the principles of the Catholic religion, by chance came upon the church where Nonnus was preaching. As soon as he saw her, he preached with such force against sinful behavior that she was moved by his words and made up her mind to convert. After having written about this intention to the prelate, she went to see him, and without indulging herself any further, she simply threw herself at his feet in front of the other bishops with whom Nonnus was conferring in the church and confessed to him her wretched state. Nonnus tried to tell her that an actress and courtesan like herself could not be baptized without first having the needed time to strengthen her resolve and to be absolutely certain of her conversion. She begged him so tenderly that her conversion appeared to him to be sincere. After her insistent appeals and a lengthy religious instruction, not only did he baptize her but he also administered to her at the same time the sacraments of Confirmation and Holy Communion, upon the advice of the patriarch or other prelates in accordance with the practices of that time. Then Pelagia gave away all her belongings to the poor, freed her slaves, and encouraged them to become Christians. She soon exchanged her white baptismal dress of innocence for penitential clothing. She wore a hair shirt, secretly left the city of Antioch, and following the advice of Nonnus shut herself up in a cave on the Mount of Olives near Jerusalem, where, disguised in men's clothing and calling herself Pelagius, she led a most austere life. She had a monastery built in Jerusalem for penitent women.

When the council assembled in Antioch ended, Nonnus returned to his church in Heliopolis. Several years later, Jacques, the deacon for this bishop, wanted to go on a pilgrimage to Jerusalem. When he left, the bishop told him to ask about a hermit called Pelagius, who had been a recluse near the city for four years by then and of whom the bishop had heard. Jacques found the anchorite on a mountain in a cell whose only opening was a small window, which was usually closed. The horrible penance in which Pelagia was engaged had changed her so much that the deacon, who in any case had not been informed of her identity, was unable to recognize her. He told her that he had come to see her on behalf of Bishop Nonnus. The allegedly male hermit answered simply that Nonnus was a holy man and that she commended him to the deacon's prayers. She then immediately closed the window, and Jacques heard her begin Tierce.[26] Jacques then heard from monks in the region so many stories about the self-mortifications of this penitent that he wanted to see her again before he returned home. But he found the penitent dead.

After Pelagius's death, according to a contemporary author, the faithful of Jerusalem and the hermits from various places came to his cell. Once the blessed body was removed, it was placed with great respect on a golden sheet richly decorated with jewels. But when his superiors decided to rub the body with myrrh, they discovered that this was a woman. The news spread quickly. All the nuns from the convents from Jericho to the banks of the Jordan, where our Lord was baptized, came with lit candles singing hymns. And the relics of Pelagia were taken by her superiors to the church of Jerusalem. Her feast day is celebrated on October 8.

Saint Marina, Eighth Century

Virgin and White Friar of Carmel, known by the name of Brother Marin

This saintly woman, a virgin and hermit, received the name of Marie at her baptism. Her father Eugene, moved by a desire for salvation, renounced the world after the death of his wife and retired in Syria to the monastery governed by the holy Abbot Eugene, leaving the child Marie in the hands of a family member. The joy and contentment of his heart in solitude would have been perfect if only the peace and tranquility of his soul had not been troubled by worry about his daughter being lost to the world. The abbot of the monastery, a witness to the progress made by his new monk, was particularly fond of him. Noticing after a while that the new monk was becoming worried, the abbot asked him why. Eugene told him that he harbored some anxiety about having left behind in the world the child he had had with his now dead wife and that the destiny of this child troubled him greatly.

The abbot, who because of the ambiguity of the word *child* thought that it was a boy, told Eugene that he could have him brought to the monastery, where he would be educated. The father immediately went off to find his daughter. He cut her hair, gave her boy's clothing, had her give up the name of Marie and assume the name Marin, and told her to keep her sex secret until she died. He brought her in that state to the monastery, where she was taught reading, writing, plainsong, the rule of the monastery, minor observances, and serving Mass. The young Marin, still at a tender age, had no difficulty learning the practices and the life of Carmel, which soon became almost natural for her. At the age of fourteen, according to Casenate, Marina took her religious vows under the name of Brother Marin.[27] Her father continued teaching her with even more care in the ways of God, inspiring in her the love of virtue while cautioning her constantly about the dangers of the flesh and of the devil, to which she would be even more exposed than the other monks.

Brother Marin lost her father three years later and remained alone in her cell, dressed as a male and seventeen years old. Her fervor in her piety, her silence, her solitude, her humility, and her obedience soon made her an example for the entire community. It was the practice at this monastery for the friars to take turns going to the market, which was three leagues away, to buy the necessary provisions for the community. The friars complained that Brother Marin always remained in his cell praying and thus avoided going to the market, as they did. The abbot chastised her and told Marin to take her turn like the others. Marin obeyed and went the next day at dawn with the monastery's cart. Unable to finish the shopping in time, she was obliged to spend the night at an inn along the way. The innkeeper had a daughter who had secretly indulged in sin with a soldier. Her father, who realized that she was pregnant, wanted her to tell him who had corrupted her. This young woman, rather than name the soldier, accused young Friar Marin of having had relations with her and having committed the sin. The father went to lodge a complaint with the abbot. Upon this accusation, the abbot summoned Friar Marin. She appeared before the full assembly of the monastery and was questioned several times: she was tortured, a practice already in usage at that time, as it is still today. The torture produced no results; she preferred to bear the pain rather than to utter a single word that would reveal her sex and her innocence. Marin, without giving any explanation, answered only that she was a sinner and that she deserved to be punished. The abbot, who did not seek further evidence, believed Marin to be guilty of the charge and had her punished according to the rigorous standards of monastic discipline. After having endured all kinds of torment, hunger, thirst, chains, and whips from which she was very bruised, she was shamefully stripped of her habit, removed from the order, dishonorably excommunicated, and driven out of the monastery.

Marin remained for three years outside the door of the monastery without saying anything to defend her innocence, as she could have easily done. She slept on the ground exposed to the ravages of the weather and the rigors of the seasons. Reduced to the ultimate wretchedness, she prostrated herself before all the monks who entered and left and asked them for their prayers and a morsel of bread in her extreme need.

Adding even more to her shame and iniquity, when the woman from the inn had weaned her child, the grandmother brought it to the monastery and left it with Friar Marin, as if she were the child's father and thus obliged to feed it. She took care of it without complaining or muttering and nourished it for five years from the alms that were given to her.

The monks were so touched by the penance of Friar Marin and her perseverance in her own humiliation that they asked the abbot to grant her forgiveness and begged him insistently to allow Marin back into the monastery. He finally agreed, but in order to impose a penance commensurate with the crime of which the abbot thought Marin guilty, he assigned to her alone the tasks of sweeping the whole monastery every day, carrying water to wherever it was needed, and serving all the friars.

Marin submitted to everything and accepted this penance willingly, although the work required was more than she could handle. For a time she was able to do it all, showing a courage not typical of her sex, until her body—exhausted by the fasting, the mortifications, and the work—finally succumbed. After several days of sickness, she died. The friars debated about whether to bury her body in holy ground or to throw it in a public waste yard. Out of compassion and without regard for Marin's crimes, the abbot ordered that her body be washed according to custom before burying her some place far from the monastery. Those who went to carry out this order recognized that she was a woman and came to inform the abbot. He wanted to see for himself. When he was convinced, he and his monks beat their breasts, gave themselves over to sorrow, and with many cries and tears asked God to forgive them for all the evils they had visited upon the saint.

The situation was revealed to the innkeeper. His daughter, embarrassed and in despair, admitted her crime and prayed to the saint that she might obtain forgiveness from her. The news spread throughout the area, and people came from far and wide to honor the tomb of Saint Marine, where several miracles took place. This monastery became renowned for the retreat and the penance of this virgin dressed as a man. Her story and her adventures are too glorious for the Carmelites not to be reported here in all the detail that I could find in the works of Church historians. Rather than leave her with the name of Marie, she is commemorated in the martyrologies under the name of Marine. Her feast day is not celebrated everywhere on the same day. The Greeks remember her on February 12. Some Roman Catholics place her feast day on the 8th of February. The Roman Catholic Church remembers her on July 17. It is reported that her body was moved from Greece to Venice around the year 1230. In Paris there is a church with the name of this saint.

Saint Hildegonde, Twelfth Century

Virgin and Bernardine, known by the name of Friar Joseph

Saint Hildegonde, a virgin in the Cistercian order in the 12th century, known by the name of Friar Joseph, had a twin named Agnès and was a native of the diocese of Cologne near the small town of Neuss. The girls were first sent to school in a convent in this town with the intention of making them nuns and thereby fulfilling the double vow made by their father and mother to consecrate their daughters to God and to make a pilgrimage to the Holy Land. After the mother of these two children died, their father had Agnès take the nun's veil and had Hildegonde accompany him to Palestine. In order that his daughter Hildegonde's purity be safe from possible attack, he had her dress as a boy and persuaded her to take the name of Joseph. They passed through France and embarked on a ship from Provence with some Crusaders. The father died during the voyage and commended the care of Joseph to a domestic in his service. Joseph, accompanied by his father's valet, continued his trip, arrived in Jerusalem, and went to Acre, which the Ancients called Ptolomede. This valet, who was responsible for the money and all the effects of the young Joseph, was so despicable that he ran away and took with him everything that his master had entrusted to him.

Joseph, in dire straits because of this theft, met a stranger who took care of her and brought her back to Jerusalem, where she remained for almost a year. They decided to return to Europe and, once they arrived in the diocese of the archbishop of Cologne, Joseph unfortunately lost this charitable companion, who in his will left Joseph his property and his money. When Joseph arrived in Cologne, she did not want to be recognized or to change her appearance. She passed herself off as a foreigner and in that role accepted the lodging that a canon of Cologne offered her. As a result, she developed such a close friendship with this canon that she went on a voyage to Rome with him. They returned together up to Spire, where Joseph remained in order to negotiate several matters for the canon.

We read in the *The Annals of Citaux*, Book 3, Year 1185, that our saint "on the way from England to Italy, encountered a thief. Since he was being pursued by archers, the thief left what he had stolen in Joseph's hands and hid in the forest. Joseph was tracked, found, arrested with the stolen goods, and condemned to death. But her innocence was soon recognized when the thief was found, and he received the death penalty. The relatives of the thief, furious about the disgrace that dishonored their entire family, took it out on Joseph and hung her from a tree. The angel of the Lord helped her in this dire situation and supported her so that she was not strangled by the rope, and also he strengthened her by his presence. Joseph remained hung in this fashion for three days. Shepherds, who were in the region, came to cut the rope and take the cadaver down from the gallows. The body fell softly to the ground. The angel of the Lord said to Joseph: 'You are free. Where do you want to go?' 'Lord,' she replied, 'I want to go to Verona.' The guardian angel immediately gave her a horse, placed her on it, and in an instant she was in Verona."

We do not guarantee the authenticity of this particular miracle, which we have only on the authority of the Reverend Père Mautique, the author of *The Annals of Citaux*. But we do know from other Church historians that Joseph finally decided to withdraw from the world and accepted the offer of a retreat that a gentleman named Bertholo offered her. They went together to the abbey of Schönau, a monastery in the Cistercian Order in the diocese of Worms, not far from Heidelberg. Hildegonde was welcomed by the monks of this monastery. After a year-long novitiate, she took her vows under the name of Joseph and conducted her life there in such a holy and prudent manner that it was noticed only at her death that she was of a different sex from those with whom she lived.

Until then, the Cistercians had accepted only men as monks, as far as

I know. But virgin women began to arrive disguised as men. They were admitted as friars. Saint Hildegonde was the first one mentioned in the annals of the order, and she paved the way for others. She no doubt had to ward off serious temptations regarding her chastity. Things could hardly have been otherwise. The friars were no less severely tested by her presence. The proud north wind, to use the language of the annals of the order, blew hard on them; a blinding and hidden fire consumed them. The voice and the eyes of the novice generated in their hearts an unchaste flame, which burned them without their knowing its source. Cupid did not wreak more havoc on the island of Calypso than Joseph did in the monastery. The friars' faces blushed upon seeing her: they were full of emotion. To deaden the impact of this fire and to repress the impulses of the flesh, they had recourse to fasting, mortification, scourging, and bloodletting.

"As long as Joseph is among you, you will burn," warned a monk from this convent, when he saw Joseph. In a loud voice, he said to those around him: "This novice can only be a woman or a devil. Never have I been able to look upon him without being tempted."[28] He told the truth, a truth acknowledged after Joseph's death. The Friars Minor would not have waited so long to clear up such a serious uncertainty. A physical examination would have soon calmed everyone and removed all doubt. The way they handled Friar John in an identical situation indicates the way they might have acted in the present circumstances.

The various martyrologists of Germany, of the Low Countries, as well as those of the Cistercians and the order of Saint Benoît, all give her the title of saint and celebrate her feast day on April 20. Her veneration, however, does not appear to be authorized by any decree from the Holy See, and we find no signs that there were legal proceedings that would lead to her canonization (Baillet, *La Vie des saints*).

Saint Athanasia

Saint Athanasia took the religious habit in a monastery in Tabenne without making known her sex. She then lived as a hermit with her husband, Saint Adonia, without his recognizing her until her death.

See Father Michel-Ange Marin of the Order of the Minims, *Vies des Pères des déserts d'Orient, avec leur doctrine spirituelle, et leur discipline monastique* (Avignon, 1761), vol. 3, p. 3, sec. 4.

Saint Catherine of Cardona, Sixteenth Century

*Saint Catherine of Cardona, virgin and hermit who, despite the
fact that her sex was known, was allowed to profess her vows
among the barefoot holy fathers of Carmel from Pastrane in
Spain. The papal nuncio wanted her to renounce being a White
Friar and to become instead a Carmelite nun. She proved to him
that heaven wanted her to be a White Friar.*

Despite foreign and domestic persecution, the reforms that Saint Theresa instituted among the Carmelites and the White Friars proceeded rapidly from the beginning. There were among both sexes amazing examples
of humility, obedience, self-denial, and chastity. Among the large number recorded by the historians of the order, the one that stands out as the
most unusual is undoubtedly the blessed and venerable Mother Catherine
of Cardona. She was born in Naples in 1519. She was of the family of the Duke
of Cardona, allied to the Salerno family, and a descendant of the house of
Aragon. We learn from Saint Theresa various edifying details about the life
of this exemplary girl. She received an education suitable to her station and
was betrothed at the age of thirteen to a Neapolitan lord, who died some
time before the marriage took place. Before she chose to leave the world,
she was highly vigilant about her own behavior, never partook in any of
the world's profane pleasures, and already observed many of the Carmelites' austere practices. She strongly wished to withdraw entirely from the
company of society in order to go into solitude and to concentrate only on
meditation of divine matters. She could not be dissuaded from this plan,
which grew ever more firm in her soul. She spoke about it often with those
who were directing her on the path of salvation. They did all they could
to dissuade her from this undertaking, which they considered to be fool-
hardy. The world, according to Saint Theresa, is so full of timidity that it
finds excess and recklessness in everything that one wants to undertake for
God, but hardly anyone remembers the extraordinary favors He bestowed
upon the men and women saints who abandoned everything to go to the
wilderness in order to serve Him.

Catherine, released from her promise by the death of her fiancé, withdrew from the world among the Capuchin nuns of Naples, with whom she

spent some time most piously and in great penance. The Princess of Salerno, who had received the order from Philip II to return home to Spain, took with her Catherine, her close relative, who found it very difficult to leave her beloved convent. Upon her arrival at Walladolic, she suffered a cruel case of gout, but she was miraculously cured by Saint Cosmo and Saint Damien, who appeared to her dressed as White Friars.[29] She was admired by the whole court of Spain because of her rare piety; and Philip II found no one in all his vast kingdom better suited to be the governess of his sons, the princes, than Catherine. At court she led a life as austere as in the strictest convent. She lived on only a few vegetables and usually fasted four days a week, and there were even some days when she did not eat at all. She did not wear fine linen but rather a rough grey serge from the Minims. She sometimes wore a hair shirt, which was so harsh and rough that the tips pierced her skin. Sometimes, to mortify herself even more, she wore around her waist a heavy iron chain. She recited daily the seven penitential psalms, the services for the dead, the hourly prayers of the Holy spirit and those of Our Lady: she scourged herself almost every day with chains made of hooks, which tore her at her flesh.

These acts of self-mortification were only preludes to those she was to practice when she was alone. She was not in her element at court; she constantly yearned to go into retreat. Catherine, through a special intercession of Providence, confessed to a monk of the order of Saint Francis, who was very enlightened about spiritual life. She revealed her plans to him, and he encouraged her to carry them out and to respond to her divine calling. She then confided her plans to a hermit from Alcala, who strengthened her resolve. She asked him to accompany her. Following the advice of the two friars, she disguised herself as a male hermit. Taking only three loaves of bread for nourishment, as did Saint Mary the Egyptian, she withdrew to the wilderness, where she lived for a while unrecognized thanks to her disguise. So as to better hide her identity, she usually spoke in a husky voice. They went together to a place where a monastery of White Friars was later built, near Villeneuve de la Xare. It was a pleasant wilderness, and they found a cavern, but it was so small that the holy woman barely had room for herself. The hermit left her there with the three loaves of bread he had brought, and he returned to his solitude.

One can hardly read without trembling just how far Catherine's spirit of penance took her. For her residence, she had only her very small cave; for a bed, she had only the ground, which was very wet in the winter and very hot in summer. For a pillow, she used a large rock. Her only blanket was her rough and coarse habit. Her furnishings were hair shirts, scourges, iron chains, and other instruments of penance. She wore under her coarse monk's habit a tunic that went down to her knees and a hair shirt made of very coarse and biting horsehair. Tight around her waist, she wore an iron chain with many sharp spikes. She scourged herself frequently for two and three hours at a time. This holy penitent's vigils were no less demanding than her other self-mortifications. After spending almost the whole day chanting prayers, she spent the night in meditation, making do with a single hour of rest. Even that hour was often interrupted, for her body was so burdened by hair shirts and chains and so beaten down by blows that her mind was constantly awake.

After she had eaten the three loaves of bread that her director had left for her at the beginning of her retreat, she chose to feed herself with roots and grass from the wilderness and made herself graze on the ground as a sheep would do, without the help of her hands. Furthermore, in the fervor of her penance, she reduced the amount of time spent grazing. In addition, she punished herself by grazing on only a limited portion of the grasses, not allowing herself to eat any of those that the donkeys ate. She lived in this fashion for her first three years in the wilderness. She made such progress that she spent forty days, in imitation of our Lord, without drinking or eating. But she was so weakened by this fast that, unable to remain standing, she leaned on a cross as she fell, crying out: "Oh, Lord! I will die if you do not help me." Our Lord visibly helped her. Such a great miracle of virtue could not remain hidden for long. A shepherd named Benites was one of the first to encounter Catherine as she was grazing on the grass. He insisted that she take some bread. But she could hardly eat any for, since she had eaten nothing but grass for three years, she had such soft and delicate gums that this new nourishment made them bleed.

Benites, unable to learn from Catherine the location of her cave, returned the next day to the same place. After inspecting with curiosity all the areas where she had grazed, he realized that near a place coming out of the mountain the grass was a bit more trampled than elsewhere. He followed this clue and came immediately upon a passageway that had been made through some large thorny hedges and blocked by a bundle of dried wood. This was the entrance to a cave carved into the mountain. The bundle of wood that served as a door was attached at the top and the bottom with ropes made from broom weed, which served as hinges, and on the inside there was another rope with which Catherine closed herself in. Benites, strongly suspecting that Catherine was in there then, did not want to enter by force or without her permission. He waited by the door as Saint Anthony had once done at Saint Paul's cave, and he made such strong entreaties with his tears and his prayers that he obtained entry into the cave. Once Catherine's way of life was revealed by Benites, the peasants in the area compelled her to moderate somewhat her rigorous living conditions. She condescended to eat a bit of bread every week, about four ounces in weight. On major feast days, she put a little bit of oil on the bread, which the inhabitants of the area brought her. On the most solemn feasts of Christmas and Easter, she took as much flour as she could hold in her fist and made a small flat cake, which she cooked over a fire. That was her greatest culinary feast.

She suffered considerably in her cave because of the devils who waged a cruel war against her. They attacked her sometimes with troublesome suggestions, sometimes with the ghosts of ferocious beasts: but she always scorned their efforts.

When she scourged herself, these clever spirits violently grabbed the whip out of her hand, and they themselves hit her brutally with it; they tore her skin with their blows and left her bloodied. After using the whip on her body, they tore at her with lions' claws, dogs' teeth, bludgeons, and snake skins. Once while she was in prayer, the devil came at her from the rear in the form of a large black dog with long hair sticking up; he attacked her with great violence and knocked her over into the thorns. Another time he appeared to her disguised as an ugly toad. Catherine, thinking that it really was a toad, took her broom and knocked it out of her cell. The devil was so indignant that he threw her down the mountains onto the rocks at the base. For a long time she bore the bruises from the blows that she received from these clever spirits.

Before she founded the monastery of the White Friars, she went to Mass with the monks of Mercy, not far from her cave. She made this voyage as a penitent, dressed in a tunic of rough cloth that covered her like a hermit such that she was always taken to be a man. After more than eight years of solitude spent observing these austere practices, her reputation spread. She was visited by several people who came to be edified by the example of her life. Her retreat became famous thanks to those who came to see her from all parts of the region. There was sometimes such a large crowd that she was obliged to climb to an elevated spot in order not to be overwhelmed. But the number of people increased along with their admiration when it became known that the hermit was a woman disguised in the hermit's habit. Her sex was learned through a letter from Prince Dom Jean of Austria, which was found in her cave, and by the prayer book that she used and on which was written: "The Princess of Evora gave this prayer book to Catherine of Cardona." From that time on, her named was changed, and she was called only the "good woman."

She fell seriously ill but did not want to leave her cavern. One day a woman whom Catherine had brought with her on a pilgrimage returned home to their cell for the night and noticed, as she pretended to sleep, that the holy woman took off her hair shirt to wash it and to remove the blood from it. Several devout women who wanted to remove the vermin that were feeding on her saw on her shoulders large bumps the size of half an orange. So many marks of austerity and so many virtues could not long remain hidden in the wilderness, and they soon came to serve as examples that touched the hearts of sinners and even those of the most faithful Christians.

The Reform of Saint Theresa was creating quite a stir at that time and had just come into force. God, who wanted to use Catherine as one of the most important supporters of Carmel, inspired in her the resolve to embrace this group. One day while she was in fervent prayer before a crucifix that she always carried, He inspired this resolve within her in a very special way. He had Jesus Christ appear to her in the habit of a barefoot White Friar, with the prophet Elias holding in his hand a habit of that order, which he presented to her.[30] Twice she received the same visit. The last was on Easter Sunday. The cave where she lived suddenly collapsed in on her. She was seriously hurt by this cave-in, for she spent the whole night with part of her body trapped under the debris. So many extraordinary signs of God's intentions for her made her travel without delay to Toledo and from there to Pastrane to the home of the barefoot White Friars. She was welcomed with joy by the fathers, who had known her for a long time; and without making any reference to her sex, which was not unknown to them, they gave her the habit of the White Friars and administered her vows.

The papal nuncio, who was in Madrid, was surprised and scandalized by this action, as were several other persons. He summoned Catherine and ordered her to no longer wear the habit of the White Friars. He told her to wear a habit appropriate for her sex and to go to a convent for women. They said that a monastery was not appropriate for her, that there was too much to fear both for her and for the monks, and that at the very least, scandal, which her presence inevitably entailed, must be avoided. But Catherine explained to him humbly that she had acted only on inspiration from heaven. "Our Lord Jesus Christ," she said, "appeared to me carrying a robe similar to the one I am wearing; the prophet Elias also visited my dreams wearing the same robe of the barefoot White Friar." The nuncio, convinced by her insistent explanations and recognizing that there was in this transformation something supernatural, yielded to Catherine's entreaties and left her with the habit of the White Friars.

When she was under the vow of obedience, she was obliged to moderate a few of her strict practices by order of the prior. He required that she eat with the community on Thursdays, Sundays, and Tuesdays, but her stomach was so weak that she was unable to eat what they did. Half of a sardine was too much for a single meal, and she had to force herself. So she was given free rein to choose her own nourishment.

After having finished her novitiate at Pastrane, she returned, with the permission of her superior, to her cave in order to found a monastery of barefoot White Friars under the name of Our Lady of Perpetual Help. Her crucifix, which she had left at the monastery, miraculously followed her in the air. Jesus Christ appeared to her disguised as a poor beggar and asked her for alms. When she answered him that she had nothing, the poor man said: "But, my mother, you could cut a piece from the robe you are wearing, which is clearly too large, and it could serve as a small hood for me."

A church and a monastery were built in the place where the cave was located, and another cave was dug for her nearby, and it is there that she spent her last five years among the White Friars, after the monastery was built, busy in the practice of all kinds of virtues and meditating day and night on eternal truths. She finished her career, which was filled with merit and good works, on May 11, 1577.

⚛ *Notes* ☙

Introduction

1. University of Leeds, Brotherton Collection, Papers of d'Eon (hereafter ULBC), file 52 and box 7, pp. 197–204. The term *Maiden of Tonnerre* (*la pucelle de Tonnerre*) is mentioned also in file 19, p. 23, file 22, p. 90, and box 8, Rough Notes II: 1026.

2. [Thomas Plummer], *A Short Sketch of Some Remarkable Occurrences During the Residences of the Late Chevalier d'Eon in England* (London, 1810).

3. "My dear Rousseau, my old colleague in politics, my master in literature, companion in my misfortune, you who, like me, had proof of the caprice and injustice of many of my compatriots," d'Eon to Rousseau, February 20, 1766, in *Correspondence complète de Jean-Jacques Rousseau*, ed. R. A. Leigh, 46 vols. (Oxford, 1965–87), 28: 313–18.

4. ULBC, file 43, p. 1191.

5. Archives Nationales, 277 AP 16, file 5, bk. 1.

6. For a fuller treatment of d'Eon's life, see Gary Kates, *Monsieur d'Eon Is a Woman: A Tale of Political Intrigue and Sexual Masquerade* (Baltimore, 2001). The best biography in French is Pierre Pinsseau, *L'Etrange destinée du chevalier d'Eon, 1728–1810*, 2d ed. (Paris, 1945).

7. Archives Nationales, 277 AP 16, file 5, contains a diary in which d'Eon jotted notes and book titles regarding viniculture.

8. Simon Linguet, "Gagure sur le sexe du Chevalier d'Eon," *Annales politiques, civiles, et littéraires du dix-huitième siècle* 1, no. 7 (1777): 383–97; ULBC, box 12, p. 32.

9. Acts 22:6–11 and 26:12–18.

10. *London Packet or New Evening Post*, May 24–27, 1771; *Public Advertiser*, April 17, 1771.

11. La Fortelle, *La Vie militaire, politique, et privée de mademoiselle d'Eon* (Paris, 1777; 2d exp. ed. 1779). It was soon translated into Italian (1779) and Russian (1787).

12. We have, however, reason to doubt d'Eon's authorship of the *Pious Metamorphoses*, or at least of some of its parts. First, the handwriting is not d'Eon's. Second, sometimes the grammar and syntax are quite different from his autobiographical writing. Third, he discusses topics such as sex and romantic love that are

almost self-consciously ignored in the autobiographical manuscripts. Nonetheless, we believe that he wrote at least the preface and that he certainly collaborated in the production of the other material, perhaps assigning it to a younger research assistant. Above all, d'Eon himself chose to include this manuscript among his writings, thereby claiming it as his own.

13. *Lettres de madame la duchesse de la Vallière, morte religieuse carmélite; avec un abrégé de sa vie pénitente* (Paris, 1767).

The Great Historical Epistle by the Chevalière d'Eon, Written in 1785

The word *epistle* invokes the New Testament writings of Paul, which were familiar to d'Eon and which set the tone for this autobiography. The Latin is a corrupted version of a citation from Virgil's *Aeneid:* "Infandum, regina, iubes renovare dolorem" (bk. 2, v. 3). These words are spoken by Aeneas when Dido requests that he recount his adventures in Troy. Literally translated, it means, "The grief you order me to revive, Queen, is too horrible to mention." D'Eon substituted "unhappiness" for "grief." Many of the persons mentioned in the autobiography are listed in the Biographical Glossary.

Chapter I

1. In d'Eon's papers at the University of Leeds, Brotherton Collection (hereafter ULBC), file 2, p. 6, d'Eon noted that Théodore-André-Timothée-Louis-Cesar d'Eon de Beaumont was baptized on February 4, 1727, and died a few months later, on August 6. He added that "Villon is a pleasant little village at the edge of the great Maulnes forest in the region of Tonnerre." It was a custom of the time to send infants to the country for wet-nursing.

2. *Née coiffée* means born with a caul. In a manuscript variant from ULBC, file 2, d'Eon claimed that he was born *la tête coiffée jusqu'au sein,* which idiomatically refers to a condition at birth in which fetal membranes cover the infant's head. *In nubibus* literally means "behind veils." D'Eon may have been referring to a condition wherein a male's testicles are not descended at birth and are thus hidden from view. In the variant mentioned above, Dr. Gueniot, who was on site for d'Eon's birth, is quoted as saying to the father: "I cannot verify if the newborn is a girl or a boy. His nature, like his head, is still *in nubibus.*" Later in the manuscript, d'Eon's father says to his concerned wife: "I cannot yet be happy or sad about the present you have bestowed. Its sex is as covered as its head, but the doctor hopes that nature will soon be developed and that it will be a good boy by the grace of God or a good girl by the virtue of the Blessed Virgin."

3. On October 7, 1728, d'Eon was baptized as Charles-Geneviève-Louise-Auguste-André-Timothée d'Eon de Beaumont. It was not unusual for a person to have male and female Christian names. His baptismal record is reproduced in Michel de Decker, *Madame Le Chevalier d'Eon* (Paris, 1987), following p. 95.

4. D'Eon used the word *cornet* to speak of his military achievement. This word was used to designate the valedictorian of a military school.

5. D'Eon explained that "this respectable lady died after the Revolution near her son in the port city of l'Orient in Brittany from the weight of old age and that of her good works, especially her charity toward the poor."

6. The *cour des aides et comptes* was one of the appeals courts in France for matters of taxation and finances.

7. D'Eon was quoting from Voltaire's letter to Rousseau of August 30, 1755, acknowledging receipt of Rousseau's *Discourse on the Origin of Inequality:* "To read your book makes one long to go on all fours."

8. A *lettre de cachet* was a warrant for arrest and seizure, often used without just cause and therefore associated with the excesses of royal power.

9. A *generalité* was a treasury subdivision used in the administration of taxes by the *ancien régime.*

10. The Thebaïds were the territories near Thebes where in antiquity pious, reflective people lived in an austere desert setting.

11. Mont St. Bernard and Mont Blanc are two of the highest peaks in the Alps.

12. The War of 1745 was part of the War of Austrian Succession (1740–48), which pitted, among others, France and Prussia against England and Austria.

13. In 1763 d'Eon won the coveted Cross of Saint Louis for military valor in the Seven Years' War. During the 1790s, d'Eon became particularly well known for his excellence in fencing.

14. D'Eon wanted to be identified as an informed student of the Enlightenment. Of course, "philosophical" in this context means stoic or frugal. After his pensions were terminated following the French Revolution, d'Eon slipped further and further into poverty. See d'Eon's account book preserved in ULBC, box 13.

15. D'Eon was playing upon a common theme in the literature of the *querelle des femmes,* celebrating the physical training women received in ancient classical education. See the anonymous pamphlet owned by d'Eon, *Female Rights Vindicated* (London, 1758).

16. The reference here is to the four trips d'Eon took between St. Petersburg and Paris between 1756 and 1761.

17. Astrakhan is a Russian city known for its sheep with tightly curled wool.

18. These somewhat enigmatic allusions possibly refer to the Prince de Conti, the Duc de Praslin, and the Comte de Guerchy.

19. D'Eon's father and uncle both died in 1749.

20. D'Eon's "Eloge du Comte d'Ons-en-Bray, Président de L'Académie des Sciences" was published in 1753 in *l'Année littéraire.*

21. The Châtelet was the seat of royal jurisdiction where notaries handled estates and wills in Paris.

22. The Aulic Council was a highly placed advisory council to the ruler of the Holy Roman Empire. D'Eon thus ironically gave himself the prestige of having highly placed advisors, such as the Prince de Conti, during his political career.

23. The French is *poule mouillée,* which literally translates as wet hen. Antoine Furetière, *Le Dictionnaire universel,* ed. Alain Rey (Paris, 1978), states that "to make fun of a coward or of a fool who does woman's work, he is called a wet hen."

24. Eighteenth-century French army officers did not share sleeping quarters with their troops but slept in individual areas apart from the enlisted military.

25. The letter *A* was an arbitrary point of reference invented by d'Eon to determine how to proceed in his prophetic reading of the Holy Scriptures. Since d'Eon believed that the Bible was inspired by God, the drawing of lots from the Scriptures was sacred. He would open the New Testament to an arbitrarily chosen page, blindly select a passage on the left and another on the right, then compare the first letter of each of the two passages. The passage whose first letter was closer to the letter *A* provided d'Eon with advice concerning the prospect of entering a convent; the passage whose first letter was farther from *A* was a commentary on joining the dragoons.

26. The passage is at the end of an episode wherein a Canaanite woman came to Jesus to ask what to do about her possessed daughter. The disciples were uncomfortable having a nonbeliever in their midst. Jesus replied with the passage cited by d'Eon and then performed a miracle to rid the woman's daughter of the devil.

27. The actual passage of Luke 3:11 has Jesus answering to a crowd of people rather than to a single individual.

28. In the Roman Catholic Church, a novena is a practice of a particular devotion for nine consecutive days. By advising d'Eon to give priority to a pilgrimage in honor of his namesake Mary, Dom Bernard was deferring to the hierarchical position of the Virgin Mary as the mother of God, vis-à-vis Saint Geneviève. In a note, d'Eon identified the location of this shrine to Mary thus: "Hautvervilliers or Notre Dame des vertus is a French village on the plain of St. Denis. It is a regular site for pilgrimages and is less than eight kilometers from Paris."

29. Actually, Mark 10:38 has Christ responding to James and John, rather than to a single person, as d'Eon cited in the passage.

30. Guy-Jean-Baptiste Target was indeed one of the great legal minds of his generation. Elected to the Estates General in 1789, he contributed to the legal reform during the Revolution and became a judge. D'Eon provided the additional comment: "More recently he believed he was acting prudently by recusing himself as the lawyer for our unfortunate King. The more bold Monsieur de Lamoignin de Malesherbes undertook the King's defense and lost his head because of it."

31. D'Eon added the following anecdote: "This preference aroused the jealousy of my classmates. They wanted to see me get into trouble along with them. They decided to trick the young chambermaid who did up our beds by throwing a blanket over her head. She complained bitterly about being jumped and gave the names of the six guilty ones, who claimed that they were from my dormitory room and that I had participated with them in jumping the young woman. In my defense, I simply said to ask the maid if I was guilty. Once she pointed out that I had defended her like a lion and that without me she could not have escaped from them,

they were all whipped soundly in front of me. Among the guilty several have since become well known: Monsieur Debrienne, the Archbishop of Toulouse and Sens as well as a cardinal; Monsieur Hue de Mirouenil, Chancellor and guardian of the seals of France; Dom Chanlate, the Abbé of Pontigny and director of the Order of Bernardines of the second chapter in Citeaux; Dom Robinet de Grignon, prior of the Carthusian monastery of Paris and since then the Director-General of the Carthusians; and the Marquis de Nonan, the Brigadier General of the carabineers, who was the first to hold me back when I incited a gentleman to draw his sword in 1752 at Comerre. Since that time, he was first at the Carthusian monastery in Paris and later guillotined on the Place de la Révolution because of his zealous devotion to the cause of Louis XVI. As for me, it's quite enough to have had my sex [literally, tail] and my passion sacrificed in the service of the King without losing my head and my neck in the affair."

32. D'Eon explained that Septfons is "the great Carthusian monastery." According to Donald Attwater (ed., *The Avenel Dictionary of Saints* [New York, 1965], pp. 123, 231), Euphrosyne and Marina may be fictional in that there is no known verification of either one's birth or death. To avoid marriage, Euphrosyne is said to have dressed as a man and then continued to lead a cloistered life. Saint Marina was disguised as a boy by her father when he entered a cloister with her. Upon his death, she continued to live disguised as a male until her death, when her identity as a woman was discovered. D'Eon devoted short chapters to both Euphrosyne and Marina in the *Pious Metamorphoses* (see Part III).

33. "Both perspectives" refer to the differing theological and hence political perspectives of the religious orders of monks, in this case, the Benedictines and the Carthusians. The Carthusian order was founded at Chartreuse, France, in 1086 by Saint Bruno under the Benedictine rule. The Benedictines, founded in 529, were in competition with the "upstart" order (the Carthusians) regarding the conduct of a retreat. D'Eon's remark about it being "dangerous" to undergo a retreat with both orders referred to his being thus enmeshed in the politics of the competition between the two orders.

34. *Essai historique sur les différentes situations de la France par rapport aux finances sous le règne de Louis XIV et la régence du duc d'Orléans* (Amsterdam, 1754) was primarily a survey of French finance ministers and their policies since 1643. The manuscript of "the short historical treatise" has apparently been lost. Perhaps d'Eon was referring to an early version of his *Mémoires pour servir à l'histoire générale des finances*, 2 vols. (London, 1758; Amsterdam, 1760). We are unaware of any work by d'Eon published in Latin.

35. D'Eon referred here to the pretender to the English throne, James III, who had been living in France since the time of England's Glorious Revolution (1689).

36. D'Eon was making a word play on the expression *dragon de vertu*, someone who strictly enforced moral precepts. A dragoon, of course, was a heavily armed cavalryman. Since Apollo fought the dragon at Delphi in the Homeric hymn to

Apollo, dragons have represented matriarchy. For d'Eon, throughout these writings, the words *dragoon* and *dragon* have thus an ambivalent association with masculine and feminine icons.

37. ULBC, file 5, pp. 1–19 includes an earlier version of these events, including an interview between the Prince de Conti and d'Eon, in which Conti was aware of d'Eon's female nature and asks him to be a spy in Russia.

38. These quarrels referred to feuds over responsibility for lost battles during the Seven Years' War. See Kates, *D'Eon*, pp. 83–86.

39. "His shield not well retrieved." Horace pretended to have been killed as a ruse to fool his enemies, the Curiacii, into inattention, which enabled Horace to defeat them in the end.

40. In 1763 Guerchy replaced d'Eon as France's Ambassador to England. D'Eon believed that Guerchy's patrons (Praslin, Choiseul, and Madame de Pompadour) wanted to sabotage his career and the careers of d'Eon's patrons (the Comte de Broglie and his brother, the Maréchal de Broglie). D'Eon's protracted feud with Guerchy (1763–67) mixed genuine scandal with petty complaints. See Kates, *D'Eon*, pp. 91–137. The feud can be followed in *Pièces relatives aux lettres, mémoires et négociations particulières* (London, 1765).

41. D'Eon explained: "This young and wholesome Arabian horse had a charming appearance and lovely movements, but he had one awful defect: he lost his sight for a week whenever the moon waned. Maréchal Ligonier, who lived near Coban, had given him to Monsieur Tynte, his neighbor at Bur Hill, an attendant to the Prince of Wales and a colonel in the Régiment des Gardes, and whom the deceased Maréchal used to praise for his military virtues in war and in peace. Monsieur Tynte, who had been my loyal friend since 1762, had given me this charming horse, making me aware of its defect. I told myself that I, who am also subject to the phases of the moon, do not fall, and so my Arabian horse—who is so polite, charming, and docile toward me when I mount him—will perhaps not fall either."

42. This story suggests that d'Eon's female genitals were discovered by those trying to aid him after this fall, thus leading to a public revelation. Nowhere do we find a contemporary account of this story, either in the press or in private memoirs or correspondence. It appears to be a fabrication invented for this autobiography. This story is repeated several times in other manuscripts, including ULBC, file 16, p. 883, file 25, p. 8, file 42, p. 1222. The London trial refers to a civil suit between two men who had gambled on the question of d'Eon's sex. The case was heard by chief justice Lord Mansfield in July 1777, shortly before d'Eon's departure for France. See Kates, *D'Eon*, 247–51.

43. The first minister in 1777 was the Comte de Maurepas.

44. Vergennes sought, through savings in certain areas, to invest heavily in rebuilding the French navy.

45. *En imposer à quelqu'un,* which means to deceive someone, is also a play on words. Hence d'Eon was also saying that he was deceived by the apparent virtues of the Archbishop of Paris and Madame Louise.

46. A *coup de théâtre* is a theatrical term referring to a sudden change of events that causes the plot to develop in a new direction.

47. Between the years 1777 and 1779 d'Eon was kept under watch at Versailles.

Chapter II

1. Throughout the autobiographical writings, d'Eon played with the meaning of the French word *dragon,* meaning dragoon or dragon. Heeding the pious tone that d'Eon sometimes adopted, Jeanne Morgan Zarucchi suggests that another reading of these first few lines could be: "Even if one casts off the skin of a Dragon, one is devoured by the Demon. He who is standing must take care not to fall." In contrast, we choose to interpret d'Eon's sense as recalling the dragoons and the military identity that went with the uniform he wore while assigned to the Russian court.

2. D'Eon provided the following commentary: "M. Tercier was, for a long time, the Chief Clerk for Foreign Affairs at Versailles. He lost this position as well as that of Royal Censor for History and Belles-lettres for having approved the publication of the well-known work by the famous Helvétius. But since he was a very knowledgeable and honest man who belonged to the Royal Academy of Inscriptions and Letters in Paris, the King secretly gave him a pension of thirty thousand tournois pounds and demonstrated his personal faith in Tercier by appointing him secretary in charge of his secret correspondence. His wife was a relative of mine and, for that and several other reasons, he considered me his friend." On Tercier see Didier Ozanam, "La Disgrâce d'un premier commis: Tercier et l'affaire de *L'Esprit* (1758–1759)," *Bibliothèque de l'Ecole des Chartres* 113 (1955): 140–70.

3. D'Eon explained that *frêle* is "the name given at the Court to the young women of the country's highest class of nobility who are chosen to be ladies-in-waiting to the Empress."

4. D'Eon described Meaux as "a very old city in France, the capital of Brie, with a rich diocese attached to the archdiocese in Paris, and which the famous Bénigne Bossuet (1627–1704, orator and bishop) controlled until his death. The choir of the Cathedral Church is considered a masterpiece."

5. There is an untranslatable sexual innuendo here. D'Eon referred to the *queue de mon uniforme dragon*. While his officer's uniform doubtless had tails, the word *queue* is also a common term for penis. The male sex organ is thus associated with the dragoon military uniform.

6. D'Eon explained: "This Princess, whose appearance is striking for the elegance of both her figure and her face, is not a woman like most others. She has the mind and the heart of a courageous man, like that of her husband who was killed in a battle between the Russians and the Turks. It was she who in 1762 escaped during the night with the Empress Catherine through the window of the imperial palace to join the group of Russian troops who were to lay siege to Peter III in his castle of Ovanienbanne, across from Croustadt, where Peter believed himself to be safe and invincible with the formidable Holstein regiment. They, in their strikingly Prussian

uniforms, spoke only German and paraded about as if they had missed their calling as monkeys. Despite all that, he was lucky to be able to scurry about and then surrender with his dear wife and the Princess Asthoff. They made him go to the citadel of St. Petersburg *relicta non bene Parmulla* [without having properly employed his shield]. Everyone knows his fate and his destiny: he was no Peter the Great with his grand and beautiful celebrations." *The Memoirs of Princess Dashkova,* trans. Kyril Fitzlyon (Durham, 1995) does not mention d'Eon.

7. D'Eon added that "my mother gave birth to me on October 5, 1728, during the grape harvest. Near the end of her pregnancy she had such a craving for large quantities of the fine grapes of Tonnerre that, when I came into this world, I had virtually drowned^f in grape julep."

8. D'Eon described Saluski as a "respected monastery for well-born girls thirty miles from Moscow in which the unfortunate Eudoxie Federossua, the first wife of Peter the Great, after exchanging her crown for a nun's veil, was obliged to take the vows of the order of Saint Basil. She was left alone with her reflections on the inconstancy of fortune, which had used her charms to elevate her to the throne, and which then used her jealousy to make her fall headlong into the horrors of a cloister."

9. D'Eon did not include the excerpts from the correspondence between the Cardinal de Bernis and the Marquis de l'Hôpital in his autobiography. The correspondence to which he referred is found in d'Eon's *Lettres, mémoires et particulières* (London, 1764), pp. 9–15. These are the letters sent to and received by the Marquis de l'Hôpital, French Ambassador to the Russian court in St. Petersburg between July 24, 1757, and August 28, 1758, regarding the appointment of d'Eon as first secretary to the French Ambassador. Cardinal de Bernis and the Jesuit priest L. de la Tour recommended d'Eon to the Marquis for the position. La Tour assured the Marquis that he would be happy with d'Eon's "energy, intelligence, personality, and virtue" (p. 10). Upon the resignation of the Marquis as ambassador, the Marquis offered d'Eon a position as attaché to the Russian court, which d'Eon refused. On June 29, 1758, the Marquis explained to the Cardinal de Bernis that d'Eon refused the position because he claimed that "he would serve no master other than the King" (p. 14). Extracts from other letters lend support to d'Eon's high ethical standards in this decision.

10. D'Eon was being coy here. Although the correspondence cited in his book establishes his important diplomatic role in Russia, nowhere do the letters imply that d'Eon cross-dressed or that his gender was questioned. Neither is there any shred of evidence for this story in the voluminous correspondence in the Archives des Affaires Etrangères. See Kates, *D'Eon,* chap. 14.

11. On Condoidi, we know nothing. The Archives Nationales contains a letter that d'Eon wrote to Poissonnier. It is reproduced in Kates, *D'Eon,* chap. 40.

12. D'Eon provided the following note: "The d'Autichamp Dragoons Regiment was also called the Caraman, formerly l'Hopital. Today the Duc de La Rochefoucauld, Liancourt, is its colonel."

13. In other words, God metes out the challenges to us according to our strengths and weaknesses.

Chapter III

1. D'Eon was making a word play here on the word *sexe,* which can also mean penis.

2. Mansfield established the legal precedent that, despite the general legality of gambling, no two parties can wager a bet on the sex of an innocent third party. See Henry Cowper, *Reports of Cases Adjudged in the Court of the King's Bench . . .* (London, 1800), 2:734–36. For a slightly different version see the newspaper article clipped by d'Eon in ULBC, case 12, large leather book, p. 202. There were actually several civil suits among gamblers who had waged insurance policies over the sex of d'Eon. For a brief recent overview, see James Oldham, ed., *The Mansfield Manuscripts and the Growth of English Law in the Eighteenth Century,* 2 vols. (Chapel Hill, 1992), 1:534–40.

3. Simon-Nicolas-Henri Linguet was indeed among the most colorful and best-known writers of the age. His opinions managed to offend everyone from Voltaire to Vergennes, and he sometimes had to hide from the authorities. His article on d'Eon was widely read. See "Sur la Chevalière d'Eon," *Annales politiques, civiles, et littéraires du dix-huitième siècle* 1 (1777): 383–97. On Linguet see Darline Gay Levy, *The Ideas and Careers of Simon-Nicolas-Henri Linguet: A Study in Eighteenth-Century French Politics* (Urbana, 1980).

4. Bucephalus was also the name of Alexander the Great's horse.

5. Although physicians testified at the various civil suits that d'Eon was female, no one told this story about a fall from a horse.

6. D'Eon used the term *Esculapes* here for physicians. Asclepius (Latin, Aesculapius) was the Greek god of medicine.

7. On male midwifery, see Adrian Wilson, *The Making of Man-Midwifery: Childbirth in England, 1660–1770* (London, 1995).

8. D'Eon noted that "the English word 'verdict' means a report of jurors on a civil or a criminal case that the Court has asked them to judge."

9. Mars was the Roman god of war, Venus the Roman goddess of love. This probably means that d'Eon had not had sexual relations as Mars (as a man) nor as Venus (as a woman).

10. D'Eon noted that he was referring to the Comte de Maurepas. On Maurepas and ministerial politics in this era, see John Hardman, *French Politics, 1774–1789: From the Accession of Louis XVI to the Fall of the Bastille* (London, 1985).

11. The reference is to Virgil, *Aeneid,* bk. 2, l. 49, and refers to Aeneas's advice to be wary of Greeks bearing gifts.

12. Adelaide and Victoire de France were the daughters of Louis XV.

13. In 1762 the Paris Parlement abolished the Society of Jesus (Jesuits) because it viewed the order as a political threat to the sovereignty of the French monarchy.

14. See Voltaire to Louis d'Eon, February 15, 1739, reprinted in *The Complete Works of Voltaire,* ed. Theodore Besterman, 135 vols. (Oxford, 1970–79).

15. "Saint James in Galicia" refers to the Spanish shrine of Saint James of Compostela, a popular pilgrimage site in the Middle Ages. "Coventry" literally refers to a British town but in this case is a colloquial expression for an exilic pilgrimage. Jean-Baptiste Vaquette de Gribeauville, as Inspector General for the Artillery Corps, made important innovations to French military technology.

16. The *datary,* which investigates candidates for papal benefices, is one of the papal government's highest offices. Several cardinals in charge of the *datary* went on to become pope.

17. D'Eon noted that "Dom Boudier came from the Percy family in Normandy, from which the illustrious Northumberland family in England also originated."

18. The Reformed Abbey was used to discipline men rejected by the military.

19. Horace pretended to run away as a ruse to divide and defeat his three opponents. D'Eon here claimed not to have acted in this way. The translation is: "He did not wisely leave his shield behind." The word *wisely* ironically refers to the expectation that a warrior take his shield with him unless he is fleeing the field of battle as a coward. Horace thus gave the impression that he was a coward by leaving his shield behind. Between 1762 and 1791 d'Eon purchased the world's largest private collection of works by Horace.

20. Saint Benoit was Pope Benedict II. The children of Saint Benoit were Roman Catholics who believed in the succession of the papacy.

21. D'Eon noted that "the Benedictines are dressed completely in black, except for the stockings, which are white wool, and they have neither beards nor mustaches. The first group prays continually while the second swears endlessly. Some eat only fish and greens while the others eat everything they find or steal. Everyone in this world does his own job. There is only the prayer: *Sanctus ivo quierat advocatus et non latro; Oras miranda.*" This is incorrect Latin. D'Eon may have meant "Pray for her, this admirable person, the holy one who asks to be a mediator and not an insidious person."

22. D'Eon noted that he called her oriental "because she was the beautiful widow of a Greek or Dragomanish physician in the Court of Constantinople."

23. D'Eon misused the term *coroner's inquests,* most likely to convey the ambience of an autopsy of the dead Chevalier d'Eon.

24. D'Eon wanted to enjoy his return to France without restrictions. The King's order to wear a dress diluted the full flavor of the metaphoric wine d'Eon earned by his diplomatic service to King Louis XV.

25. On Bertin, see Emile Langlande, *La Marchande de modes de Marie-Antoinette: Rose Bertin* (Paris, 1911). D'Eon noted that a trousseau is clothing above and beyond a dowry given to a young woman when she marries.

26. D'Eon's official duties involved being an expert at encoding and decoding diplomatic secrets. Although the others on the diplomatic staff entrusted him with

these duties, they did not suspect nor were they skilled enough to decode his gender, which he had encoded.

27. D'Eon noted: "Calpin: the name of the editor of the large, old French dictionary called the *Calpin*." Hence Mademoiselle Bertin determined the style and kind of dresses d'Eon would wear before the King.

28. *Draguées de chicoton* were medicinal lozenges made from the sap of the aloe.

Chapter IV

1. The *Eau de la Reine de Hongrie,* according to Furetière, was a distillation made with rosemary and "spirit of wine." It received its name from the marvelous effects of this concoction upon a seventy-two-year-old Hungarian queen.

2. D'Eon noted: "Being in a bad mood, Mademoiselle d'Eon uses the word Harpies to describe those doctors, matriarchs, jurists, and judges of the Court who, in London, declared him to be a woman and who, at Versailles, declared him to be a maiden. No matter where she turns, she is condemned to wear a dress."

3. Jean-Jacques Rousseau's *Emile* advocated that children be brought up in the country and that boys learn a handicraft so that they might have a place within the society.

4. The reference to nether regions was a double entendre, referring to her private parts and her willingness to defend them.

5. "Fat in the wrong place" means pregnancy.

6. The rest of the passage is a quotation from the Mansfield letter and is in English in the memoirs.

7. The motto of the Jesuits is "To the greater glory of God."

Chapter V

1. D'Eon noted that "Monsieur Amelot was the Ministre de la Maison du Roi [minister of the King's household] and Monsieur de Sartine was the Ministre de la Marine [minister of the navy]."

2. A louis was a denomination of gold money in eighteenth-century France, roughly equivalent to twenty francs.

3. D'Eon noted: "The house of De Vivier is one of the oldest families of the nobility in the area of Tonnerre. In the army I was a close friend of Monsieur De Vivier, major of the Régiment de Picardie, aide to the Major General of the whole infantry of Maréchal de Broglie's army in Germany. Monsieur De Vivier died as Major General of the Strasbourg garrison, which is usually composed of ten thousand foot soldiers. He was a courageous, prudent, and virtuous man. Before that, I had sold, with the right to buy back, the largest of my houses in Tonnerre to his uncle the Comte De la Salle, a major in the musketeers who died as Maréchal of the King's Encampments and Armies. At the Battle of Fontenoy, De la Salle re-

ceived four saber wounds and seven bayonet wounds without surrendering either his saber or his spirit to the enemy. He was a worthy son of the town and region of Tonnerre."

4. This wordplay contrasts *calotte,* meaning an ecclesiastical head covering, and *culotte,* meaning pants or drawers.

5. An écu was a French coin worth about $4.50 in the eighteenth century.

6. D'Eon erroneously cited Mark 13:14 as the source for this biblical quote.

7. D'Eon erroneously cited Luke 6:29 as the source for this biblical quote.

8. The Caloyers were a group of Greek Orthodox monks founded by Saint Basil. Mount Athos is a Greek mountain on which, beginning in the eleventh century, were founded monasteries of about four hundred monks whose role was to transcribe and thus save the written documents of Western civilization.

9. D'Eon explained: "In the past, *grabataires* were those who put off being baptized until their death."

10. D'Eon noted that "many scholars have confirmed that Thomas à Kempis is the inimitable author of *The Imitation of Jesus-Christ.*"

Chapter VI

1. D'Eon noted that "M. Bertier had a great number of land holdings in Burgundy as well as around Paris."

2. D'Eon indicated explicitly his intention of placing a copy of the letter here. A copy of this letter, dated October 12, 1777, is in the Archives de Ministère des Affaires Étrangères, Correspondance Politique, Angleterre, Supplément 17:51.

3. As far as we know, d'Eon did not receive any major injuries in battle, but rather he broke his leg and sustained other injuries traveling as a courier between the Russian Empress Elizabeth and Louis XV during the Seven Years' War.

4. The relationship was perfectly normal in the sense that Louis XV approved of de Broglie's spy network, of which d'Eon was an important part.

5. Alcantara, a military and religious order, was founded in 1156 in imitation of the Templars.

6. We have not found the original of this letter in any archival collection.

Chapter VII

The passages referred to in the epigraph source are "He who has ears to hear let him hear" (Mark 4:9); "What does thou say of him who opened my eyes? He is a prophet" (John 9:17); and "He who does not love abides in death" (John 1, 3:14). These biblical references underscore the inspiration for d'Eon's piety, which influenced the tone and attitude of Christian charity in his narrative. Despite the disjunction between d'Eon's text and these references, d'Eon constantly attempted to ground his autobiography in the Christian Gospels, much as Augustine did in his *Confessions.*

1. The Rubicon was the boundary between Cisalpine Gaul and Italy. When Caesar crossed the Rubicon, he put himself above the law in his decision to invade Rome.

2. D'Eon noted that "Rollet senior [was] a lawyer in the Parliament and on the King's Bench." Voltaire wrote a scandalous mock-heroic epic poem entitled *La Pucelle,* which ridicules Joan of Arc. Voltaire did not publish this work, but it was read frequently at social gatherings.

3. Saint Thomas was celebrated for his role as the "doubting Thomas," who would not believe the apostles who told him about the resurrected Christ. Thomas insisted that he would not believe unless he could place his hands in the wounds of Christ's risen body. Upon seeing Christ, Thomas did place his hand in the wounded side of Christ. Christ's response was: "Blessed are they who have not seen, and yet have believed" (John 20:29).

4. The French term *parties* refers both to the sides in a conflict and also to parts, a polite reference to genitals. D'Eon was playing on this double meaning, combined with the equally ambiguous *pays bas* to make a sexual innuendo. (*Pays bas* also refers to the Netherlands, the territory that today comprises Belgium and Holland.)

5. This is a reference to the Blessed Virgin Mary.

6. The great seal is the seal of the King, the small seal that of the Queen.

Chapter VIII

1. In the Roman tradition, Vestal Virgins were women dedicated to caring for the inner sanctum of the temples to their gods. In Christianity, the Vestal Virgin was symbolic of the condition of nuns who took the vow of chastity and dedicated their lives to the service of God.

2. The simple tonsure is the less drastic variation of the ecclesiastical practice of shearing one's hair in preparation for taking the vows of a religious order.

3. Mademoiselle Bertin assumes that d'Eon will shortly join a convent. The marriage refers to the ceremony whereby a nun becomes the bride of Christ. The breviary is a prayer book used daily by those who enter religious orders. Since canon law is the law of the Church, "canonically approved" is the Church's blessing for the precedent of d'Eon's joining a convent. Mademoiselle Bertin also alludes to d'Eon's being beatified by the Church as the prior step to sainthood. Since the official process of beatification requires a miracle to be produced in the name of the person being beatified, Mademoiselle Bertin implies that d'Eon's change has been a miracle and warrants d'Eon's beatification and ultimate sainthood.

4. The Sanhedrin was the highest council of the ancient Jews, consisting of seventy-one members.

5. D'Eon noted that Mademoiselle Bertin, who dresses the Queen, also dresses the most important women of the court, including the Duchesse de Montmorenci.

6. D'Eon noted: "The oldest daughter of Monsieur and Madame Genet, the first lady to the Queen, married Monsieur Campan, a man of great merit and secretary of the Queen's Cabinet. The second daughter married Monsieur Rousseau, the major-domo of Monseigneur le Comte de Provence and fencing master of the King's pages. The third daughter, Adelaide, who was as sweet and beautiful as she was likeable, married through my agency Monsieur Augué, the director of a war office, to whom the Queen gave the position of Collector General of Taxes, despite the opposition of Monsieur de Calonne, the Comptroller General. The fourth daughter married a rich financier with the protection of our august Queen. He only had one son, as intelligent as the father, who was the Plenipotentiary Minister of France to America. Unfortunately for him, he quarreled with the famous General Washington and retired to New York where he married the daughter of the English general who commanded the army."

7. D'Eon was doing a riff on the word *heroine*. From *héroïne* he went to *zéro*, to *héron*, to *hermine*, to *fouine*, to *colombe*, to *columbine*, going through a series of animals (mostly birds) to end at *concubine*.

8. The Hesperides were the nymphs of Greek mythology in whose garden were found trees bearing the golden apples of immortality.

9. D'Eon explained that *trabee* was "the name for a dress worn by the Roman generals in their triumphant processions."

10. This is a conflation of John 15:5 ("I am the vine, you are the branches. He who abides in me, and I in him, he it is that bears much fruit, for apart from me you can do nothing"), John 6:44 ("No one can come to me unless the Father who sent me draws him; and I will raise him up at the last day"), and John 6:55 ("And he said, 'This is why I told you that no man can come to me unless it is granted to him by the Father'").

11. D'Eon explained: "Mademoiselle Bertin was born in the district of Amiens, the capital of Picardy. The peace treaty that she arranged with Mademoiselle d'Eon overshadowed the famous peace treaty of Amiens and will overshadow yet many another. Amiens is the birthplace of Jacques Silvius, Jean Riolan, Vincent Voiture, Jacques Rohault, Charles du Fresne — the patron saint of Le Lange, and Hugues d'Amiens."

12. D'Eon noted: "Mademoiselle Bertin lodges in her home forty working women from her dress shop and keeps them in order just as if they were in a well-disciplined convent."

Chapter IX

1. As if providing proof for his fear, d'Eon noted that the families of his religious and political patrons joined together: "The Marquis de Lostange, nephew of the Archbishop of Paris [Christophe de Beaumont], married the eldest daughter of the Marquis de l'Hôpital, my patron and France's ambassador in Russia."

2. D'Eon explained that the word *archiâtre* was a title taken by the principal physicians of the Roman emperors and the kings of France. The French word *cornet* was used in Chapter I to refer to d'Eon's success in military school. He added the feminine ending to the word *cornet*. *Cornette* also refers to the headdress worn by nuns.

3. D'Eon remarked about Crete that "the Ancients mention several famous labyrinths, the most renowned being that of Crete, which Daedalus constructed and which contained the Minotaur."

Chapter X

1. In the biblical Acts of the Apostles, Ananias was sent by God to Damascus to reveal God's plans for Saul of Tarsus, the bitter anti-Christian who had been blinded for three days after being struck from his horse in the year 44. Saul eventually became the Christian evangelist Paul, the writer of the biblical Epistles.

2. The *épistémonarque* in the Greek Church was an ecclesiastical officer responsible for the inspection of everything that pertained to faith.

Chapter XI

1. This saying exemplifies a symmetrical principle of d'Eon's historical moment.

2. Loosely taken from Acts 9:10–16. Saul is the Jewish identity of Paul, the composer of the epistles in the New Testament, before he was converted to Christianity.

3. Loosely taken from Acts 9:21.

4. D'Eon noted that "Bur Hill near Cobham is 19 miles from London, noteworthy for Paine's Hill, the home with a beautiful porch and gardens belonging to the late Mr. Hamilton and the late Mr. Hopkins. It was the site of frequent walks by Lieutenant-Colonel Honslaw, the courageous Colonel Tynte, the great John Wilkes, Humphrey Cotes, and the lowly Chevalier d'Eon."

5. D'Eon used the word *Esculapes* to refer to doctors. Aesculapius was a son of Apollo and god of medicine.

6. D'Eon cited his source as the "original depositions in the English language and appellant's evidence."

7. D'Eon provided the following sources: Deut. 17:6, 7:15; Matt. 18:16; John 8:17; 1 Cor. 15:1; Heb. 10:28.

8. The French word *on* is a third-person pronoun referring to others without designating any person in particular. It can be translated as "one" in such expressions as "one says" or "one does."

9. D'Eon probably meant the great French Revolution of 1789, which resulted in the loss of his pension. D'Eon identified the treasurer as "M. Duruey, the Guard of the Royal Treasury, who was guillotined with my cousin M. le Prince."

10. These are slang terms for diarrhea.

11. Numidia is an ancient name for what today comprises Algeria.

12. This section must have been written in 1805, when d'Eon was seventy-seven years old.

13. These two sentences are in English in the original.

14. D'Eon remarked that "this monastery belongs to the famous Abbey of the Ladies of Fontevrault."

Other Autobiographical Writings and Fragments
D'Eon's Second Visit to Christophe de Beaumont

This narrative can be seen as a sequel to Chapter X of d'Eon's autobiography.

From the Letter to the Duchesse, May 1778

The verse used for the epigraph actually comes from Rom. 8:31.

1. D'Eon adds: "During this period d'Eon retired frequently among these nuns. Her usual home in Versailles was in the house of the ladies Genet and Campan, attendants to the Queen. In this house she did her first novitiate in a white shift, a short or a long dress, with the decorum required in the place where she lived. It was mandated by the King that she remain in Versailles under the watchful eye of Monsieur Amelot, the King's Secretary of State; she could not come or go without his personally written and signed permission. That was the great freedom she enjoyed in the kingdom of the Franks and Gauls!"

2. The simple tonsure did not apply to women; this appears to be a joke by d'Eon.

3. For more on the Popess Joan, see Part III.

4. *Possessoire* and *petitoire* are legal terms referring to d'Eon being the landlord and absentee resident of the estate that d'Eon's mother left him in Tonnerre. D'Eon is debating here whether the Church has a legal right to take away his property since he did not take a vow of poverty in conjunction with his simple tonsure in the convent.

5. "Packed up my sack and skittles" is an allusion to his male genitals being trussed up for his entry into the convent.

6. These words are not exactly repeated in all the references; the Hosea citation should be 2:24.

7. D'Eon is probably referring to Acts 1:7–8: "It is not for you to know about dates or times, which the Father has set within his own control. But you will receive power when the Holy Spirit comes upon you."

8. D'Eon is probably referring to Isa. 4:1: "Then on that day seven women shall take hold of one man and say, 'We will eat our own bread and wear our own clothes if only we may be called by your name; take away our disgrace.'" Paul's conver-

sion is first described in Acts 9:1–30 and retold in 22:6–11 and 26:12–18. Nowhere, however, does Acts mention the Baradi Bridge incident.

9. This is a reference at least to the Comte de Guerchy, with whom d'Eon feuded.

Letter to the Duchesse, June 1789

1. In northwest Turkey, the Strait of Marmara connects the Black Sea and the Aegean Sea.

2. This is not an accurate citation for the reference.

3. Although d'Eon placed this passage in quotation marks and referred to Paul's Epistle to the Hebrews, it is only loosely derivative from Heb. 1.

4. This is not an accurate citation for the reference.

5. Hypothetical translation of a poor Latin construction.

6. Apoc. 9:3: "And there was given to them power, as the scorpions of the earth have power."

7. Apoc. 7:14: "And I said to him: 'My Lord thou knowest.' And he said to me: 'These are they who have come out of the great tribulation, and have washed their robes and made them white in the blood of the Lamb.'"

8. There is no Rom. 10:31. D'Eon was probably confusing Hebrews 10:31 ("It is a fearful thing to fall into the hands of the living God") and Rom. 14:9 ("For to this end Christ died and lived again, so that he might be Lord of both the dead and the living").

9. D'Eon identified himself as the male *chevalier* here to play on the dual meanings of the word as knight and servant within the army of the Church's faithful.

10. When d'Eon returned to France in 1777, he left some six thousand British pounds with his close friend, Washington Shirley, the fifth earl of Ferrers. When Ferrers died in 1778, his younger brother refused to give the money to d'Eon, ostensibly forcing d'Eon to return to England in 1785 to initiate civil proceedings to claim it.

Reply from the Duchesse

In the manuscript we find not the original of this letter but a copy in d'Eon's hand. In fact, no original has been found, leading to speculation that this letter is in fact a piece by d'Eon.

1. Hypothetical translation of imperfect Latin.

2. Hypothetical translation of imperfect Latin.

3. Hypothetical translation of imperfect Latin.

Christian Reflections

1. D'Eon wrote "Agrippé," which means gripped, with an untranslatable play on the words *Agrippa* and *agripper*, meaning to grab.

A Special Request

1. D'Eon played on the French word *queue,* meaning both tail and penis.

2. D'Eon used the English word *bills,* which he explained in a note as "the English word meaning the note for the collection of goods delivered or for an expense."

3. Christophe de Beaumont told d'Eon to dress in female clothes because he believed that d'Eon was a biological female raised as a male. D'Eon here is practically admitting to us that this story is a "legend."

4. *Folio* refers to a large book in which one sheet is used per page; *duodecimo* refers to a smaller book in which sheets have been folded so that each page is one-twelfth the size of a full sheet.

5. D'Eon noted that "the deceased Comte de Haux was promoted to Maréchal de France after his victory in the small kingdom of Corsica, and if he were still living he would be among the greatest of them."

6. Here William Serran is compared to Aristarchus, the ancient Greek astronomer who was the first to argue that the earth revolves around the sun.

7. Col. 3:11: "Here there is neither 'Gentile nor Jew,' 'circumcised nor uncircumcised,' 'Barbarian nor Scythian,' 'slave nor freeman'; but Christ is all things in all."

Historical Precedents Found by d'Eon
Pious Metamorphoses

The sense of the passage quoted at the beginning of Part III is "The one who dreaded failure stayed home. Fine!" It follows the famous line from Horace: "It is not everyone who gets to go to Rome."

1. This selection is missing from the manuscript.

2. D'Eon owned a rare manuscript copy of this early feminist text of the 1440s. The *Roman de la Rose* is one of the most popular epic poems of the late Middle Ages.

3. D'Eon remarked that André Tiraqueau was "a legal advisor whose pen was as prolific as his wife was fertile. It was observed during his time that every year he produced a book and she a child."

4. Æthelwulf ruled Wessex from 839 to 858; Alfred ruled Wessex from 871 to 899; Pope Leo IV led the Church from 847 to 855. Ockley (more commonly, Aclea) is an unidentified battleground in Surrey or Hampshire. The battle occurred around 851.

5. The *romescot* was an annual tax to the Papal See.

6. Joan was so impressed with Louis II that she gave him a one-hundred-year dispensation from Gratian's canon laws. He was thus exempted from those laws and was not held accountable for the sins or crimes committed under them.

7. D'Eon remarked: "*Papa pater patrium,/Papiface pondito partum;/Et tibi tunc*

edam;/De corpore quando recedam. These verses are cut or changed by most scholars. The way they are presented here is the most complete and the most reasonable. One must agree that this possessed man was a very clever and learned devil to be able to compose three such diabolical verses on the spot. They are quite typical of fourteenth-century taste."

8. Rogation Day is the Thursday that falls forty days after Easter.

9. D'Eon commented that, "according to the opinion of most scholars, she had occupied the papal seat for two years, five months, and several days."

10. D'Eon added the following reference: "*Dejecta, mitellam mulierem lam devenisse querbatur* [Dejected, she complained to have now become an extremely weakened woman] (Boccaccio, *De Flavis mulieribus*)."

11. This is probably Nicolas Lenglet Dufresnoy, *De l'usage des romans. Où l'on fait voir leur utilité et leurs différents caractères,* 2 vols. (Amsterdam, 1734). D'Eon owned a copy of Lenglet's popular biography of Joan of Arc. See also d'Eon's "Notice sur l'abbé Lenglet Dufresnoy," *l'Année littéraire,* 1 (1754): 219. D'Eon added the following reference: "Angel Manrique, *Cisterciensivm sev verivs ecclesiasticorvm annalivm a condito Cistercio* (Lugduni, 1642), chap. 11."

12. This is probably the second volume of *Histoire du calvinisme & celle du Papisme mises en parallèle: ou apologie pour les Réformateurs, & pour les Réformez, divisée en quatre parties* (Rotterdam, 1683).

13. D'Eon added the following reference: "Adrien Baillet, *La Vie des saints, composée sur ce qui nous est resté de plus authentique et de plus assuré dans leur histoire,* vol. 3 (Paris, 1704), p. 307, note xxv. He places Saint Eugenia in the third and fourth centuries."

14. D'Eon remarked: "On page 323 in volume 2 of *The Lives of the Holy Fathers of the Wildernesss and the Holy Monks of the East and the West* [Joseph François Bourgoing de Villefore, *Les Vies des S.S. Pères des déserts et saintes solitaires D'Orient et d'Occident,* 4 vols. (Anvers, 1714)], published in 1714 in Anvers (Amsterd), can be found a Saint Eugenia of the second century who was disguised as a man and who, with two eunuchs, entered a monastery not far from Alexandria. One has to look carefully in Baillet and other reliable authors to determine whether these two saints are different or the same."

15. D'Eon's reference: *Paradis. Carmel.,* anno 257, chap. 4. l. 3b; *Histoire des ordres monastiques,* tom. 1er, 2e partie, p. 344.

16. D'Eon's reference: Ibid., chap. 39.

17. D'Eon's reference: Ibid., p. 133, anno 440.

18. D'Eon's reference: Ibid.

19. D'Eon's reference: *Hist. Carmel.,* vol. 4, chap. 12, pp. 309–10.

20. D'Eon's reference: *Paradis. Carmel.,* chap. 129, anno 392.

21. D'Eon's reference: Ibid., chap. 161, anno 423.

22. D'Eon's reference: *De sacru antiquatate ordinis B. V. Marie de monte Carmelo,* chap. 10; *Ordres monastiques,* vol. 1, chap. 11, p. 390.

23. D'Eon's reference: *Paradis. Carmel.,* Ib.

24. D'Eon's reference: Ibid., chap. 24, anno 290.

25. D'Eon's reference: Ibid., chap. 22, anno 471.

26. *Tierce* is the third of seven canonical hours reserved for prayer in the ecclesiastical prayer day. These canonical hours are recommended for religious communities and hermits.

27. D'Eon's reference: *Paradis. Carmel.*, chap. 10.

28. D'Eon's reference: R. V. Maurique, *Cistercian History,* chap. 6, anno 1188.

29. D'Eon's reference: Francisco de Santa Maria, *Histoire générale des Carmes Deschaussez et des Carmelites Deschaussees,* bk. 2, chap. 6.

30. D'Eon's reference: *General History of the White Friars,* bk. 12, chap. 12.

Biographical Glossary

Æthelwulf. Anglo-Saxon King of Wessex, 839–58.

Agabus. New Testament prophet. In Acts 11:28, Agabus predicts a severe world famine.

Alfred. 849–99. Anglo-Saxon King of Wessex, 871–99.

Amelot de Chaillou, Jean Antoine. 1732–95. French minister for the Maison du Roi, 1783–87.

Archbishop of Paris. *See* Beaumont.

Aristarchus of Samos. Ca. 312–230 B.C.E. Greek astronomer. He was the first to maintain that the earth revolves around the sun.

Aristotle. 384–22 B.C.E. Greek philosopher.

Armstrong, John. 1709–79. British physician, poet, and essayist. He may have known d'Eon through their mutual friend, the politician John Wilkes.

Augustine, Saint. 354–430. Bishop of Hippo, theologian, author of the autobiographical *Confessions.*

Autichamp, Jean Thérèse Louis de Beaumont, Marquis d'. 1738–1831. Dragoon colonel. He fought in the War of the Austrian Succession and the Seven Years' War under the Duc de Broglie.

Bayard, Pierre Terrail, Chevalier de. 1473–1524. Military hero. He accompanied the armies of Charles VIII into Italy.

Beaumont, Christophe de. 1703–81. Pious and conservative Archbishop of Paris, 1754–81.

Bellisle, Charles-Louis-Auguste-Foucquet, Duc de. 1684–1761. Minister of war during the Seven Years' War.

Benedict II, Pope. Served as pope 684–85.

Bernis, François Joachim de Pierre de. 1715–94. Served as foreign minister, 1757–58; created cardinal in 1758; served as Ambassador to the Vatican, 1769–91.

Bertier de Sauvigny, Louis Bénigne. 1737–89. Intendant of Paris, 1776 until his death at the hands of a revolutionary mob in July 1789.

Bertier de Sauvigny, Louis Jean. 1709–88. Intendant of Paris, 1744–76.

Bertin, Rose. 1744–1813. A common seamstress who rose to become Marie Antoinette's dress designer and fashion advisor.

Bestuchev, Comte DuDrumin, Alexis Petrovitch. 1692–1767. As Russian Chancellor, 1744–58, he favored an anti-French policy. He was banished to Siberia by Empress Elizabeth in 1758 and restored by Catherine in 1762.

Blondel, David. 1591–1655. Protestant scholar.

Boileau, Nicolas. *See* Despréaux.

Boisrobert, François le Metel. 1589–1662. Playwright and founding member of the Académie Française.

Boudier, Pierre François. 1704–87. Benedictine author and savant.

Broglie, Charles François, Comte de. 1719–81. Diplomat, statesman, and foreign policy advisor to Louis XV. He was d'Eon's most important patron.

Broglie, Victor François, Maréchal de and Duc de. 1718–1804. Older brother of the Comte de Broglie. They jointly commanded the army of the Rhine during the Seven Years' War, 1756–63.

Campan, Jeanne Louise Henriette Genet, Mme. 1752–1822. Lady-in-waiting to Marie Antoinette.

Charlemagne. 742–814. Emperor of the Holy Roman Empire and King of the Franks.

Charles the Bald (Charles II). 823–77. Emperor of the West, King of the West Franks, 875–77.

Chavigny, Anne-Théodore Chevignard, Chevalier de. 1687–1771. French Ambassador to Venice, 1750–52, and to Switzerland, 1752–63.

Chétardie, Joachim-Jacques Trotti, Marquis de la. 1705–59. French Ambassador to Russia, 1740–42.

Choiseul, Comte de. *See* Praslin.

Choiseul, Etienne François, Comte de Stainville and Duc de. 1719–85. Foreign minister, 1758–61. He served as minister of war until 1770 and of the navy until 1766.

Cicero, Marcus Tullius. 106–43 B.C.E. Roman statesman and writer.

Colbert, Jean-Baptiste. 1619–83. Key minister under Louis XIV, known for his economic reforms.

Conti, Louis-François de Bourbon, Prince de. 1717–76. First cousin of Louis XV, with whom he feuded during the Seven Years' War. He was known for his good looks, gallantry, philosophical curiosity, and military heroism. He was an important patron of d'Eon during the 1750s.

Dashkova, Catherine Vorontsov, Princess. 1743–1810. Lady-in-waiting to Catherine the Great. Her *Memoirs,* ed. K. Fitzlyon (London, 1958), do not mention d'Eon.

Despréaux, Nicolas Boileau-. 1636–1711. French poet, literary critic, and royal historiographer under Louis XIV. In 1694 he published an antifeminist satire, "Satire X." (The title "Against Women" does not appear in some editions and may be a later addition by an editor.)

Douglas, Alexander Pierre MacKensie, Count and Baron of Kildin. 1713–65. Scotch Jacobite who supported the Pretender during the 1745 rebellion. He emigrated to France in 1747, where he performed diplomatic missions to Russia on behalf of the Prince de Conti and Louis XV.

Dryden, John. 1631–1700. English poet and playwright.

DuDrumin. *See* Bestuchev.

Durey d'Harnancourt. 1690–1765. Intendant of Grenoble. In 1763 he published *Dissertation sur l'usage de boire à la glace.*

Elizabeth, Empress. 1709–62. Ruled Russia, 1741–62.

D'Eon de Beaumont, Françoise de Charanton. 1708–92. D'Eon's mother. She married Louis in 1723.

D'Eon de Beaumont, Louis. 1695–1749. D'Eon's father. He served as mayor of Tonnerre and as subdelegate of the Paris intendant.

D'Eon de Beaumont, Marguerite-Françoise. Born 1718. D'Eon's sister. She married the Irish nobleman Thomas O'Gorman in 1757.

D'Eon de Beaumont, Théodore-André. 1727. D'Eon's brother. He lived only from February to August.

D'Eon de Tissey, André-Timothée. 1683–1749. D'Eon's uncle, with whom he lived during his high school years in Paris. He served as secretary of the police of Paris.

Falconet (Falconnet), Amboise. Died 1817. Paris lawyer who pleaded several famous cases before the Paris Parlement.

La Fontaine, Jean de. 1621–95. Author of the *Fables.*

Fréron, Elie. 1718–76. An opponent of Voltaire and the *philosophes*. He founded *l'Année littéraire* (Literary Yearbook).

Genet, Jacques-Edme. 1726–81. Chief administrator of the Ministry of Foreign Affairs.

Gribeauville, Jean-Baptiste Vaquette de. 1715–89. Military officer. After rising in the French artillery corps, Gribeauval fought for Russia during 1758–62. Returning to France, he eventually became the Chief Inspector General for the artillery corps.

Guerchy, Claude Louis François Régnier, Comte de. 1715–67. French Ambassador to England, 1763–67.

Hôpital, Paul-François de Galucci, Marquis de l'. 1714–88. French Ambassador to Russia, 1763–69.

Horace (Quintus Horatius Flaccus). 65 B.C.E.–8 C.E. Latin poet. While living in England, 1762–77, d'Eon purchased the world's largest private collection of books by Horace.

Joan of Arc, Saint. 1412–31. French national hero who helped save the nation from the English.

Joan, Popess. An apocryphal figure from the Middle Ages who supposedly served as pope during 855–58.

Jurieu, Pierre. 1637–1713. Protestant scholar.

Kaestner, Abraham Gotthelf. 1719–1800. German mathematician.

Languet, Jean-Joseph. 1677–1753. Archbishop of Sens.

Lenglet Dufresnoy, Nicolas. 1674–1755. French writer.

Ligonier (Ligonnier), Jean-Louis. 1680–1770. French Huguenot military officer. He fled to England following religious persecution in 1724 and rose to the rank of field marshal. He was later pardoned by Louis XV.

Linguet, Simon-Nicholas-Henri. 1736–94. French editor of the influential *Annales politiques, civiles, et littéraires du dix-huitième siècle* (Political, Civil, and Literary Yearbook of the Eighteenth Century).

Lothair I. 795–855. Grandson of Charlemagne, King of Bavaria, crowned Emperor in 823.

Louis II. 846–79. Awarded Italy and the imperial Crown by his father, Lothair I, who divided the Holy Roman Empire among Louis and his two brothers.

Louis XVI. 1754–93. King of France, 1774–92. He was executed January 1793.

Louise de France, Madame. 1737–87. Daughter of Louis XV. She retired to a Carmelite convent in 1770.

Luckner, Nicolas, Baron de. 1722–94. Prussian general during the Seven Years' War. In 1763 he joined the French, becoming a marshal during the Revolution in 1791, and General Chief of the Army in Germany in 1792.

Malagrida, Gabriel. 1689–1761. Italian missionary and preacher known for his work in Brazil.

Malebranche, Nicolas. 1638–1715. French philosopher and priest.

Mansfield, Lord. 1705–93. Chief Justice of King's Bench, England. He judged d'Eon's legal battles as well as several civil suits over his sex.

Maurepas, Jean-Frédéric Phélypeaux, Comte de. 1701–81. Minister of the Interior, 1774–81.

Merlin. Legendary magician and wise man of the medieval Arthurian story.

Monica, Saint. 331–87. Mother of Saint Augustine. She was prominently featured in his *Confessions*.

Montmorenci-Bouteville, Duchesse de. Married into one of France's established noble families. D'Eon lived in her home for some months during 1778, where perhaps the drafts of the autobiography were begun. According to d'Eon, her husband, the Duc de Montmorenci, held the title of First Baron and Prince of the Holy Roman Empire.

Montmorency-Laval, Guy-André, Duc de. 1723–98. Became Maréchal de France in 1783.

Nivernais, Louis Jules Barbon Mazarini Mancini, Duc de. 1716–98. Chief of the diplomatic team that negotiated the Peace of Paris with England at the conclusion of the Seven Years' War.

Nostradamus. 1503–66. French astrologer and physician.

Ons-en-Bray (or Onsenbray), Louis Léon Pajot, Comte d'. 1678–1753. President of the Paris Academy of Science. D'Eon wrote his eulogy in *l'Année littéraire* in 1753.

Orléans, Louis, Duc d'. 1703–52. Chief of the Council of State during the regency of his cousin, Louis XV.

Orry, Comte de Vignori, Philibert. 1689–1747. Intendant of Soissons and Lille and Controller General of Finances, 1730–45.

Petrarch, Francesco. 1304–74. Italian poet, scholar, and humanist.

Philip the Evangelist, Saint. Mentioned in Acts 8 and 21.

Pitt the Elder, William. 1708–78. First earl of Chatham. He was British prime minister, 1756–61 and 1766–68, during the Seven Years' War.

Pitt the Younger, William. 1759–1806. British prime minister, 1783–1801, 1804–06, during the epoch of the French Revolution.

Poissonier, Pierre Isaac. 1720–98. Went to Russia in 1758, where he and d'Eon became friends. Through d'Eon's mediation, he published an anti-Rousseauian, pro-science discourse in *l'Année littéraire,* 1759. See also d'Eon to Poissonier, July 15, 1775, in the Archives Nationales, Papiers d'Eon, 277 AP/1, 4: 235, reprinted in Gary Kates, *Monsieur d'Eon Is a Woman: A Tale of Political Intrigue and Sexual Masquerade* (Baltimore, 2001), pp. 224–25.

Poitiers, Duchesse de Valentinois, Diane de. 1499–1566. Mistress of Henry II. She had great influence in his court.

Pompadour, Jeanne Antoinette Poisson, Marquise de. 1721–64. Mistress of Louis XV. She was tolerated by the royal family and generally detested by the court.

Praslin, César-Gabriel de Choiseul-Chevigny, Comte de Choiseul and Duc de. 1712–85. Minister of foreign affairs, 1761–66; minister of the navy, 1766–70. He followed the policies of his more powerful cousin, the Duc de Choiseul.

Prévost, Abbé Antoine François. 1697–1763. Author of the novel *Manon Lescaut,* 1731.

Quintilian (Marcus Fabius Quintilianus). Ca. 35–96. Roman scholar of rhetoric.

Raynal, Guillaume Thomas François. 1713–96. Liberal philosopher.

Regulus, Marcus Atilius. Died 250 B.C.E. Third-century B.C.E. Roman general who commanded troops in the First Punic War, 264–41 B.C.E.

La Rochefoucault, Marquis de Surgères, Alexandre Nicolas de. Born 1709. Military officer who served under the Prince de Conti during the War of the Austrian Succession. He also wrote comedies.

Rousseau, Jean-Jacques. 1712–78. Published *Emile* in 1762, developing novel notions of child rearing. D'Eon read and analyzed Rousseau's works and considered him a mentor. See d'Eon to Rousseau, February 20, 1766, in Rousseau's *Correspondance complète,* ed. R. A. Leigh, 46 vols. (Oxford, 1965–87), 28: 313–18.

Sartine, Comte d'Aby, Antoine Raymond de. 1729–1801. Head of police of Paris, 1759–74; minister of the navy, 1774–80. He retired to Spain at the beginning of the Revolution.

Saxe, Hermann Maurice, Comte de. 1696–1750. Military general and theorist. He led troops in the War of the Austrian Succession. Louis XV appointed him Maréchal in 1747.

Semiramis. Legendary Queen of Assyria and Babylonia. As a widow, she waged war throughout the Near East to India. She is said to be responsible for such monuments as the Hanging Gardens of Babylon.

Soubise, Charles de Rohan, Prince de. 1715–87. Co-commander of the army of the Rhine during the Seven Years' War.

Spanhem, Friderich. 1650–1712. Catholic scholar.

Stormont, David Murray, seventh Viscount of. 1722–96. British Ambassador to Saxony, 1756–59; Poland, 1761; France, 1772–78.

Sully, Maximilien de Béthune, Duc de. 1560–1641. French statesman and key minister under Henri IV.

Tacitus, Publius Cornelius. 56–ca. 120. Roman statesman and historian.

Target, Guy-Jean-Baptiste. 1733–1806. Among the best legal minds in late eighteenth-century France.

Tercier, Jean-Pierre. 1704–67. Director of Louis XV's ring of spies, known as le Secret du Roi, which after 1763 included d'Eon.

Theresa of Avila, Saint. 1515–82. Spanish mystic.

Tynte, Charles Kemys. 1710–85. Served in British House of Commons, 1745–74.

Vallière, Louise-Françoise de la Blume le Blanc, Duchesse de la. 1644–1710. Mistress of Louis XIV. After he dropped her, she spent the rest of her life in a Carmelite nunnery. D'Eon owned a devotional work that she wrote.

Vergennes, Charles Gravier, Chevalier de, then Comte de. 1717–87. Minister of foreign affairs, 1774–87.

Voltaire (François-Marie Arouet). 1694–1778. French writer.

Vorontsov, Michael Ilarianovitch, count. 1714–67. Russian Vice-Chancellor, 1744–58; Russian Chancellor, 1758.

Walpole, Robert, first earl of Orford. 1676–1745. Often regarded as the first British prime minister. He held that office for an extraordinary two decades: 1721–42.

Wilberforce, William. 1759–1833. British politician and abolitionist. His hatred for slavery and the slave trade stemmed at least partly from his evangelical Christianity.

⋘ Index ⋙